OTHER BOOKS BY MARSHALL HOUTS

Art of Advocacy — Appeals

Art of Advocacy — Cross Examination of Medical Experts

Courtroom Toxicology — Environmental Toxins, Industrial Poisons & Drugs (7 vols.)

Who Killed Sir Harry Oakes?

King's X — Common Law and the Death of Sir Harry Oakes

They Asked for Death

Proving Medical Diagnosis and Prognosis (14 vols.)

Cyclopedia of Sudden, Violent and Unexplained Death

Where Death Delights

Lawyers' Guide to Medical Proof (4 vols.)

Photographic Misrepresentation

Courtroom Medicine: Death (3 vols.)

Courtroom Medicine

The Rules of Evidence

From Arrest to Release

From Evidence to Proof

From Gun to Gavel

TRAUMA — Personal Injury — Medicine — Surgery (creator and editor — 30 vols.)

For amen, I say to you, till Heaven
and earth shall pass away, not
one jot or one tittle shall be
lost from the Law . . . . . .
[Jesus in] Matthew 5:18

JESUS' TWO SANHEDRIN ACQUITTALS

Their Legacies Of Due Process Of Law

BY
MARSHALL HOUTS, J.D.

Swallows™
BOOK PUBLISHERS
31878 Del Obispo, Suite 608
San Juan Capistrano, CA 92675

Library of Congress Catalog Card Number 89-092049

ISBN 0-9624234-0-8

to

MARY

again with love

TABLE OF CONTENTS

ILLUSTRATIONS

PROLOGUE:
FORMAT AND APPROACH

Our 1900-year misreadings of the sketchy reports of Jesus' legal trials by *gospel* writers *Matthew, Mark, Luke* and *John* continue to confuse us all; so it's high time we take a fresh look at what happened to this itinerate Jewish preacher (as his fellow Jews saw him during his lifetime), in Jerusalem, perhaps around 30-33 A.D.

To find out what really took place, we must reconstruct at least eight separate but tightly meshed segments of the broad picture:

(1)   The Jewish Temple-State;

(2)   The synagogue preachers;

(3)   The sophisticated Jewish legal system: Jesus' Small Sanhedrin trial for sabbath-breaking;

(4)   Jesus' Great Sanhedrin trial for false prophecy;

(5)   The Roman presence in Judea;

(6)   Jesus' night-time interrogations by the High Priests after his Gethsemane arrest;

(7)   The imperial Roman legal system: Jesus' trial before Pilate for sedition; and

(8)   Jesus' missed "due process of law" message.

Although nothing like "transcripts" of Jesus' trials ever existed (neither Jews nor Romans made running, verbatim records), we can create safe facsimiles, *provided* we use our source materials correctly, weighing both the positive and negative fact-finding values of each tool, neither overplaying nor underplaying its true worth.

GOSPELS

I approach the *gospels* in the posture of an objective historian digging for the facts, nothing more, nothing less, carefully steering clear of anything theological.

Our only direct sources of Jesus' legal trials come from the non-lawyer *gospel* writers; but they leave us skimpy facts only (*Appendix 1*). They wrote to advance a common *theological* theme

(*Appendix 2*), not to explain the niceties of either the Jewish or Roman legal system.

Striped down to its bare bones, Christian interpretation of that theme runs:

(1) A Jew with the Hebrew-Aramaic name of Jeshua ben Joseph (Joshua bar Joseph; later, *Greek* = Jesus Christ: "Joshua, the Anointed") lived and preached in the Galilee and surrounding areas, including parts of Judea;

(2) He developed such a great following that he became a threat to the Bureaucrats who ran the Temple-State in Jerusalem;

(3) Following God's preordained plan for the world's salvation, "the Jews" decided that he must go, so "they" plotted his death;

(4) "The Jews" conspired with the Romans to arrest Jesus at night so they could give him a secret, kangaroo trial, and condemn him to death;

(5) Since "the Jews" could not execute any accused without the Roman governor's permission, they took Jesus before Praefectus Pontius Pilate early the next morning, and accused him of sedition;

(6) Though really wanting to save Jesus, Reluctant Dragon Pilate finally approved Jesus' immediate crucifixion;

(7) Three days later, Jesus rose from the dead, to become Christianity's Risen Lord;

(8) By his death on the cross, he took on the sins of the world, arranging God's pardon; and

(9) Jesus will redeem from sin and grant life everlasting to anyone who accepts him as the Risen Lord, becomes "reborn," and leads a new life following the commandments of Christ Jesus the Lord.

This Book's Only Goal

My sole thrust is to correct the misinterpretations of what the *gospels* say — more correctly, hint — about Jesus' legal trials. I work only with what Christian theologians call "Jesus' human side," "Jesus' humanity" or the "human Jesus," purposely staying away from anything else about him.

I make no effort to rewrite any part of the *gospel* accounts; instead, you and I together will pull out the legal clues the writers give us, then insert them into safe, *non-gospel*, historical sources, so we can reach correct conclusions.

The Great Timetable Error

First off, why the centuries-old garble of what the *gospel* writers try to tell us about Jesus' legal encounters with both the Jewish and Roman rulers? We can sum it up crisply with the label: "The Great Timetable Error!"

In lantern-slide quickness, the *gospel* writers flash us the *separate* judicial and executive events which led to Jesus' execution. They would be shocked to know how we mistakenly compact these distinct incidents into a single, continuous episode which lasted no more than twelve to fifteen hours.

It did not happen that way!

It could not happen that way!

Professor Robert Grant's *Historical Introduction to the New Testament*[1] explains our problems with chronology:

> While we have indicated that Luke regarded himself as a historian, we should bear in mind that his conception of history was to a considerable degree 'rhetorical.' *He felt free, as other ancient historians felt free*, to give an arrangement to his materials which was not necessarily chronological but brought out their meaning as he understood it. Thus in Luke 9:31-18:14 we have an account of a journey towards Jerusalem which the evangelist has used to provide an occasion for including materials of various sorts, mostly without precise indications of time or place.

We continue to ignore a much earlier warning of the dangers of attempting anything resembling a "timetable" approach to the *gospels*, particularly Jesus' trials. Scholars consider Papias, Bishop of Hierapolis (*Asia Minor* = present-day Turkey), a key bridge between the *gospel* writers and the Church fathers. His life probably overlapped *Matthew, Mark, Luke* and *John*, although no evidence exists that he knew them personally. Some of his writings suggest that he did know Jesus' disciple John (not the *gospel* writer), as well as the daughters of Phillip the Evangelist, one of the early Church Fathers in Jerusalem after Jesus' death (Acts 6:5; 8:26 – 40; 8:9).

An avid collector of oral traditions about Jesus, Papias gave us five volumes entitled *Interpretation of the Lord's Oracles* (125-150 A.D.), and sounded the alarm on *Mark* which we need to read carefully:[2]

> Mark became Peter's interpreter and wrote accurately all that he remembered, *not, indeed, in order*, of the things said or done by the Lord.

> For he had not heard the Lord, nor had he followed him, but later on, as I said, followed Peter, who used to give teaching as necessity demanded; but not making, as it were, an arrangement of the Lord's oracles; so that Mark did nothing wrong in thus writing down single points as he remembered them.

Chronology, as we know it, means the arrangement of past events in the order of their occurrence; but all four *gospel* writers handled it flippantly by our standards:

> At that time . . . .
> Matthew 14:1

> In those days . . . .
> Mark 8:1

> Now as he was teaching in one of their synagogues
> . . . .
> Luke 5:2

> While he was in one of the cities . . . .
> Luke 5:2

After this, he went to Capernaum . . . .
John 2:12

A first-sight reading of the *gospels* alerts us to many built-in confusions when we try to apply present-day chronology: *Matthew, Mark* and *Luke*, for example, place the eating of the "Passover meal" (Last Supper) on what we now call Thursday evening; but *John* puts it on Friday. *John's* "chronology" throughout differs entirely from the other three writers. Great bodies of literature try, unsuccessfully, to reconcile the conflicts; but to date, the exact time of the Last Supper remains up for grabs, some scholars even arguing plausibly for Tuesday or Wednesday instead of Thursday or Friday.[3]

Chronology Real Key to Understanding Jesus' Trials
These problems with the order of events do no harm *until we come to Jesus' trials*. Then, we commit serious errors of analysis by suddenly assuming that the gospel writers did intend to give us a "timetable" of events, something totally foreign to their theological goals, or to their approach to chronology in general.

Ancients' Concept of "Time"
The concept of "time" itself as the Jews and gospel writers knew it also wipes out anything akin to a "timetable" reading of the gospel accounts of Jesus' trials. *The Interpreter's Dictionary of the Bible* explains:[4]

> It has been observed again and again how closely the Hebrew conception of time is bound up with its content, or even identified with it.
>
> In order to underline the precedence of the time content as opposed to the chronological statement of time, it has often been pointed out that the Hebrew verb does not have any real tenses. Actions are determined primarily by the content-aspect of being completed or not being completed, not by the time categories of past, present, and future.
>
> The Old Testament possesses a conception of time

which is entirely unlike ours and therefore a completely different understanding of reality.

Individual events . . . are arranged not according to their position in chronological sequence, but according to the nature of their content, fixed by God or psychologically perceived.

Matters which are widely separated with reference to time can, if their content coincides, be identified and regarded as simultaneous. The linear scale of time is replaced by the rhythm of time with the incessant return of the same time content.[5]

Must Construct Our Own Order of Events

Since *Matthew* and *Luke* rely heavily on *Mark*, and *John* uses his own separate order of events, with *Luke* following the ancient historian's free license with "time and place," we must construct our own "timetable" of the separate events which scholars, theologians and preachers erroneously call the *"trial"* (singular) of Jesus.[6]

THE JEWISH SOURCES

A highly sophisticated, full-bodied Jewish legal system operated for centuries before Jesus' time; and it is absurd to say that it suddenly ceased to function for a single twelve-to- fifteen-hour period while "the Jews" railroaded Jesus.

The Torah

The *torah*[7] (Pentateuch),[8] the "Five Books of Moses — *Genesis, Exodus, Numbers, Leviticus* and *Deuteronomy* — held the Covenant Constitution Moses worked out with God at Mt. Sinai around 1250 B.C., as well as the great Law Codes which grew over a minimum of 1200 years before Jesus' trials.[9]

The *torah's* great Codes clearly spelled out the Law's "due process" mandates, all expressly reaffirmed in *Deuteronomy*,[10] the most beautiful law book ever written. It dated from at least the time of King Josiah (640-609 B.C.). Its statutes and court decisions set out the controlling precedents for both of Jesus' Jewish trials, the first in the Small Sanhedrin of the Temple Mount, the second before the Great Sanhedrin in the Hall of the Hewn Stone, inside the Temple proper.

The Talmud

The *talmud*[11] reports the Common Law of the Jews: Decided cases, history, parables, sermons, legends, customs and stories, in its 2-1/2 million words, divided into 63 separate volumes (tractates), with 524 chapters, classified in six major categories (orders) by Hillel the Elder, *before Jesus' time*.

Some writers say that we cannot be sure the detailed legal rules of substance and procedure described in the *talmud* operated during Jesus' lifetime, since our present written *talmud* dates from 180-200 A.D.

They do not understand how legal systems require centuries to evolve in painful slowness, always looking back for case precedents and guidance from experience, reluctant to make changes, especially on such basics as "due process."

I answer these arguments in detail in *Appendix 3*: A group of men did not sit around a table and concoct an abstract legal system, then make up thousands of decided cases to flesh it out decades *after* Jesus' death.

The entire posture of the *talmud* is one of nostalgia, of recapturing the times before the burning of the Temple around 68-70 A.D. The *talmud* describes Temple years and pre-Temple eras, the way things worked then, Temple practices and legal rules and procedures.

The Baritot and Midrashim[12]

Among other things, the *baritot* consist of thousands of decided cases, many cumulative rather than creative, which the editors of the *mishna* portion of the *talmud* did not include. We do not know how many of these cases came down from the courts before Jesus' time, but can safely assume from their content, quite a few.

The *midrashim* contain parables, legends, sermons, homely illustrations and pithy sayings which helped explain the Law and its ethical teachings to the people. These go back as far as Jewish memory, to the time of creation, and worked their way into every person's vocabulary and thinking processes, no doubt giving Jesus some of his most moving figures of speech. Much of this *[h]aggadah* (narration) literature helps interpret the *torah's* Covenant Constitution and the great Law Codes, the *halachah (halakah.)*

Josephus

Flavius Josephus,[13] born in 37 A.D., four to seven years after Jesus' crucifixion, lived to the year 100. The son of a priestly family in Jerusalem, he boasted "royal blood" through his mother, and joined the Pharisees at age nineteen.

Shortly after the great Jewish revolt against Rome in 66 A.D., Josephus became the commanding general of the Jewish forces in the Galilee. Debate continues over his exact mission; but two years later, he defected to the Romans. By 70 A.D., he sat as protege to Roman Emperor Vespasian and spent the rest of his life in Rome writing four priceless books, totaling over 1 million words:

> *The Wars of the Jews* (75-79 A.D.)
> *The Antiquities (Histories) of the Jews* (90-94)
> *Against Apion* (probably before 96)
> *Life of Flavius Josephus* (shortly before his death)

I find him one of the most brilliant writers of all time, every bit Shakespeare's equal in the soliloquy format, and in dramatizing legal, family and political confrontations.

Without Josephus, we would be considerably less informed on all phases of Jewish history from 400 B.C. to his death. The family of Herod fascinated him much like Abraham Lincoln captured Carl Sandburg's time and talents, which leaves us with far more biographical data on Herod than any other ruler during Rome's long history.

Old and New Testament scholars rely heavily upon Josephus to help them develop the real meaning of ambiguous passages, and give them their *sitz im leben* ("life setting").

ON TO OUR RECONSTRUCTIONS

We can now be off and running with our reconstructions, *to search out only the legal events, avoiding completely anything theological, staying away from all matters of "faith" or probes into "why" Jesus lived, and the nature of his "mission."*

We start with the Jewish Temple-State.

Jesus' preaching ministry covered most of Palestine, including the Decapolis, parts of Syria, and finally Jerusalem where he met his death by crucifixion after a summary trial before Roman Governor Pontius Pilate.

PART 1

THE JEWISH TEMPLE-STATE

And ye shall be unto me
a kingdom of priests,
and an holy nation . . . .
Exodus 19:6

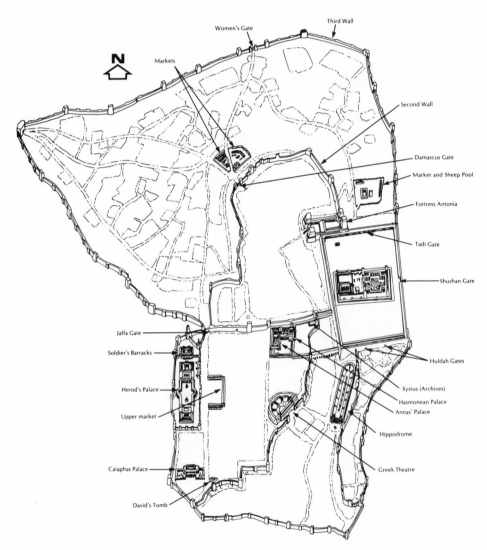

Jerusalem's principal structures at the time of Jesus' trials. The imprint of Herod the Great gave the city its character, and lasted until the destruction of the Temple in 70 A.D., and its final plowing under in 135 A.D.

Chapter 1

YOM KIPPUR: DAY OF ATONEMENT

Our best feel for the Temple-state will come from attending the all-day *Yom Kippur* (Day of Atonement) celebrations in the Temple around 29 A.D., along with Joshua bar Joseph (Jesus) and his close associates, the *talmud's* 480-page tractate *Yoma* serving as our chief guide.[1] Other *talmud* tractates also contain details of *Yom Kippur's* rituals.

All the Temple sounds could be heard as far away as Jericho, especially the "sound of the 'shovel' (*magrepah*)...the singing of the Levites..." and "...the clashing of the cymbals."[2] Only abject poverty, serious illness or personal catastrophe prevented male adults (those twenty and above) from celebrating this most sacred of all the Festivals in the Temple at Jerusalem.[3] Joshua bar Joseph would be there, unless some compelling reason held him back in the Galilee.[4]

Torah required every man's presence in Jerusalem!

Josephus estimates the crowds at three million[5]; but even if he exaggerates (as many scholars claim), one-tenth that number produced a press of bodies difficult to control.

The "shovel" played a key role,[6] helping the rulers of the Temple move along the tedious, exhausting rituals. From its perch in front of the Temple's Porch, it overlooked the Court of the Priests, the Great Altar, the Slaughter House for the sacrificial animals, and out to Nicanor's Gate separating the Court of the Israelites from the Court of the Women. This bellows-operated air pipe with ten holes, each one emitting ten different sounds, permitting 100 separate combinations, directed the hundreds of thousands massed within the Temple Promenade (*hel*),[7] on the Temple Mount,[8] inside the walled city,[9] as well as those camped upon the surrounding hillsides: "People could not hear one another speak in Jerusalem from the noise of the 'shovel'."[10]

The "shovel" served three purposes: "When a priest heard the sound of it, he knew that his brother priests were going in to prostrate themselves; and he would run to join them. When a Levite heard the noise of it, he knew that his brother Levites were going into chant; and he would run to join them. And the head of the priests on duty used to make the lepers stand in the East Gate, awaiting the sprinkling of the blood."[10]

Joseph Caiaphas[11] presided as High Priest, holding that office from 18 A.D. to 37 A.D. I see him short, obese, haughty, of limited intellect, and a dupe of the Committee of Ten.

He cringed at the next deafening blast from the "shovel," his deep sighs of submission coming almost as sobs between his labored pantings. Jonathan ben Annas,[12] Captain of the Temple (*sagan*) and Caiaphas' brother-in-law, with two special assistants, helped him reach a prostrate position atop his bloated belly just north of the Altar, his head facing the Sanctuary.[13]

Although the worshipers could not hear it, all presumed that Caiaphas pronounced "The Ineffable Name." In turn, they roared out their response: "Blessed be the Name; the glory of His kingdom is for ever and ever."[14]

In truth, for several centuries, the High Priests and Temple Bureaucrats assumed a monopoly over the *pronunciation* of the Divine Name as part of their rote to keep total control over Judaism, lock, stock and prayer.

Everyone presumed the correct pronunciation to be something like *Yah-Weh* or *Ye-HO-vah* ("He who will always be"), which came from the tetragrammaton (*Greek* = "four letters") of the four consonants, variously written JHVH, IHVH, KHWH, YHVH and YHWH (written Hebrew vowels did not appear until the Seventh Century A.D.), But the Temple Bureaucrats used God's name as a naked power play: "Those who 'know the name of God' (Psalm 9:10, 9:11, 91:14) know His identity and personal character and therefore, in contrast to the heathen (Psalm 79:6; Jeremiah 10:25), trust and hope in Him."[15]

The Bureaucrats taught that if the people could not pronounce God's name correctly, they could not reach Him directly. Of necessity, they must go through the High Priest and his Bureaucratic lackeys who forced themselves as mediators and agents, interveners and negotiators, manipulating the Name of God into a fraternity password which they alone controlled.

Bar Joseph and his Galilean followers joined Caiaphas and the other worshipers in a prone position on the marble floor in the Court of the Israelites.

Caiaphas rocked back and forth in his white linens: Drawers, tunic, mitre and girdle, carefully described by God to Moses in the Book of *Exodus*, elaborated in the centuries that followed, and now preserved in the *talmud*.[16]

For "the Day,"[17] all ritual garments of the whitest linen symbolized the search for purification, the regular vestments[18] of golden thread and rich embroidery temporarily put aside.

The prostrate worshipers, at least those who knew the ritual at all, presumed that Caiaphas next began the first of endless confessions: "May it be Thy will that I sin no more, and what I have sinned wipe away in They mercy, but not through suffering . . . ."[19]

The continuing, compelling theme of repentance rang out so that each man as a person, and the group as a Nation, could be restored whole before God, who forgave man's sins through His Goodness and Mercy. Repentance figured in God's plan even before He made the earth: "Seven things were created before the world was created, and these are they: The *torah*, repentance, the Garden of Eden (Paradise), Gehenna (Hell), the Throne of God, the (Heavenly) Temple, and the name of the Messiah . . . ."[20]

Each time the congregation dropped to the Temple's floor, it produced "one of the ten miracles which were wrought in the Temple," that ". . . though the people stood closely pressed together, they still found wide spaces between them to prostrate themselves."[21]

Jonathan ben Annas and his aides raised Caiaphas to his feet, pointing him in the direction of the Slaughter House, as the chorus of Levites,[22] standing on the steps below Nicanor's Gate,[23] began their haunting wail of *Psalm 51*:

> Have mercy on me, O God, according to Thy steadfast love; according to Thy abundant mercy, blot out my transgressions.

> Wash me thoroughly from my iniquity, and cleanse me from my sin!

The chant became a soul-deep dirge, all nuances of tenor and bass urged heavenward by the orchestra of forty-four separate kinds of instruments:[24] Harps and lutes, violins and guitars, zithers and lyres, reed horns and woodwinds, square drums and round drums, shaking bells and rattling clappers:

> For I know my transgression, and my sin is ever before me.

> Against Thee, Thee only, have I sinned, and done that which is evil in Thy sight . . . .

The director of the chorus and the orchestra leader temporarily suspended their Bureaucratic rivalries, their selfish dissensions converted into a temporary goal of majestic perfection:

> Purge me with hyssop, and I shall be clean; wash me, and I shall be whiter than snow.

Both music directors, caught in the heavenly swell of their powerful anthems, also submerged their secret bickerings against the Committee of Ten who denied them uniforms of a rank equal to the priests:[25]

> Create in me a clean heart, O God, and put a new and right spirit within me.

Caiaphas completed the second of his five total immersions[26] in the golden lavers[27] west of the Great Altar, and the next of his ten sanctifications;[28] but his pantings now came so fast his aides feared he might not last out the entire day. They quickly dressed his shivering body, partially shielded from the curious eyes of the worshipers by a translucent linen sheet, so that all witnesses could testify that nothing "unclean" interposed itself between his bare skin and the new, white garments of the nation's sanctification.[29]

Caiaphas' deep sigh, almost a groan, melted into the other noises as he accepted the knife from Jonathan's hand, preparing for the kill of the first bullock, his second confession already made, or was it the third? He assumed that Jonathan would keep everything in proper ritual order; otherwise, the Pharisees[30] would force him to start anew: "Concerning every ministration of the Day of Atonement, if one service was done out of order before another one, it is as if it had not been done at all."[31]

At best, the killing of the animal always became a tricky maneuver;[32] and two Pharisees monitored his every move with zeal, making certain that he ". . . lay his two hands between him and the sacrifice."[33] They also checked to see "if he stood upon any vessel, or upon his fellow's foot,"[34] since any "interposing between the floor of the Sanctuary and the priest" would invalidate the entire Day of Atonement service.[35]

Caiaphas looked to his brother-in-law who returned a hopeful nod, the other attendants set with their golden bowls poised and ready. Caiaphas' sigh this time came out a shout; but with surprising deftness, he pulled the razor-sharp blade across the bullock's throat, his one stroke severing gullet, windpipe and carotid artery, so that the "life-blood"[36] gushed out: "The blood coming forth in a jet, with which life leaves the body of the animal."[37] For generations, the sages taught that "only the life-blood sanctifieth." The attendants played a key role in the ritual: Catch the blood in the bowls and prevent even the slightest spurt from staining Caiaphas' white garments, which would produce a defilement.[38]

Even so, before he climbed the steep *ramp*[39] to the top of the Altar, Jonathan and the attending priests stripped off Caiaphas' clothing to the skin, immersed him once more in the golden laver, and redressed him in fresh, snowy-white garments.[40] The immersions alone sapped his strength, to say nothing of the additional stoopings and bendings of the ten washings of his feet and hands.[41]

Before it began, he came to "the Day" in a state of near collapse from his ordeal of preparation which started seven days earlier.[42]

They confined him in the Cell of the Counsellors,[43] on the second floor overlooking the Temple Mount proper, to make him "Levitically clean" for the Day of Atonement, one goal to separate him from his wife: "His wife might become menstruant during intercourse . . . . He as one having congress with the menstruant would be Levitically impure for seven days, thus prevented from officiating on the Day of Atonement."[44]

Accidental contact with a corpse,[45] or with the spittle of a Levitically ignorant person,[46] could also create defilement, and keep him from functioning on the Day of Atonement.

They kept his diet tasteless and simple "in order to produce speedy elimination."[47] He could not eat or drink white wine, citron, fat meat, purslane, eggs or garden-rocket, since these might produce sexual excitement and cause a "pollution" (nocturnal emission; "wet dream").[48]

The "Elders of the Priesthood" read to Caiaphas during his seven-day retreat, drilling him in the Day of Atonement rituals prescribed by the Pharisees, after extracting an oath from him " . . . . that you do not change anything of what we've said to you."[49]

They also segregated Caiaphas' deputy (*sagan*), Jonathan ben Annas, in a separate cell, to make him ready to take over on "the Day," should Caiaphas become defiled.[50] If Jonathan could read the scriptures himself, he did not need readers; but both he and Caiaphas must be kept awake all night long to avoid the risk of a "pollution":[51] "If he sought to slumber, young priests would snap their middle finger before him and say: Sir High Priest, arise and drive the sleep away this one time on the pavement . . . . Show us the *kidah* (pressing both big toes against the floor, bowing and kissing the pavement, and rising without moving the feet - this difficult performance was called the *kidah* - the bowing to the ground.)"

The Temple ceremonies dragged on, and Caiaphas, aided by Jonathan and eight lesser priests, struggled up the *ramp,*[52] an inclined plane 48 feet long by 24 feet wide, to reach the "circuit" around the Great Altar of Burnt Offering. It stood fifteen feet above the ground,[53] its top measuring forty-eight feet square,[54] the priests' targets the four-and-one-half foot horns"[55] on the corners of the Altar, each one a straight, square, hollow prominence. They would sprinkle it with blood from the bowls. All told, Caiaphas would make forty-three separate sprinklings of blood.[56]

Looking out through the blue smoke arising from the burning flesh mingled with incense, Caiaphas and Jonathan could see Joshua bar Joseph standing in the Court of the Israelites in a cluster of two dozen other Galileans, all dressed in superb, white linen, a trade mark of the Galilee.[57] Seeing Joshua bar Joseph perhaps reminded them of Samuel's description of Saul, Israel's first king: "And when he stood among the people, he was taller than any from the shoulders upward. And Samuel said to all the people, 'Do you see him whom the Lord has chosen? There is none like him among all the people.' And all the people shouted, 'Long live the king'!"[58]

Caiaphas next prepared for his first entry into the Holy of Holies to make the incense offering,[59] this privilege his alone of all Israel, and this only on this one Day.[60]

The Temple Bureaucrats' passion for "ritual purity" evolved ten "degrees of Holiness" (Circles of Holiness), each one progressively more exclusive than the other:[61]

(1)   The land of Israel (*erez Israel*);
(2)   The City of Jerusalem;
(3)   The Temple Mount;
(4)   The *hel* (promenade around the Temple area proper, with its latticework wall (*soreg*), beyond which no Gentile could go without evoking the death penalty);
(5)   The Court of the Women;
(6)   The Court of the Israelites;
(7)   The Court of the Priests;
(8)   The area between the Porch and the Altar;
(9)   The Sanctuary; and finally
(10) The Holy of Holies.

Everything coned down to this Holy of Holies (*debir*) inside the Sanctuary proper; ".... unapproachable, inviolable, invisible to all,"[62] the sacred receptacle of the Ark of the Covenant which, at one time contained the Law Tablets that God gave Moses at Mt. Sinai. The Ark and the Tablets long ago disappeared, some said when the Babylonians burned the First Temple; others, that the Ark of the Covenant came empty when David brought it to Jerusalem,[63] even before Solomon built the people their First Temple.

The Pharisee monitors dared not let Sadducee Caiaphas out of their sight until he actually disappeared behind the sacred veil guarding the Holy of Holies. They forced him to an oath to follow their Pharisee ritual, but did not trust him: The Sadducees held firmly to their literal interpretation of ".... the cloud of incense may cover the mercy seat," saying this meant that the incense must be lit *outside* the Holy of Holies, so that the smoke could rise up as the High Priest entered.[64] Against this argument, the Pharisees ruled that the incense must be lit only *after* the High Priest entered the Holy of Holies and stood before the mercy seat. The Pharisees' popular support among the common people forced the Sadducean Bureaucrats to follow their Pharisee rituals throughout the entire service.

His aides exhorted Caiaphas to make his prayer inside short, ".... So as not to frighten Israel": One High Priest once prolonged his stay inside the Holy of Holies, terrifying "all Israel" who feared he could not obtain forgiveness for their sins, or that he suffered some personal mishap, their ancient protocols not flexible enough to provide for saving the nation from such an awesome emergency.[65]

Caiaphas swayed on the verge of physical collapse as the limitless prostrations, immersions, washings and sprinklings continued. All told, he must kill fifteen sacrificial animals (bullocks, rams, and goats),[66] and be ritually perfect in each Act, else they would need to start all over again.

Throughout "the Day," the chorus of Levites sang and chanted, the orchestra supporting them and playing separately, the "shovel" shaking the heavens and earth with its blasts; and through it all, Joshua bar Joseph and his fellow Galileans participated with Phariasaic correctness.

Not many penitents made efforts to remember the number of times they fell to the marble pavement, knowing only that the ear-rending blast from the "shovel" preceded the scramble to reach the prone position; and each knew that when the music of the Levites came up to a deafening pitch, the High Priest pronounced "The Ineffable Name." They did not question the right of the priests to make certain that the worshipers could not hear it, and so maintain the password to God for their own private use.

Reaching the scapegoat part of the ceremony,[67] the congregation struggled to its feet, a sort of mass lurch of one against another.

Caiaphas watched Jonathan draw lots over two identical he-goats, one to be selected "for the Lord," the other "for Azazel."[68] Caiaphas placed both hands upon the head of the "sin" goat,[69] chanted the "confession," tied the crimson thread of wool between its horns;[70] and again the Temple "miracle" took place:[71] Although at least 100,000 people stood compacted together, each could prostrate himself when ". . . the fully-pronounced Name came forth from the mouth of the High Priest."

Caiaphas next tied another crimson thread to the door of the Hall leading inside the Temple,[72] delivering the sin-laden "goat for Azazel" to a priest who led it out through the eastern (Shushan) Gate, across the arched bridge which spanned the Kidron Valley, on to the Mount of Olives, through Gethsemane, and then along the twelve-mile path in the rugged mountains toward Jericho. There Priests would push the goat over a cliff, bearing the sins of Israel on its back.[73]

The Levite chorus sang again from the depths of Israel's soul:[74]

> Then I will teach transgressors Thy ways, and sinners will return to thee.

Relay stations three-quarters of a mile apart next picked up the signal of waving towels: The "goat for Azazel" lay dead at the bottom of the cliff![75] Caiaphas and Jonathan carefully inspected the crimson thread tied to the door in the Hall of the Temple, to see another miracle happen: The crimson thread atop the door turned "white."[76]

Israel stood purified before the Lord!

They moved back to the Slaughter House where Caiaphas skillfully cut the throat of the he-goat "for the Lord"[77]; more sprinklings followed.[78] Caiaphas, once more and alone, entered the Holy of Holies with the goat's blood mixed ritually with the blood from the bullock, "all Israel" prostrating themselves again until he backed out unscathed.[79]

Priests carried severed limbs, entrails, organs, sides and tails of the sacrificial animals up the *ramp* to the main Altar for the burning.[80] All told, 500 priests worked the ceremonies.[81]

Through it all, Joshua bar Joseph and his company of Galileans continued their letter-perfect partakings, no one able to find the slightest fault in his performance.

Caiaphas reeled from hunger: The perpetual statute "afflict yourselves"[82] meant abstention: "On the Day of Atonement, it is forbidden to eat, to drink, to wash, to anoint oneself, to put on sandals, or to have marital intercourse,"[83] the rationale for the fasting that ".... he might be purged of all food and drink in his bowels so as to make him equal to the ministering angels."[84] For gluttonous Caiaphas, giving up food and drink for even a few hours equaled the torture of death itself.

They neared the end of the tedious regimen. Caiaphas, coming out of his last immersion, now wore his regular golden vestments,[85] to offer up the sacrifice of his own ram, the ram of the people, and the seven unblemished one-year-old lambs.[86]

As the priests accompanied the exhausted Caiaphas up the *ramp* for the final sprinklings about the horns of the Altar, they saw a near riot break out to the west of the Slaughter House, in the Priests' Court in front of the Porch: The priest who offered the sacrificial animal could claim its hide which he sold as his own.[87] For as long as anyone could remember, the claim to the hides took place in the Parwah Chamber;[88] but about the time of Annas' High Priesthood,[89] the priests of the lower castes (course) quit paying the traditional graft for the hides to Annas and the Committee of Ten.[90] This meant that the chief priests' agents (the Temple Police) must seize the hides in the Court of the Israelites, before the officiating priests could rush them to the safety of the Parwah Chamber, where they protected them through a

Bureaucratic fiction called "dedicating them to the Temple."[91] If the Police could not lay hands on the hides in the Priests' Court, Annas and his Committee of Ten could not collect their graft. Fights for the hides broke out often.

The Bureaucrats next pointed Caiaphas toward Nicanor's Gate, to let him end the services with the Eight Beatitudes: "Blessed be the glory of the Lord from the place of His abode . . . ."[92]

His voice and heavy breathing slurred into the chorus of the Levites, as they responded: "Let the words of my mouth and the meditation of my heart be acceptable in Thy sight, O Lord my rock and my redeemer."[93]

Jonathan shouted his final promptings to Caiaphas, whose barely audible voice mumbled: "Blessed be the Lord who day by day bears our burden. He is the God of our salvation, the Lord of hosts be with us . . . ."[94]

The Levites answered in song and music, the worshipers with their "Blessed be the Name; the glory of His kingdom is for ever and ever!"[95]

Mercifully, for the weary Caiaphas, it ended!

The Temple Bureaucrats began their slow, barefooted procession back to Caiaphas' house for the post-Temple feast:[96] Out from the Court of the Gentiles through the western gate, toward the upper City;[97] across the arched bridge that crossed the Tyropoeon ("Cheese Makers") Valley; above the marble court of the Xystus which surrounded the Archives Building; in front of the Hasmonean Palace which Herod's sons used as their guest house on their visits to the Holy City; past the lavish palace which old Annas built for himself immediately after buying the High Priesthood in 6 A.D.; before Herod's ornate Palace where Pontius Pilate and his soldiers stayed when they came down from Caesarea to Jerusalem to police the Pilgrimage Festivals. Several of its great rooms could sleep as many as 100 men at a single time.[98]

Finally, the Bureaucrats reached Caiaphas' own luxurious Palace,[99] the promise of food and drink drawing them on.

Joshua bar Joseph — later to be called Jesus — would cover much of this same route after his *third* arrest, in the Garden of Gethsemane some months, perhaps years, later.

Chapter 2

THE TEMPLE:
BUREAUCRACY'S POWER SEAT

Annas and his fellow members of the Committee of Ten knew that their hold on the nation rested on a blend of raw, secular power, coupled with the spiritual zeal of the people for the Temple rituals, everything and every second in the life of the orthodox Jew sacred, nothing secular, "Temple" fused into their genes ever since David conquered Jerusalem a thousand years earlier.

They really did not need this *Second* Temple where Joshua bar Joseph came to worship. Their forefathers erred in building it, and it evolved as a millstone around their individual and national necks, stifling Judaism's spiritual flowering, finally causing the demise of the Jewish nation.

Why?

How?

Who let it happen?

In hindsight, did their forefathers misunderstand God's will?

In 586 B.C., the Babylonians trampled them in battle for the third and final time, burning King Solomon's magnificent *First* Temple[1] (Solomon = 972-931 B.C.), carrying away the leading citizens and all the priests of the Kingdom of Judah.[2] They could not know in advance that this tragedy would become the maturing stage for Judaism, and develop the base for our Judeo-Anglo-American Common Law system.

A great anonymous poet marched with the crushed survivors into their Babylonian Exile, and wrote what became *Psalm 137*, one of the most poignant works of all time:[3]

By the rivers of Babylon, there we sat down, yea, we wept, when we remembered Zion.

We hanged our harps up on the willows in the midst thereof.

For there they that carried us away captive required of us a song; and they that wasted us required of us mirth, saying, Sing us one of the songs of Zion.

How shall we sing the Lord's song in a strange land?

Their doom appeared sealed, their brethren in the Northern Kingdom of Israel long gone when the Assyrians captured Samaria in 721 B.C.:[4] To Assyria went the "Ten Lost Tribes,"[5] scattered and absorbed by the Pagans into total extinction.

The possibility that Judaism could survive in this "strange land" of Babylon appeared so remote that the Babylonians became careless. The captors could not know the Jews' national yearnings, as deep-seated as the genes on their red blood cells:

If I forget thee O'Jerusalem, let my right hand forget her cunning.

If I do not remember thee, let my tongue cleave to the roof of my mouth; if I prefer not Jerusalem above my chief joy.[6]

The Babylonians let the Jews live together and worship their strange God who could pose no threat:[7] Invisible, not requiring a physical icon of rocks or stones, wooden or graven images, carved animals or erotic statuettes, sun or planet, fetish or puppet, mannequin or model.

So the Jews learned to "sing the Lord's song in a strange land"; but they also remembered Zion.[8]

They worshiped their "strange" God in what the Prophet Ezekiel called "the little sanctuary,"[9] the beginning of the synagogue; and though not a single word survives to describe the physical appearance of these first synagogues, the deep spiritual format of its service[10] honed Judaism itself. Since the people knew that their God would never permit them to escape their Exile until they made themselves whole in Him, salvation through repentance and atonement became the compelling goal of every soul among them: They must be restored "in Him," as persons and as a nation.

With Solomon's great Temple gone, animal sacrifices could be no more; so they made the greatest substitution in all history: *Prayer for animal sacrifice!*[11] This "a*vodah* (service) of the heart"[12] began the great evolution of group worship, as no other people ever used it,[13] combining song and dance, praise and petition, lecture and responsive readings, rhythm and symbolism. Liturgy took form, every combination designed to help man reach his God, to lift him up, to strengthen him, to control and fulfill him.[14]

So on each Sabbath, the Jews in the disgrace of their demeaning Captivity,[15] met in their "little sanctuaries" to praise God and hasten their freedom, their return to Jerusalem they knew would come as soon as they purified themselves.

The synagogue evolved; the Sabbath matured.

And it worked!

Cyrus I[16] and his Persians crushed the Babylonians; and in 538 B.C., he told the Jews that those who wished it could go home.[17] Many did, although great throngs of the most prosperous remained in Babylon.[18]

All during the long Exile, urged on by the prophet Ezekiel, they "remembered Zion" as they knew it before their forced departure. They thought "Temple," the heart of their nation, the center of their national dreams; so they built the "Second" Temple, finished around 515 B.C., even though they could not afford it.

They could not guess that the synagogues would grow in this restored Israel, nor could they foresee the rise of the Bureaucratic cult of the Temple-State that would all but destroy the true essence of Israel's God, with His master creations of Time, Goodness and the Law.

In less than two centuries, the Temple debased itself into the seat of political power: Rigid, heartless and exclusive, the High Priest possessing almost unrestrained control:[19] Only the independent judges remained to call him to account for his most flagrant abuses of God's Law.

During Joshua bar Joseph's lifetime, the Committee of Ten outwardly ruled the country; but the nation of Abraham, Isaac and Jacob became the private fiefdom of the four great families: *Annas, Boethus, Phiabi* and *Kamithos*.[20]

German scholar Joachim Jeremias describes them in detail:[21]

> These families, so suddenly raised to the nobility, who came partly from abroad, partly from the provinces, quickly formed a new and powerful, if illegitimate, hierarchy.
>
> There were essentially four families in this hierarchy, each of which strove to keep the highest priestly office to itself for as long as possible. Of the twenty-five illegitimate high priests of the Herodian-Roman epoch no fewer than twenty-two belonged to these four families: eight from the family of Boethus, eight of Hannas, three of Phiabi and three of Kamith. It can be assumed that the three remaining high priests had some connection with these families.
>
> Originally the most powerful of the four families was that of Boethus. This family came from Alexandria. Its first representative was the high priest Simon, the father-in-law of Herod. This family managed in time to come to produce seven further members for the high priesthood, and its powerful influence can be seen, too, in the name 'Boethuseans' by which a section of the Sadducees, and probably even the whole party, was known.
>
> In the following period, the family of Boethus was overtaken by the house of the high priest Annas whose five sons, along with his son-in-law Caiaphas and his grandson Matthias (AD 65), held the premier rank.
>
> The house of Kamithos, like that of Phiabi, provided

three high priests according to Josephus; but the legendary account of the Talmud says seven, who were said to have been brothers, of whom at least one, and possibly two, must have held office as deputy for his brother who was prevented from officiating by ceremonial defilement.

The four families bought, sold and traded the High Priesthood more or less at will, the successful bidders sometimes so ignorant of Jewish history that they could not even read the Holy Scriptures with understanding. They knew practically nothing of Judaism's immense past, or its hopeful future to become the Redeemed of God.

This corruption of the High Priestly office[22] appalled the orthodox Jew, educated in the traditions of basic Judaism. It no longer operated as God ordained it: "Wherefore it is also a tradition that none should hold God's high priesthood save him who is of Aaron's blood, even if he happened to be a king . . ."[23]

Many, particularly the Pharisees and Essenes, claimed that the tenure of Israel's last legitimate High Priest ended in 174 B.C., when Greek (Selucid) King Antiochus IV sold the office to Jason, not of Aaron's family;[24] Jason soon lost it to Menelaus, who outbid him by three hundred talents.[25] The Hasmoneans (Jewish freedom fighters who overthrew the Greeks) toyed with the High Priesthood until they eventually merged it into the kingship (104-103 B.C.),[26] Herod and his son, Archelaus, manipulated it for their own political and financial fortunes; and when the Romans assumed direct rule of Judea and Samaria in 6 A.D., they held the High Priest liable for the only two items that interested them: (1) public order, and (2) taxes,[27] In short, the High Priest became the political dictator of the Jews, answerable to Rome through its on-site military governor, the *praefectus* (*procurator*).

But Rome never understood the Jews' Law and the Covenant Constitution, or the spiritual values which produced their legal procedures.

The political theft of the highest religious office continually galled the people: If the appointing "Gentile"[28] king or Roman agent ever heard of "Aaron's line," he completely ignored it.

The *talmud* and *Josephus* give us the names and reigns of the

High Priests from Herod's time to Joshua bar Joseph's trials: Fourteen different members of the four great Hellenized families[29] bullied their way in and out of the office:[30]

High Priest:	Appointed By:	Dates in Office:
Ananel	Herod the Great	37-36 B.C.
Aristobulus III (Mariamne's 17-year-old brother)	Herod the Great	35 B.C.
Ananel (second term)	Herod the Great	34 B.C.
Jesus, son of Phiabi (Phabes)	Herod the Great	c. 34-22 B.C.
Simon, son of Boethus (Boethos)	Herod the Great	c. 22-5 B.C.
Mattaiah, son of Theophilus (Matthias) (Theophilos)	Herod the Great	5 B.C.-12 March, 4 B.C.
Joseph, son of Elam	Herod the Great	5 B.C.
Joezer, son of Boethus (Joazar) (Boethos)	Herod the Great	4 B.C.
Eleazar, son of Boethus (Boethos)	Archelaus (Herod's son who ruled as *ethnarch*)	from 4 B.C.
Jesus, son of See (Sie)	Archelaus	until 6 A.D.
Annas (Ananos)	Quirinius (Roman governor of Syria)	A.D. 6-15

Ishmael, son of Phiabi I (Phabi)	Valerius Gratus (Roman procurator of Judea)	c. A.D. 15-16
Eleazar, son of Annas (Ananos)	Valerius Gratus	c. A.D. 16-17
Simon, son of Kamithos (Camithos)	Valerius Gratus	A.D. 17-18
Joseph Caiaphas	Valerius Gratus (confirmed by Praefectus Pontius Pilate, 26-36 A.D.)	c. A.D. 18-37

The profits of the great families became enormous, since they apportioned the nation's economy among themselves: Monopolies in incense,[31] songs and the art of writing.[32] The ceremonial operations of the Temple produced uncounted by-products: The blood from the animal sacrifices, sold to the gardeners for manure, brought in substantial sums,[33] especially during the three great Pilgrimage Festivals of Passover (*pesah*), Pentecost (*shavuot*) and Tabernacles (*sukkot*), when "it is praiseworthy for the sons of Aaron [the priests] to walk in blood up to their ankles."[34]

The powerful families made cartel contracts with favored sections of the country for wine, oil, wood and wheat,[35] all with kickbacks to the Committee of Ten.

Any Bureaucracy quickly moves to the "Buddy System": If the non-Bureaucrat "outsider" develops a "buddy" at the power seat, he gains lucrative contracts for goods and services. In practical effect, the "buddy" almost confers a "we-insider" status on the "outsider" merchant or purveyor of services; but not quite, since the "outsider" remains in grace only as long as his "buddy" carries clout within the tightly closed circle.

Capernaum and Chorazin,[36] on the Sea of Galilee, admittedly grew the finest wheat in all the land; but Annas and his Temple

32

confederates awarded the Temple contracts to their favorites around Jerusalem for Judean wheat.

Operating skillfully through Bureaucracy's machinery, Annas and the great families controlled every facet of the nation's economy:[37] Nails, flax (linen), sandals, asphalt, weaving, tailoring, tanneries, candles, bronze and iron works, potteries, butchers, spice making, baking, winemaking, ointments, jewelry, all the building trades for new construction and for maintenance, the practice of medicine, the barbers.

Not a single product escaped their ruthless greed!

From time to time, "outsider" rebels challenged them, many before Joshua bar Joseph; but they responded with the usual Bureaucratic put-down: They discredited the "outsider's" work product, vaguely and without specifics, by branding it "not innovative" or "poor quality."

The small tradesman and artisan, craftsman and shopkeeper, independent farmer or sharecropper, lived helpless against the iron rule of the Bureaucrats, particularly when they ran up against "the Bazaars of the sons of Annas":[38] Stores set up on the Mount of Olives and the Temple Mount itself, ". . . . for the supply of pigeons and other commodities required for the sacrifices, and owned by the powerful priestly family, to whom they proved a source of wealth."[39]

All the common people suffered, but not entirely in silence: They sang a derisive sort of folk ballad dramatizing their plight at the hands of the hovering Bureaucracy:[40]

> Woe is me because of the house of Boethus;
>   woe is me because of their staves!
> Woe is me because of the house of Hanin (Annas);
>   woe is me because of their whisperings!
> Woe is me because of the House of Kathros (Kamithos);
>   woe is me because of their pens!
> Woe is me because of Ishmael, the son of Phabi (Phiabi);
>   woe is me because of their fists!
> For the High Priests, and their sons are Temple treasurers;

> And their sons-in-law are trustees; and their
> servants beat the people with staves!

The sad but accurate parody told of a people enslaved by their Bureaucratic rulers, who beat them physically, slandered them without cause, and held secret cabals to devise ever more oppressive ways of continued control.

No one knew exactly how many people lived directly "on-Temple"; but realistic estimators can account for 18,000 priests and Levites;[41] their wives, children and other dependents added another 30,000 or 40,000 to the clergy's roles:[42] At least one-tenth of the nation's 500,000 to 600,000[43] people moved under Annas' personal command, almost all of Jerusalem's non-festival population of 25,000.[44]

Annas and the Committee of Ten also ran the country's welfare programs,[45] and the public building projects, many sequels to Herod's building ambitions of fifty years earlier.[46]

Jerusalem lived primarily on its tourism forced upon the 5,000,000 Jews dispersed throughout the Roman Empire (one in ten Jewish): The "second tithe" must be spent in the Holy City, all male Jews (Joshua bar Joseph most certainly included) obligated to come to Jerusalem for the Pilgrimage Festivals[47] each year. It all gave Annas a domineering hand over every innkeeper, shopkeeper and merchant in the area.[48]

Judaism survived the Bureaucrats' corruptions only because of the synagogues and their schools for *torah* and *talmud*. At the time of Joshua bar Joseph's trials, 394 synagogues[49] flourished in Jerusalem alone. God inflicted the Babylonian Captivity on their ancestors to let the synagogue develop, and preserve His Goodness and Law, and with it, the Covenant Constitution.

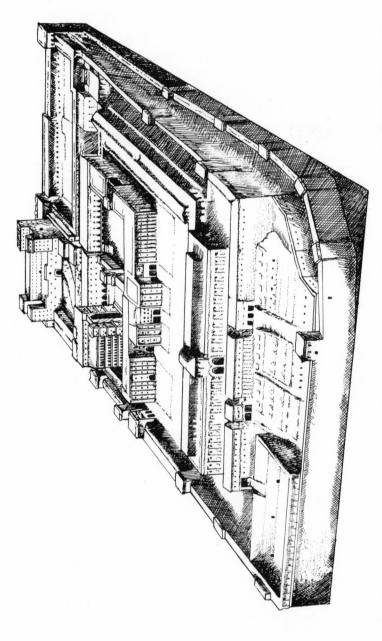

Herod's Temple in Jerusalem, perhaps the most imposing religious complex of all time (viewed from above). The fortress Antonia, another of Herod's massive building projects, dominates it and all of Jerusalem. Jesus' Roman trial before Pilate for sedition took place inside the Antonia.

Chapter 3

THE TEMPLE
AND TEMPLE MOUNT

The Committee of Ten ran the nation from the *Second Temple*, really the "Third",[1] above all else, Herod's Temple! The *talmud* leaves no doubt of the pride the Jews took in it: "He who has not seen the Temple in its full construction has never seen a glorious building in his life."[2]

The editors of the books of *Kings*[3] and *Chronicles*[4] describe the elaborate details of the building of the "First" Temple, King Solomon's Temple: Its workmen, physical dimensions, lavish furnishings and golden treasures. It became the nation's heart until the Babylonians burned it to the ground in 586 B.C.,[5] after Israel forgot her Jehovah and went whoring with the gods of the neighboring nations.[6]

We learn of the real "Second" Temple from both the *talmud* and *Josephus*, an all too abbreviated, primitive copy of the First,"[7] built by the impoverished Exiles after their return to Jerusalem from the Babylonian Captivity in 538 B.C. Without resources to duplicate Solomon's plush details, this "Second" Temple embarrassed[8] them constantly, until Herod enlarged it into one of the great architectural feats of all time, even though he made it more a testament to Herod than to God: "He got ready a thousand wagons, that were to bring the stones for the building and chose out ten thousand of the most skillful workmen, and brought a thousand sacerdotal garments for the priests, and had some of them taught the arts of stonecutters, and others of carpenters, and then began to build."[9]

As a first step, he created a massive artificial base, which they called the Temple Mount, lifting everything Heavenward, silhouetting all against the dazzling blue of the Judean sky: "He also built a wall below (the present "Western Wall"; "Wailing Wall"), beginning at the bottom which was encompassed by a deep valley."[10]

The earthen fill atop the immense stone foundations created a plateau which Herod paved with white marble.[11] Trapezium-shaped, the north side of the Temple Mount ran 1,020 feet; the east side, 1,530 feet; the south, 910 feet; and the west 1,578 feet (more than five American football fields).[12]

Blocks of matched limestone, some weighing up to 100 tons, enclosed the Temple Mount. Skillfully laid by master masons, the south wall and its footings towered 450 feet (45 floors) above the southward sloping Lower City.[13]

Five gates[14] through the walls led from outside the Temple Mount into the Court of the Gentiles: The double Hulda Gate[15] served the priests who lived in the Ophel, the suburb at the southeast corner of the Temple Mount.[16] They passed through its vaulted archway and forty-five-foot-square vestibule, to enter a subterranean double tunnel two hundred feet long.[17] This led to a flight of stairs opening into the Court of the Gentiles close to where the priests could enter the Temple proper to perform at the daily sacrifices.[18]

Four walls[19] encased the Temple Mount, each lined on the inside by porticoes and cloisters, their roofs supported by hundreds of marble columns,[20] for the most part Corinthian pillars cut from single blocks of marble, each one rising 37-1/2 feet high,[21] arranged in double rows.

Herod attempted to ingratiate himself with his subjects with the southern wall by reproducing Solomon's "Royal Porch,"[22] its 162 pillars[23] positioned in four rows of forty each (the two extra pillars forming a sort of screen) to support the elaborately carved cedar roof 100 feet[24] (ten stories) above the paved floor. Also called the "Basilica," it housed "the Bazaars of the Son of Annas":[25] The shops of the merchants, stalls of the moneychangers, and others of the "insider" Bureaucracy beholden to Annas.[26]

The outer Square within the walls of the Temple Mount, the Court of the Gentiles,[27] stood open to Jews and Gentiles alike.

During the great Pilgrimage Festivals,[28] it easily accommodated crowds of 100,000, all becoming waves of ranting noise and babbling confusion. Any day of the year, dozens of scribes argued the Law, and preachers harangued clusters of listeners in separate pockets in the crowds, one group not knowing what others discussed.

Joshua bar Joseph debated and preached many times[29] to crowds of varying size in this rowdy, raucous Court of the Gentiles,[30] when he came up to Jerusalem to participate in the great Festivals.

The Sanctuary proper sat in the west-central area of the Temple Mount,[31] reached through a series of steps, walkways and gates.

Fourteen steps led up from the Court of the Gentiles to a seventeen-foot-wide walkway (*promenade*) called the *hel*.[32] A five-foot-high, stone latticework wall called the *soreg*[33] enclosed the *hel*, with openings to let the Jewish people inside.

Plaques in Greek and Latin attached to the *soreg* clearly spelled out Annas' exclusive, nationalistic concept of Judaism:[34]

> "No foreigner (non-Jew) is permitted to pass through this grating into the Sanctuary and its surroundings. If discovered there, he has brought the punishment of death upon himself."

Nine separate gates[35] through the hel led to the Temple area proper: A single one in the east called the Gate Beautiful,[36] opened on to the paved Court of the Women.[37] This Court stood uncovered, except for its four corners which contained the Chamber of the Lepers in the northwest,[38] the Chamber of the Wood in the northeast,[39] the Chamber of the Nazarites in the southeast,[40] and the Chamber of the Oils in the southwest.[41]

A covered, arched gallery ringed the second story of the walls above the Court of the Women so that they could visit together and look down upon portions of the cultic rituals: ". . . for women were not permitted to enter nor yet to pass by way of their own gate beyond the partition wall."[42]

The special Nicanor Gate separated the Court of the Women and the Court of the Israelites, special in many respects: It ". . .

was of Corinthian bronze, and far exceeded in value those plated with silver and set in gold."[43]

Fifteen half-circle steps at the base of Nicanor's gate led up from the Court of the Women, serving as the stage for the Chorus of Levites, the luster of the closed double gate giving them a glittering theatrical backdrop.[44]

From the Court of the Women and the hel around the other sides of the Temple proper, the male Jews moved into the Court of the Israelites, which ringed the inside walls of the main Temple structure whose facade towered 150 feet high.[45] Moving inward came the Court of the Priests,[46] an inside parallelogram of the Court of the Israelites, the two Courts separated only by a "... low stone parapet, fair and graceful, about a cubit high."[47]

The great Altar of Burnt Offering overshadowed the Court of the Priests:[48] "In front of it stood the Altar, fifteen cubits high (cubit = 18-20 inches), and with a breadth and length extending alike to fifty cubits, in shape a square with horn-like projections at the corners, and approached from the south by a gently sloping acclivity (ramp)."[49]

An aura of "ritual purity" ("ritual cleanliness") hovered about the Altar, even the slaughtering areas for the sacrificial animals which abutted it.[50]

Everything fused down to the Holy of Holies inside the Sanctuary proper, the magnetic center of the Ten Circles of Holiness which sustained Annas' concept of Judaism as an exclusive, Bureaucratic cult.

The *lishkat ha-gazit*,[51] the "Hall of the Hewn Stone," loomed as the most impressive of all the great Temple rooms: Here sat the Great Sanhedrin (*bet din ha-gadol*), administering the sophisticated system of Law that grew from the Covenant Constitution over more than a thousand years. Joshua bar Joseph's trial for false prophecy took place in this great Basilica, where he heard the High Priest announce a "favorable verdict" ("not guilty").

Chapter 4

THE COMMITTEE OF TEN

While *John* mentions a few names, he is content to tell us that "the Jews"[1] plotted Jesus' (Joshua bar Joseph) death.

Matthew describes "the chief priests and the elders of the people."[2] *Mark* talks about "all the chief priests and the elders and the scribes"[3]; and *Luke* adds "the whole company," "they" and "the people" to the terms "elders," "scribes" and "chief priests."[4]

A Committee of Ten[5] wielded the real power in the Jewish Temple-State, and Joshua bar Joseph spoke out against them. They saw him a threat to their way, their "thing," and moved to get rid of him, the plot line as simple as that; but we must flesh it out with the details.

Professor David Flusser, Hebrew University, a leading Jewish authority on Jesus and the New Testament, confirms a "Committee" ruling the Jewish Temple-State throughout Jesus' lifetime, and still controlled the country at the time of the Temple's destruction in 70 A.D.: "The phrase ('chief priests and the scribes with the elders') is thus a formal designation for the *temple committee*: the elders were the elders of the temple and the scribes were the temple secretaries."[6]

Other scholars find support for the "Temple Committee" in several statements in the *talmud*,[7] these citations describing a group of "priests," "sons of the High Priests," and "the court of the priests," separate and distinct from any of the judicial courts (*bet din*; *bet din ha-gadol*; or *Court of Three*). This appears abundantly clear in *talmud: Rosh Hashanah* 22a, where this group of "priests" is overruled by the *bet din* (Small Sanhedrin).

German historian Emil Schurer spells out a "Committee of

Ten" which he calls the *dekaprotoi*.[8]

Bo Reicke, Professor of New Testament at Basle University, Switzerland, is even more explicit in his treatment of the "Committee of Ten":[9]

> In the New Testament, the plural 'high priests' refers, contrary to a common misapprehension, in typical Hellenistic fashion, to a consistory made up of priests and laymen (a body with a fixed membership; this was first shown, on the basis of rabbinic texts, by J. Jeremias in his *Jerusalem zur Zeit Jesu*, II B 1 (1929), pp. 33-40.)

> Such a committee of the assembly of elders is first mentioned in a diplomatic note from Jerusalem to Sparta about 144 B.C. (*Josephus Ant.* XIII:166), where it is called "council of the priests" (Greek = *koinon ton hiereon*).

> Greek analogies confirm that the so-called high priests were a common administrative board responsible for the temple and sacrificial system of the particular region, such as 'the high priests of the island' (*scil.* Cyprus); 'the high priests of Asia' (cf. Acts 19:14); 'the high priests of the Galatian league.'

> Because supervision of the temple and sacrificial system at Jerusalem was complicated after the time of Herod, the high priest on duty was supplemented by such a consistory, which was given the usual technical name, 'the high priests.' As a consequence of the broad impact of the cultic law and the service of the altar, the authority of the Jerusalem consistory extended to various areas of domestic politics in general.

> Its members were therefore also called 'the rulers' (I Macc. 14:28; Acts 4:5, 8; Josephus Bell. II. 405, 407).

> Another term for this governing body was 'the ten

foremost men' (Josephus Ant. XX. 194), an expression that shows it was composed of approximately ten wealthy and distinguished citizens.

This suggests yet another Hellenistic analogy, for several Greek and Roman cities had a ten-man committee of wealthy and distinguished, primarily aristocratic councilors (Greek *dekaprotoi*, Latin *decemprimi*); this was even true of Tiberias, the capital of Galilee (Josephus Vit. 69. 296) (Schurer, Vol. 2 (4th ed., 1970) pp. 172, 201 f.).

In other words, the 'high priests' at Jerusalem made up an aristocratic committee of the High Council, a consistory that functioned as the executive government of the Judean temple-state.

Herod I (The Great) is the real genesis of this Committee of Ten. After he firmed up his hold on his Judean kingdom in 37 B.C., he ordered the massacre of forty-five members of the Great Sanhedrin who had threatened to convict him of murder some fifteen years earlier, when he ruled as governor of the Galilee. These murders decimated the Sanhedrin's political and executive powers, though not its traditional judicial role.[10]

Herod then appointed a Greek-style privy council of wealthy aristocrats called a *gerousia*, in theory to advise him and help him rule; but it existed in name only, Herod ruling as unrestrained dictator.

When Herod died in 4 B.C., this subdued but eager *gerousia* jumped into the power void and quickly became the Committee of Ten, the new dictators of the Jewish nation; but try as Herod and the Committee did, they never succeeded in usurping the ancient *judicial* functions of Israel's three independent courts: Court of the Three; Court of the Twenty-Three (*bet din*); and Court of the Seventy-One (Great Sanhedrin; *bet din-ha-gadol*).

Years earlier, this group of Sadducean aristocrats chose "ten" as their number, not "seven" or "twelve," since for centuries, "ten" held symbolic meaning for the Jews: *minyan* ("number"), the word for the quorum of "ten" male adults needed for public synagogue service and other religious ceremonies.[11] "Blessed under ten

... "[12] became a symbol of cosmic perfection; and the Old Testament and *talmud* both used "ten" as a favored number.[13]

The members of this tiny club governed all of Israel, the overlords of the Jewish people, masters of every fact of life, save one: *They could not control the independent judges!* The aristocrats-Bureaucrats came as part of Herod's legacy:[14] Uncultured, crude, conceited, totally selfish, and pathetically ignorant of basic Judaism's great traditions.

Annas undoubtedly ruled as dominant member of the group, directing the internal operations of the Temple-State ever since he first bought the High Priesthood in 6 A.D.,[15] the year the Romans took over direct rule of Judea and Samaria, after deposing Herod Archelaus (son of Herod the Great). He held the High Priestly office himself from 6 to 15 A.D.; became father-in-law to Joseph Caiaphas, the current High Priest; and before the demise of the Temple-State in 70 A.D., five of his sons and one grandson would also serve as High Priest.[16]

Joseph Caiaphas undoubtedly belonged to the Committee of Ten, perhaps presided over their sessions with old Annas watching cunningly from the background.

Jonathan ben Annas, as *sagan* ("Captain of the Temple"), Annas' son and Caiaphas' brother-in-law, would be a Committee member, as would representatives from the three other great families: *Boethus, Phiabi* and *Kamithos.*

Regrettably, neither the *talmud* nor our other sources leave us much in the way of physical descriptions of the principal actors, the sources content to describe what these people did or said; still, scholars know a surprising amount about physical appearance, dress, hair style and other day-to-day activities of the various classes of the population.

Most Jewish aristocrats adopted Greek dress and other customs;[17] so we can expect that Annas, the leading Hellenizer of them all, would set the mode in both dress and hairdo.

I picture him well into this seventies, using a hair style to give him a much younger look: Meticulously trimmed once a week, combed forward without part in the Greek mode, with semi-circular ringlets plastered tightly against his head. His regal, haughty carriage, even with his sloping shoulders which no robe could drape well, made him appear taller than his average height.

Mostly, he sat in deep reflection, alternately turning the gaudy amulet[18] on the golden chain around his neck, ninety degrees forward and then back, until it fell flush against the embroidered robe covering the chest. The charm gave clear evidence of his character: One side contained a Chnoubis, the confused human body with the head of a lion, holding a snake whose head poured out solar radiations, seven rays of light from the seven planets, one of the favorite magical symbols among the Hellenized Jews. On the obverse side, the signs of the Jewish zodiac surrounded a pulsing sun, the Greek letters for "God" arched in clockwise fashion around the rim, to meet the transliteration of the Hebrew phrase "Chnoubis bound with incantations" flowing in the opposite direction. The marginal lettering, again in Greek, on the obverse side, translated "Renderer of giants." In culture, Annas acted more Greek than Hebrew; in theology, more pagan than Jew.

As with all Bureaucrats, regardless of era or place, the Committee of Ten labored under the delusions that they rendered public service, working for the people instead of for themselves. They could not appreciate their own warped motives, nor redirect their distorted goals.

The Committee of Ten probably planned Joshua bar Joseph's prosecution while sitting on stone benches and carved chairs in the Cell of the Counsellors, one of thirty-eight "chambers" surrounding the Sanctuary of the Temple.

The *talmud*[19] uses "cells" interchangeably with "chambers" or "rooms": The "Cell of the Lambs," "Cell of the Seals," "Cell of the Fireplace," "Cell of the Shewbread," "Cell of the House of Abtinas," "Cell of Parwah," "Rinsing Cell," and "Cell of the Vessels."

The frequent descriptions of the Cell of the Counsellors clues us to its importance in the executive hierarchy of the Temple Bureaucracy.

The members of the Committee of Ten, then, are "the Jews" whose stranglehold on the Jewish people Joshua bar Joseph threatened, the "bad guys" who plotted his death, certainly not the Jewish people as a whole.

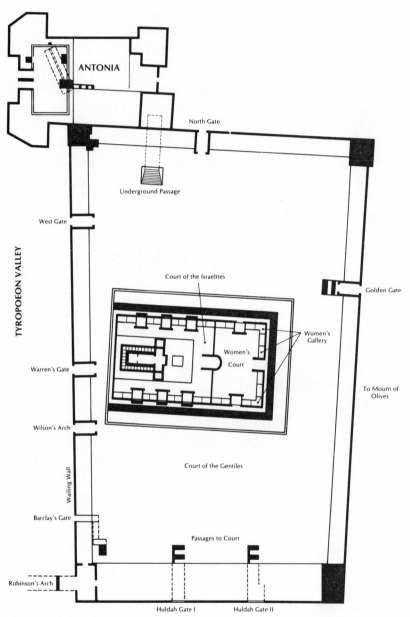

The Temple Mount at the time of Jesus' trials. Herod created its artificial base with blocks of matched limestone, some weighing up to 100 tons. Over the earthen fill, he paved this plateau with white marble. The south wall and its footings towered 450 feet (45 floors) above the sloping Lower City.

PART 2

THE SYNAGOGUE PREACHERS

And Jesus went all about
Galilee, teaching in their
synagogues, and preaching
the gospel of the
kingdom . . . . and his fame
went throughout all Syria!
Matthew 4:23-24

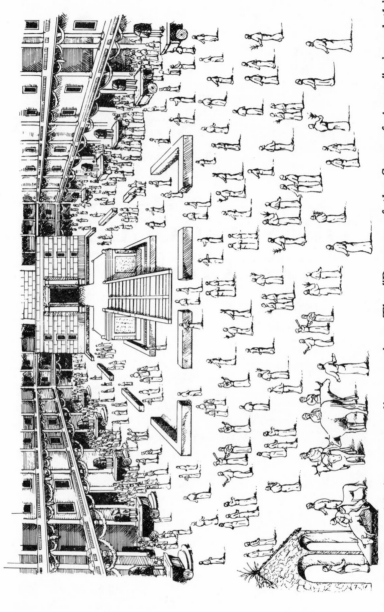

The Court of the Gentiles with its surrounding porticos. The "Bazaars of the Sons of Annas" ringed this Court. Here, Jesus overturned the tables of the money-changers as one of his final provocations of the Temple Bureaucrats who felt threatened by his preaching.

Chapter 5

THE SYNAGOGUE AT CAPERNAUM

We must next attend a Sabbath service in the synagogue at Capernaum (*Kfar-Nachum*),[1] on the northwest shore of the Sea of Galilee, sometime around 29-32 A.D., recognizing at once that the liturgy for this service is the foundation of all Christian liturgies, whether Catholic, Orthodox or Protestant.

Each worshiper came that Sabbath morning with the same goal in mind: A passionate love affair with God![2]

The reader stood on the raised pulpit (*bimah*), slightly to the east of center of the rectangular nave, laid out on an azimuth of 165 degrees, almost due south, so that the main entrance door faced the Temple of God in Jerusalem,[3] Herod's Temple: All men must be reminded always of the Eternal Fire of their faith that burned there; yet, the synagogue did not serve as a sub-Temple. No animal sacrifices took place; no High Priest ever appeared; the Temple's rigid rituals did not apply; no Temple Police spied on the synagogue services to keep everything "Levitically clean."

The synagogue stood totally independent of Temple, in tension with it; still, both Temple and synagogue lived as parts of the same Judaism that evolved under the Covenant Constitution. "Good" Jews went both to Temple and to synagogue, Joshua bar Joseph among them.

The musical voice of the reader from the congregation echoed off the polished limestone slabs of the floor,[4] supporting the sixteen, two-storied, white limestone columns that carried the roof, its open beams and cedarwood trusses combining to hold the flat terra-cotta tiles:[5]

> How goodly are thy tents, O Jacob, thy dwelling places, O Israel!
>
> In Thine abundant love have I come into Thy house, O Lord, and in reverence do I worship Thee in Thy holy Sanctuary.
>
> O Lord, I love the habitation of Thy house and the place where Thy glory dwelleth.
>
> Therefore I will bow down and pray unto Thee, O Lord, my Maker.
>
> Accept my prayer, O God, and in Thy great mercy, answer me with Thy saving truth.

All joined in the loud "Amen," the men standing around the pulpit in the nave, the women in the women's gallery[6] in the northwest corner of the second floor to which they climbed by an outside stairway.

The children studied their Bible lessons in the House of Study (*bet-ha-midrash*)[7] to the east. The honored elders[8] sat on the room's only benches or seats, the reader's intonations continuing:[9]

> How precious is Thy loving-kindness, O God! The children of men take refuge under the protection of Thy sheltering care.
>
> They shall be abundantly satisfied in Thy house; and Thou shalt refresh them with Thy living waters. For with Thee is the fountain of life; in Thy light do we see light.
>
> O continue Thy loving-kindness unto those who know Thee, and Thy righteousness to the upright heart.

The "amens" of the congregation rose louder as the *cantor*[10] replaced the reader in the pulpit, his deep baritone stirring ancient longings within them all, and they raced to join audibly in the martial beat of the tone:[11]

> Who shall ascend the mountain of the Lord? And who shall stand in His holy place?
>
> He that has clean hands, and a pure heart; Who has not set his mind on what is false, and has not sworn deceitfully.
>
> He shall receive a blessing from the Lord, and righteousness from the God of his salvation.

The honored elders[12] knew the hours-long service by heart, but still thrilled in a new communion each Sabbath and festival morning.

The worshipers swayed, stepped forward then backward, looked up, bowed down, rolled first to the left and then to the right.[13] The overflow crowd fought to get in because they heard that Joshua bar Joseph would preach the sermon of the morning.[14]

All the worshipers joined with feeling, Joshua bar Joseph especially, in the recitation of the *sh'ma,*[15] the Jews' capsulated creed of faith, Israel's simple doxology (*Deuteronomy* 6:4-5):

> Hear, O Israel: The Lord our God is one Lord; . . . .

The *cantor* descended the pulpit, the reader replacing him, the next responsive reading establishing the first of the service's three main themes: "The God of Creation!"

God's credibility rested entirely upon the premise that He made all things (Psalm 95:3-6):

> For great is the Lord,
> A King greater than all the mighty.
>
> In His hands are the depths of the earth;
> His also are the heights of the mountains.
>
> The sea is His for He made it.
> And His hands formed the dry land.

> Come, let us worship and bow down;
> Let us bend the knee before the Lord, our Maker.

"Bending the knee,"[16] a technical phrase, came from the root *b'rakhah* ("spring"; "oasis"): As a man bends the knee to drink life-giving water from the earth, so should he do the same when he sups his spiritual waters during his love match with his God. David said it a thousand years earlier: "All my bones praise the Lord,"[17] so the worshipers danced and chanted, singing the words instead of speaking them.

The reader moved to his second theme: "The God of History!" (*Nehemiah* 9:6-11):

> Thou alone are the Lord. Thou art the Lord God, who didst choose Abram . . .

> Thou madest a covenant with him to give his descendents the land of the Canaanite . . .

> Thou didst see the affliction of our fathers in Egypt, and didst hear their cry by the Red Sea; and didst perform signs and wonders upon Pharaoh, and on all his servants . . .

> Thus didst Thou make Thy name great to this day.

> Thou didst divide the sea before them, so that they crossed the sea on dry land, whereas their pursuers didst Thou cast into the depths like a stone in the mighty waters.

By this time, almost two hours into the service of song and responsive readings, chant and dance, vocal prayer and silent meditation, the worshipers reached a first-name basis with God.[18] No longer a restrained, formal approach, it became a grand opera of praise and thanksgiving: For God, for life, for themselves, for each other, for friendship, both divine and human.

The thrust of the service built to the third main theme: "God's Demands Upon Man!" Seven members of the congregation came up to read sections of the *torah*, first a *kohan* (a descendant from

Aaron), then a man whose genealogy ran back to the tribe of Levi, and five others.

Ezra and Nehemiah set the basic format of the service as early as 450-400 B.C., within the century after the Jews returned from Babylon.

The "ruler of the synagogue" (*archisunagogos*),[19] in his raised seat of honor in the corner of the nave where the western and south walls met, faced the worshipers: His joyous singing made him a sort of assistant director, cheering on the *reader* and *cantor* as they performed in the pulpit.

The *torah* readers paused at the end of each verse to let the interpreter[20] translate the Biblical Hebrew into Aramaic.

As one learned in the Law, Joshua bar Joseph frequently served as interpreter in this "his own city" and favorite synagogue.[21]

The Jews began using Aramaic soon after their Return from Babylon, it the official language of their Persian overlords. Also a Semitic language, it bore a similar relationship to Hebrew as modern Spanish to Italian: Some words identical; others completely different. For example, *ben* meant "son of" in Hebrew, while *bar* carried the same meaning in Aramaic. The Temple Bureaucrats prided themselves in their use of pure Biblical Hebrew, another haughty separation from the common people.

By 30 A.D., Aramaic had replaced Hebrew throughout Palestine as the common language of conversation.

As our educated Jew, Joshua bar Joseph spoke both Biblical Hebrew and Aramaic, and undoubtedly handled with ease both the written and spoken *koine*, the "common" Greek language of the area.

A challenging rule of thumb plagued the synagogue translators: "He who translates a verse literally is a liar, while he who adds anything thereto is a blasphemer."[22]

The readings from the Prophets (*haftorahs*) followed, with the interpreter allowed more latitude: He could translate the equivalent of three verses at a time of the Prophets, instead of one only of the *torah*.[23]

A hush settled over the crowd, both inside and out. The lessons of the children in the House of Study in the east portico ceased, their teachers pressing toward the central door into the nave, the only sounds the chirping of the sparrows. In this brief hallelujah of silence, a sudden rush of the wind quieted the birds.

In the traditions that began during the Babylonian Captivity 600 years earlier, the reader called for itinerant preacher Joshua bar Joseph to ascend the pulpit and preach the sermon.[24]

Chapter 6

THE PREACHER FROM NAZARETH

Joshua bar Joseph's first three sentences cast a spell over his listeners in the Capernaum synagogue: "And he said:[1]

> There was a man who had two sons; and the younger of them said to his father, 'Father, give me the share of the property that falls to me.'

> And he divided his living between them.

The worshipers tensed as they heard the start of bar Joseph's favorite teaching tool, the parable,[2] its great worth its ambiguity: Each hearer would give it his own meaning, fit it to his own need, work it into his own experience.

The fathers in the audience thought of their roles with their own sons, in varying hues of love and pathos. They understood the Jewish laws of property and inheritance.[3] The father in bar Joseph's parable went considerably beyond what the Law required when "he divided his living among them," the younger son demanding and receiving not only the right of possession, but the right to dispose of the property during the father's lifetime:[4]

> Not many days later, the younger son gathered all he had and took his journey into a far country, and there he squandered his property in riotous living.

Called *marshal* in Hebrew, the parable format included allegories, similitudes, obscure sayings, figurative discourses, folk stories and fables, the *scribes* (rabbis) — particularly the

Pharisees — developing the parable into a precise formula over the centuries, with key introductory words:[5] "I will relate a parable to you," or "With what shall the matter be compared?" or "It is like . . . ." or "He is like . . . ."[6]

> And, when he had spent everything, a great famine arose in that country, and he began to be in want.

Many "younger sons" in the synagogue well remembered how they, too, once hoped for independence, to go into a "far country." By the year 30 A.D., ten times as many Jews lived throughout the Mediterranean world as in Palestine itself; and the *diaspora*[7] ("the scattering"; "the dispersion"; "the dispersal") held great economic appeal.

Mothers standing in the women's gallery thought with heavy heart of their own sons in Alexandria or Rome, Damascus and Athens, identifying with this specific mother never once mentioned in Joshua bar Joseph's story:[8]

> So he went and joined himself to one of the citizens of that country, who sent him into his fields to feed swine.

Everyone within hearing entered the drama, made more awesome by their feel for the Jewish law against swine: "It is not right to breed pigs any place whatsoever . . . ."[9,10]

> And he would gladly have filled his belly with the pods that the swine ate; and no one gave him anything.

> But when he came to his senses . . . .

Now began the Hebrew-Aramaic idiom that stood for "repentance,"[11] known to every listener in the synagogue.[12]

> . . . . he said, 'How many of my father's hired servants have bread enough and to spare, but I perish here with hunger!

> 'I will arise and go to my father, and I will say to him, Father, I have sinned against heaven and before you; I am no longer worthy to be called your son; treat me as one of your hired servants.'

The worshipers heard public story-telling in its finest hour: Joshua bar Joseph did not let the son say a drab, "I'll go home"; rather he used a phrase of action, of spontaneous charge: "I will arise and go to my father!" This Galilean audience could interpret the vivid imagery in their own cultural setting, remembering the Jewish proverb: "When Israel is reduced to the (bean pods of the) carob tree, they become repentant":[13,14]

> And he arose and came to his father.

> But while he was yet a great way off, his father saw him and had compassion, and ran and embraced him and kissed him.

The crushed, bereaved father watching and waiting with heavy heart for months and years, now violated the Eastern sense of propriety: An aged man should not run!:[15]

> And the son said to him, 'Father, I have sinned against heaven and before you; I am no longer worthy to be called your son!

By this time, the listeners could barely keep their feet on the floor, wanting to shout and dance for joy for the return of the lost sinner:[16]

> But the father said to his servants, 'Bring quickly the best robe, and put it on him; and put a ring on his hand, and shoes on his feet; and bring the fatted calf and kill it; and

> 'let us eat and make merry; for this my son was dead, and is alive again; he was lost, and is found.'

> Any they began to make merry.

The symbolism conveyed substance, making bar Joseph's parables different from the rest: The surprise ending that cut through the tedious deadwood of the traditional case arguments up in the Temple, which usually began,[17] "Our Rabbis taught," or "Rabbi Jonathan said . . .," "but Rab Simeon b. Eleazar said that . . ."

The Capernaum congregation expected bar Joseph to relate a stern lecture by the father to the son: The rebellious son's disrespect for parental authority; his consorting with harlots; the riotous living; the disgrace of working with pigs; requirements of penance and restitution; his reduced, embarrassed family status; and the superior, model role of the elder brother who stayed home.[18]

But bar Joseph gave it all a new twist: A father whose love and compassion for a lost, dead son knew no limits, not a Pollyanna rejoicing that signaled flippant approval of the son's errant ways, but the "God is good" of fundamental Judaism that featured forgiveness and restoration.[19]

The worshipers could puzzle out their own meanings of putting the costly robe[20] on the son; the signet-ring, a symbol of authority,[21] on his finger; the shoes worn only by free men;[22] the fatted calf in a culture that could not afford meat except on great occasions;[23] and the symbolic brotherhood dance of the men.[24] It all meant total forgiveness, complete reinstatement.[25]

But why? How?

This charismatic preaching moved the heart of every pious Jew who heard it, in the Galilee, across the Jordan, as far north as Tyre and Sidon, and under the noses of the Temple Bureaucrats in Jerusalem: Jesus the fundamentalist, radical only in urging a return to the basic Judaism of "God is good!" and man's ability to go directly to Him, without the need for the intervention of the Temple Bureaucrats.

Goodness and the Law arose as special forces of God's creation: Both physical, real, hearty, robust and corporal. As agents of God Himself, they too possessed creative powers: Inspiring and prodding while guiding and leading, licensing man to his unique self, but checking him from abuses. Goodness and the Law clasped man's hands to pull him upward toward God, then broke his fall when he forgot his purpose; they inflated his talents to the heights of the heavens, but saved him from the despair of his self-centered defaults, God's own arms that alone gave life a meaningful pattern.

Joshua bar Joseph preached God's Goodness as the heart of Judaism's true message. The substance of Judaism lay not in the doctrine of one God against many, but in the character of that one God.[26]

Bar Joseph moved his parable toward its ending:[27]

> Now this elder son was in the field; and as he came and drew near to the house, he heard music and dancing.
>
> And he called one of the servants and asked what this meant.
>
> And he said to him, 'Your brother has come and your father has killed the fatted calf, because he has received him safe and sound.'

Now, Bar Joseph jolted his listeners from thoughts of the "prodigal" to the feelings of the "good" son who never left his father's love or family duties:[28]

> But he was angry and refused to go in. His father came out and entreated him, but he answered his father, 'Lo, these many years I have served you, and I never disobeyed your command; yet you never gave me a kid, that I might make merry with my friends.'

What of the actions of the father, or the elder son, or both?[29]

> 'But when this son of yours came, who has devoured your living with harlots, you killed for him the fatted calf!'

He did not say, "when my brother came," but rather, "this son of yours," the caustic epithet for a hated stranger.

Each listener in the synagogue needed to decide the meaning for himself, then debate the lesson at home with his family! The parable format put the burden squarely on the hearers to ponder the reactions of the elder son, to see what it meant to them, if they could pull out some personal guidance.

They now saw the older son's anger rushing toward hatred; and Joshua bar Joseph continued with Judaism's theme of "God is good!" leaving no room for hatred of any hue:[30]

> And he said to him, 'Son, you are always with me, and all that is mine is yours.

> 'It was fitting to make merry and be glad, for this your brother was dead, and is alive; he was lost and is found.'

No wonder the crowds following Joshua bar Joseph often ran into the thousands,[31] overflowing the synagogues, out to the rocky hills around the Lake. His pull lay both in the new twist of their old message and the spellbinding power of his delivery: A restatement of ancient truths in new imagery, to let them live once more, fresh, spontaneous, dramatic and entertaining, full of hope for the day and promise of the morrow, not sapped of life by the 313 rules of "thou shalt not!"

The message cut through the legalistic, semantic exercises so dear to the hearts of the Temple Bureaucrats in Jerusalem who profaned Judaism into their own stagnating Bureaucratic tool.[32]

The Temple Bureaucrats forgot—if they ever knew—that Goodness and the Law could only operate as parallel powers, each supporting, each checking the other, the two great forces losing their might if not used in tandem.

Joshua bar Joseph's national reputation[33] spread across the country side by word-of-mouth, grew by leaps and bounds, filling the desperate needs of the people for physical solace and spiritual lift: "And they were astonished at his teaching, for he taught as one who had authority, and not as the scribes."[34]

(From this point on, we will begin to merge together Jeshua ben Joseph's (Joshua bar Joseph's) Hebrew-Aramaic names into his Greek name, "Jesus," even though "Jesus" did not develop until

perhaps two decades after his death, when the Church Fathers began to use "Jesus" to broaden the base of followers of the new religion to include Gentiles as well as Jews.)

Nicanor's Gate as viewed from the Court of the Women. The chorus of Levites stood on the fifteen semicircular steps in front of the forty-five-foot-wide doors, hauled to Jerusalem from Egypt. The Jews took great pride in the special beauty of this Gate, more so than all of the other gates even though they were covered with gold.

Chapter 7

JESUS' FELLOW-GALILEANS: THE "PEOPLE OF THE LAND"

Josephus knew the Galilee well, and wrote in-depth of its 204 cities and villages:[1,2]

> Galilee, with its two divisions known as Upper and Lower ... although surrounded by powerful foreign nations, have always resisted any hostile invasion, for the inhabitants are from infancy inured to war, and have at all times been numerous; never did the men lack courage nor the country men. For the land is everywhere so rich in soil and pasturage and produces such variety of trees, that even the most indolent are tempted by these facilities to devote themselves to agriculture. In fact, every inch of the soil has been cultivated by the inhabitants; there is not a parcel of waste land.

Only 50 miles in north-south length and 22 east and west, it lay north of Judea and Samaria, bounded by the Jordan River flowing through the Sea of Galilee on the east, ancient Phoenicia and the Mediterranean on the west, and "composed of a hundred hills, each with its little plain."[3]

Plentiful rainfall, guaranteed by the mountains of the Lebanon, caused walnuts, figs, vineyards and all manner of fruits to flourish:[4, 5]

> It is a paradisal country, rivalling Egypt in its grain and cereals, and, although small, surpassing her in wine and oil and fruit.

Around Nazareth and Cana, Capernaum and Chorazin,[6] flowers of every color waved out to meet the pink and white oleanders that bordered the sand-bottomed wadis.[7]

But the People!

A great Rabbi from Jerusalem once summed it up: "Galilee, Galilee! Thou dost hate the *torah*."[8]

Animosity between the two districts of the Galilee and Judea boiled for centuries:[9] "Why then are Judea *and* Galilee particularly specified? To show us that Judea and Galilee are normally reckoned to be on hostile terms."[10]

Their enmities seethed in a raw, vengeful history, the two Galilees part of the original Promised Land awarded to the tribes of Asher and Zebulin, Naphtali and Issachar. Together with parts of six other tribes, they made up the Northern Kingdom of Israel, after the country split at Solomon's death in 931 B.C. This left only Benjamin and Judah (which earlier absorbed Simeon) as the Southern Kingdom of Judah (Judea) after the "Assyrians came down like a wolf on the fold" in 722 B.C. and carried away the people of the Kingdom of Israel into slavery, forever erasing these "Ten Lost Tribes."[11] Only Judah remained.

When the Judean refugees returned to Jerusalem from Babylon, they found the lands of the former Northern Kingdom overrun by foreigners: Samaritans, Aramaeans, Philistines and Mesopotamians, giving rise to its title, *Gelil ha-Goyim* ("Galilee of the nations"),[12] or its more recent label: "Galilee of the Gentiles,"[13] "Gentile" meaning "non-Jew."

From about 330 B.C. onward, Alexander the Great brought in the Greeks, his driving goal to impose Greek culture upon the entire world, his tool the formation of Greek cities everywhere, settled by Greek soldiers and specially trained immigrants from the Greek homeland.

Alexander's heirs scattered their cities throughout Palestine: Totally Greek in physical lay out, political structure, religious practice and everyday language (*koine* = common Greek), in no way Jewish.[14]

The *Decapolis*[15] (*Greek* = "ten cities") ringed the Galilee east of the Jordan (Hippo, Gadara, Pella, Philadelphia, Gerasa, Dion, Canatha, Damascus and Raphana), the tenth, Sythopolis (*Beth-*

Shan), actually inside the Galilee, west of the Jordan. Acre[16] (Akka; Acco; Ptolomais) became the great Greek port on the Mediterranean, twenty-five miles northwest of Nazareth, with Sepphoris, "the largest city in Galilee."[17] This capital of the whole Galilee dominated the area, the Hellenic influence of the Greek cities prevailing all along the Mediterranean coast, through Caesarea and as far south as Gaza.[18] The name now became *Gahil-ha-Goyim*, "Circle of the Gentiles":[19] The schools (*gymnasia*) Greek; thinking Greek; human knowledge (reason) became God; Greek *soter* ("savior") religious sects to make life bearable for the great bulk of the people.

The mystery cults flourished, man's nature demanding something more than intellectual approaches alone; and Greek streams of thought fought hard against the Hebrew of those who practiced orthodox Judaism:[20]

THE GREEK THRUST	THE HEBREW THRUST
Motto:	
Know thyself!	Know thy God!
Emphasis:	
Wisdom and Knowledge	Justice and Mercy
Approach:	
Probing questions; logical arrangement, slogans and labels	Love of God = Love of neighbor = moral demands on all men
Method:	
Truth comes from reason	Truth is revealed by God

Scheme:

Eternal Source (God) can be contacted only through mediators: *logos*; *nous*; *soter* ("savior")	Personal God must be contacted directly without use of mediators

Goals:

To obtain truth in this world: Culture; beauty; form; harmony; symmetry; proportion. (No base on which to build individual freedom or personal morality)	To obtain righteousness, finally salvation: Doing God's will (His Law). Personal morality and individual freedom follow as byproducts

Chief Concerns:

Learning: Art; literature; philosophy; science	Personally communing with the God of Creation, the God of history, and exploring man's direct relationship to Him
Civic life with its political, social, intellectual and aesthetic interests	Daily life "in God," with its religious, moral and social concerns

Prospects:

Flourishes in times of prosperity	Flourishes in times of adversity

Great political stresses raged throughout the area. In 6 A.D., when Jesus bar Joseph probably reached his tenth year, Judas the Galilean plunged the country into a bitter rebellion against Rome. *Josephus* tersely sums up the destructive war:

> Quirinus, a Roman Senator . . . arrived in Syria, dispatched by Caesar to be governor of the nation

and to make an assessment of their property.

Coponius, a man of equestrian rank, was sent along with him to rule over the Jews with full authority (including the infliction of capital punishment).[21]

But a certain Judas, a Gualanite from a city named Gamala, who had enlisted the aid of Saddok, a Pharisee, threw himself into the cause of rebellion.

They said that the assessment carried with it a status amounting to downright slavery, no less, and appealed to the nation to make a bid for independence. They urged that in case of success the Jews would have laid the foundation of prosperity, while if they failed to obtain any such boon, they would win honor and renown for their lofty aim . . . .

Since the populace, when they heard their appeals, responded gladly, the plot to strike boldly made serious progress; and so these men sowed the seed of every kind of misery, which so afflicted the nation that words are inadequate . . . .

Some were slain in civil strife, for these men madly had recourse to butchery of each other and of themselves from a longing not to be outdone by their opponents; others were slain by the enemy in war.

In this case certainly, Judas and Saddok started among us an intrusive fourth school of philosophy . . .[22]

The followers of this new philosophy called themselves *zealots*, dedicated freedom fighters of the traditions of the Maccabees 175 years earlier:

As for the fourth of the philosophies, Judas the Galilean set himself up as leader of it. This school agrees in all other aspects with the opinions of the Pharisees, except that they have a passion for liberty that is almost unconquerable, since they are convinced that God alone is their leader and master. They think little of submitting to death in unusual forms and permitting vengeance to fall on kinsmen and friends if only they may avoid calling any man master.[23]

Throughout Jesus bar Joseph's years in the Galilee, the Zealots maintained fierce guerrilla warfare[24] against the Romans, robbing traders and caravans, and terrorizing foreigners and native collaborators alike. Jesus knew many of the fighters personally, heard them report their forays and raids, their successes, their losses; and when he chose his own Apostles years later, he included Simon the Zealot.[25]

Ideas clashed in the Galilee, every bit as violent as the banging heads and flying fists, the swords and staves of the guerrilla wars.

The Galilee actually came to Judaism only quite late, probably at about the same time that Hasmonean King Alexander Jannaeus (Yannai) forced circumcision upon Herod the Great's ancestors in Idumea (104 B.C.), the conversion process slow and reluctant: The masters of the Temple-State and doctors of the Law back in Jerusalem[26] still suspected the Galilee's conversion as less than genuine. They called the Galileans *am-ha-arez*[27] ("people of the land"[28]), by this time a term of contempt for a religious ignoramus. Even the gentile Hillel said: "The *bor* ("empty-headed man") cannot be sin-fearing nor the *am-ha-arez* pious."

Dozens of cruel obscenities put down the *am-ha-arez*: "Let him [a man] not marry the daughter of an *am-ha-arez*, because they are detestable and their wives are vermin, and of their daughters it is said, *Cursed be he that lieth with any manner of beast* (Deuteronomy 27:21)."[30]

The vicious prejudices mounted: Contact with the spittle of an *am-ha-arez* created a ritual (Levitical) defilement (pollution).[31]

Further, "If a man has taken upon himself to be trustworthy, he must tithe (send a portion to the Temple) whatever he eats and whatever he sells and whatever he buys; and he may not be the guest of an *am-ha-arez* (an uninstructed person, in the Galilee or any other place, who is indifferent to tithing of produce and to the observance of clean and unclean)."[32]

Tithing helped sustain the Bureaucrats in Jerusalem; but Annas and the Committee of Ten did not trust the *am-ha-arez* to deliver up the tithes.[33] They labeled as *dem'ai* anything that came from an *am-ha-arez*: "Dubious, suspicious = produce concerning which there is a doubt as to whether the rules relating to priestly and Levitical dues and ritual cleanness and uncleanness were strictly observed. Any produce bought from an *am-ha-arez*, unless the contrary is known, is treated as *dem'ai*."[34]

They treated untithed produce as unclean, the orthodox user required to tithe a portion of it to remove the potential impurity, even though it meant double taxation if the *am-ha-arez* producer or seller actually tithed it initially.

Through the years, the slanders from Jerusalem against the "people of the land" in Galilee grew more vicious: "The garments of an *am-ha-arez* possess *midras* ('place of pressure' denoting Levitical impurity arising in an object in contact with a gonorrhoeist who sits, lies, rides upon or leans against it)."[35]

The orthodox Jews also discriminated against the *am-ha-arez* in matters of employment:[36]

> Beth Hillel holds that it is not permissible to employ an attendant who is *am-ha-arez*, while Beth Shammai holds that it is permissible to employ an attendant who is an *am-ha-arez*.

Different laws stressed great differences in the customs of the people:[37]

> An unspecified reference to the terumah ("heave offering"; tithe) in Judea is binding, but not in Galilee, because the Galileans are unfamiliar with the *terumah* of the temple-chamber.

Countless distinctions existed in their laws of marriage,[38] widow's rights,[39] the wording of the betrothal contract[40] and the bride's virginity:[41]

> "He who frequently eats (visits) at his father-in-law's house between the time of betrothal and the time of marriage, in Judea, without witnesses, cannot after the marriage raise the claim of loss of virginity, because he is alone with her. In Judea, he cannot raise this claim; but in Galilee he can raise it."

They used different weights and measures:[42]

> "The weight of five *sela's* of warp in Judea which is ten *sela's* in Galilee (the Gaililean *sela* being equal to half that of Judea)."

Years later, when Jesus bar Joseph recruited followers in the Greek city of Bethsaida ("House of Fisheries") along the north shore of the Sea of Galilee, a skeptic named Nathanael summed up the consuming prejudice against the *am-ha-arez* in bar Joseph's village when he asked in mockery: "Can anything good come out of Nazareth?"[43]

With all their ridicule of the *am-ha-arez*, the Temple Bureaucrats feared the Galilee, remembering the revolt by Judas in 6 A.D. which ended with 2,000 rebels crucified by the Romans, a rebellion that threatened the status quo of the Temple-State. They vowed never to let it happen again; and anyone who developed a serious following immediately became suspect.

Chapter 8

THE NAZARETH THREAT

The Galilee[1] lent itself to the rise of fakirs, faith healers, miracle workers, false prophets and, of course, the Zealot guerrillas, the *am-ha-arez* particularly prone to any sort of vain promise. Usually, these rabble rousers, as Jerusalem saw them, thrashed themselves out in short order, though some stirred great commotions. *Josephus* describes an earlier one:[2]

> Now some of the Jews thought that the destruction of Herod's army came from God, and that very justly, as a punishment of what he did against John, that was called the *Baptist*; for Herod [Antipas, son of Herod the Great] slew him, who was a good man, and commanded the Jews to exercise virtue, both as to righteousness towards one another, and piety towards God, and so to come to baptism;

> for that the washing [with water] would be acceptable to him, if they made use of it, not in order to the putting away [or the remission] of some sins [only], but for the purification of the body; supposing still that the soul was thoroughly purified beforehand by righteousness.

> Now when [many] others came in crowds about him, for they were very greatly moved [or pleased] by hearing his words, Herod, who feared lest the great influence John had over the people might put it into his power and inclination to raise a rebellion, (for they seemed ready to do anything he should

advise,) thought it best, by putting him to death, to prevent any mischief he might cause, and not bring himself into difficulties, by sparing a man who might make him repent of it when it should be too late.

Accordingly he was sent a prisoner, out of Herod's suspicious temper, to Macherus, the castle I before mentioned, and was there put to death. Now the Jews had an opinion that the destruction of this army was sent as a punishment upon Herod, and a mark of God's displeasure to him.

This new *am-ha-arez* Jesus bar Joseph looked to Annas and the Committee of Ten like another John, the crowds following him growing every day. Word reached them that he preached to 5,000[3] at one sitting, and then somehow fed the multitude by multiplying five loaves of bread and two small fishes.[4]

Many claimed they saw him order a lame man to rise up and leave his bed and walk.[5] He gave sight to a man blind since birth,[6] voice to another who never before uttered a single word.[7]

Once on the Sea of Galilee, a violent storm threatened bar Joseph's boat and his companions. He spoke to the winds, and stilled the waters.[8] He healed the servant of a Roman Centurion from a distance, without even seeing him.[9] He cast out evils,[10] and withered a fig tree with his curse.[11]

Wild tales, of course, but the type that stirred up the ignorant *am-ha-arez*!

Then, something more threatening began: Jesus bar Joseph attacked the Temple Bureaucrats directly, calling them "a generation of vipers,"[12] "a wicked and adulterous generation seeking after a sign,"[13] "hypocrites,"[14] "blind guides who strain at a gnat and swallow a camel,"[15] who "omit the weightier matters of Law, judgment, mercy and faith,"[16] who "are like whited sepulchres which indeed appear beautiful outward, but are full of dead men's bones, and of uncleanness!"[17]

"Ye who build the tombs of the prophets and garnish the sepulchres of the righteous!"[18]

He pulled no punches in his salvos against the Temple cult:

"If you had been in the days of your fathers, you would have been partakers with them in the blood of the prophets."[19]

"How can you escape the damnation of hell? . . . O Jerusalem, Jerusalem, thou that killest the prophets, and stonest them which are sent unto you . . . your house [Temple] is left unto you desolate."[20]

He debated both the Pharisees and the Sadducees – primarily the Pharisees – on their stifling, technical rulings on the Law: On divorce, he championed the rights of the woman whose husband could put her away by merely handing her a bill of divorcement.[21] On Levitical purity, he ate with publicans[22] (tax collectors) and drank at the table with sinners.[23] On the forgiveness of sins, he argued that the sinner could go directly to God, so did not need to go through the priests and pay the sin offering.[24] On skipping the ceremonial washing of hands before eating, he taunted his Pharisee critics: "Now do ye Pharisees make clean the outside of the platter; but your inward part is full of ravening and wickedness."[25] On the choking technicalities around the Sabbath, he taught: "The Sabbath is made for man, and not man for the Sabbath."[26]

His practical approaches to the Sabbath particularly shocked them.

Then, the news hit Annas and the Committee of Ten like a thunderbolt: The crowds tried to seize Jesus and make him a king.[27]

They dared wait no longer. As Herod Antipas did earlier with John the Baptist, they must act now before all the Galilee rose up against them and the Romans; so they sent down spies[28] from Jerusalem, from the ranks of both major parties – Pharisees and Sadducees – to see how best to dispose of the menace from Nazareth.

The Sadducees,[29] the priestly, aristocratic party controlling the Temple Bureaucrats under Annas and the Committee of Ten:

(1) Collaborated politically with the Romans ruling the Temple-State for them;

(2) Wanted, above all else, to resist change and preserve the status quo;

(3) Acknowledged only the Laws expressly included in the

torah, and rejected the "oral Law" (interpretations; case decisions) that the Pharisees developed over the centuries;

(4) Denied the doctrine of the resurrection of the body;

(5) Denied the coming of future rewards and punishments in an afterlife, holding that the "soul" perished with the body;

(6) Denied the role of Fate in man's affairs, saying that each man controlled his own destiny;

(7) Denied the existence of angels and spirits; and

(8) Denied the traditional concept of a "personal" God who took interest in man's day-to-day affairs.

Their beliefs evolved more Greek than Jewish, almost anti-Jewish.

The Pharisees[30] challenged the Sadducees on most issues, claiming direct descent from Moses and Ezra. The largest of the parties, they enjoyed enough support from the people to let them force their rulings on all matters of Law and Temple ritual on to the Sadducees, while standing passive on matters of politics: They believed the nation should submit peaceably to Roman rule, as long as Rome did not interfere with their inward religious life, thinking that unbridled rule by the Temple Bureaucrats would be every bit as impious, possibly worse, than the status quo under the Romans.

They developed the "Oral Law," the great body of case decisions, interpreting the Law Codes of the *torah*, saying their rulings came from God through Moses, at the time He gave them the *torah*. Their constructions gave Judaism its life, and saved it from total oblivion after the Temple's fall in 70 A.D.

The Pharisees[31] believed in:

(1) The resurrection of the physical body;

(2) The doctrine of future rewards and punishments;

(3) The coming of the "Kingdom of God," when the "good times" of David's reign would return;

(4) The coming of a "Messiah" from David's line;

(5) A combined role of Fate, free-will and Israel's idea of a "personal" God, who could be talked to and called upon for help;

(6)   Angels and spirits; and

(7)   Three foundations of the World: (a) The Study of the Law, (b) The worship services of both Temple and synagogue, and (c) Acts of kindness (charity).

Pharisee fought with Sadducee on all shades of Temple ritual; Pharisee argued against Pharisee on interpretations of the "Oral Law;" Sadducee against Sadducee on the divisions of the Temple spoils and how best to get along with Rome; but they all closed ranks to march in lock-step when anyone threatened their "thing" in the Temple status quo.

They sent their agents into the Galilee to gauge firsthand the strength of the Jesus menace, and found out soon enough, as Matthew (12:9-14) reports:

> And when he was departed thence, he went into their synagogue:
>
> And, behold, there was a man which had his hand withered. And they asked him, saying, Is it lawful to heal on the sabbath day? that they might accuse him.
>
> And he said unto them, What man shall there be among you, that shall have one sheep, and if it fall into a pit on the sabbath day, will he not lay hold on it, and lift it out?
>
> How much then is a man better than a sheep? Wherefore it is lawful to do well on the sabbath days.
>
> Then saith he to the man, Stretch forth thine hand. And he stretched it forth; and it was restored whole, like as the other.
>
> Then the Pharisees went out, and held a council against him, how they might destroy him.

And held a council against him!

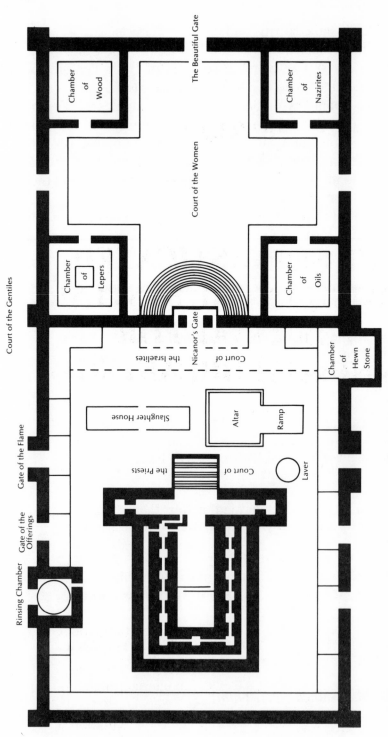

The layout of the Temple proper. The Hall (Chamber) of the Hewn Stone is particularly important. Called the *lishkat ha-gazit*, it loomed as the most impressive of all the Temple rooms. Here sat the Great Sanhedrin, Israel's highest court.

PART 3

THE SOPHISTICATED JEWISH LEGAL SYSTEM: THE TRIAL FOR SABBATH-BREAKING

. . . . so that the fugitive may
not be killed, until he has
stood in the presence of the
congregation [a jury] for
trial.
Numbers 35:12

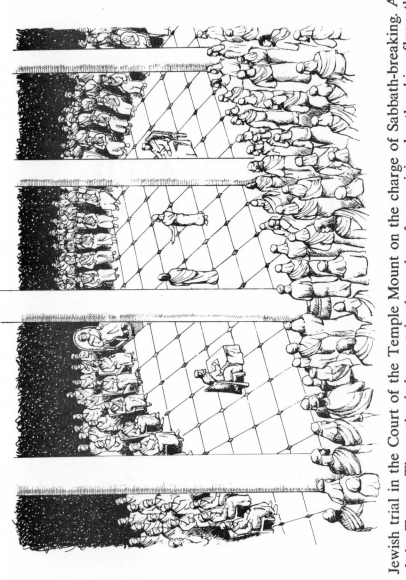

Jesus' first Jewish trial in the Court of the Temple Mount on the charge of Sabbath-breaking. Also called the Court of the Twenty-Three, the judges sat in the order of a semicircular threshing floor, the accused standing directly in front of the Ha-Nasi (president of the Court), the prosecuting witness testifying to his right. Disciples-probationers stand behind the judges, with curiosity seekers watching the proceedings through the openings between the columns from the Court of the Gentiles.

Chapter 9

THE FIRST JEWISH TRIAL

Matthew's throw away line in the King James version, ". . . *and held a council against him,*"[1] alerts us to a trial in a Jewish court!

"Held a council," "gathered the council," are technical legal terms, and do not mean merely a "conference," "discussion," "debate" or "exchange of views."

John (11:47-51) also reports the fact of a Jewish trial some time before Jesus' final arrest in Gethsemane:

> So the chief priests and the Pharisees gathered the council, and said, "What are we to do? For this man performs great signs. If we let him go on thus, every one will believe in him, and the Romans will come and destroy both our holy place and our nation."
>
> Caiaphas who was high priest that year, said to them, "You know nothing at all; you do not understand that it is expedient for you that one man should die for the people, and that the whole nation should not perish."
>
> . . . So from that day on they took counsel how to put him to death.
>
> Jesus therefore no longer went about openly among the Jews, but went from there to the country near the wilderness, to a town called Ephraim; and there he stayed with the disciples.
> *Revised Version*

Other translations use "Council" and "Sanhedrin" interchangeably:

Then the *Sanhedrin,* or Great Council was called together . . . .
　　　　　Norlie's Translation

Then the priests and the Pharisees called a meeting of the *Sanhedrin* . . . .
　　　　　Moffatt's Translation

So the chief priests and Pharisees called a meeting of the council (*Sanhedrin*) . . . .
　　　　　Amplified New Testament

Consequently the chief priests and the Pharisees gathered the *Sanhedrin* together . . . .
　　　　　New World Translation

Then the chief priests and the Pharisees called a meeting of the *Sanhedrin* . . . .
　　　　　New International Version

Consequently the chief priests and the Pharisees gathered the *Sanhedrin* together and began to say . . . .
　　　　　Kingdom Interlinear Translation

So the head priests and Pharisees convened the *Sanhedrin* and said, ...
　　　　　The Original New Testament

The phrases "Sanhedrin called together," "called a meeting of the Sanhedrin," "gathered the Sanhedrin together," "convened the Sanhedrin," used by the non-lawyer *gospel* writers give us *the fact of a trial in the Jewish courts.* Other translations of *Mark* (3:2) and *Luke* (6:7) confirm it with technical legal jargon (*The New Testament from 26 Translations, et al*):

". . . that they might inform against him"

". . . in order that they might lay an information against him"

". . . that they might accuse him"

". . . so that they could bring a charge against him"

". . . so as to have a complaint to bring against him"

". . . find how to accuse him"

". . . hoping to have a charge to bring against him"

". . . so that they might trump up some charge against him"

Accuse him to whom, or to what?
For what? Not to themselves! What good would that do?
Not to the Committee of Ten!
They already knew their minds.

They searched for evidence to "accuse him" before a Court of the Twenty-Three (Small Sanhedrin; *bet din*), of a death penalty offense so "that they might destroy him," these Sadducees, Pharisees and scribes (as the writers vaguely call them) seeking to become a "set" of "prosecuting witnesses," as the strict rules of Jewish Law demanded for a criminal charge against any accused.[2]

The trial which *Matthew* and *John* specifically describe, and which *Mark* and *Luke* confirm by their legal terminology, stands separate and apart from the last events in Jesus' life: He went off into the wilderness after the episode ended to let things cool off in Jerusalem. This presumes a verdict of acquittal which Caiaphas damns: Only a "death sentence" would save "the whole nation" and "our holy place [Temple]," to let the Bureaucrats maintain their lucrative status quo.

Our mistakes in interpreting these *gospel* reports of Jesus' two Jewish trials stem from our forgetting the mechanics of how the New Testament took shape.[3]

The writers of the first "books" used reed pens and nutgall (lampblack pigment) ink, and wrote on papyrus, a plant in abundance along river banks. They cut its white, pithy core into thin strips, wove them into layers, pressed them together to squeeze out the moisture, dried and polished them.

Vellum, a fine parchment from calf, kid and lamb skin, did not replace papyrus until the 4th and 5th century A.D. We now work primarily with vellum copies of the originals, made at least 200-300 years after *Matthew, Mark, Luke* and *John* wrote their *gospels.*

The writers put each episode in Jesus' life on a separate papyrus sheet called a *pericope*[4] (Greek = "cutting"), but made no efforts to arrange them in anything like chronological order, nor did they ever try to tell a running, unified story. They wrote in narrow columns, without space or other separations of individual words. They did not use punctuation; and the concept of sentences and paragraphs came many centuries later. We do not know how they stacked or filed their loose papyrus sheets.

Only in 1250 A.D. did Cardinal Hugo de Sancto Caro divide both Old and New Testaments into chapters,[5] and this quite arbitrarily;[6] and the separation into verses came in 1557, by a printer named Robert Stevens as he rode horseback from Lyons to Paris:[7] Printing expedience produced the verse divisions, not biblical scholarship!

Bible scholar Clarence Craig sums it this way:[8]

> In the instruction of converts, in the controversy with opponents, and in cult devotion, the stories and sayings of Jesus were formulated. No connected narrative was called for in the preaching of the gospel message. The sayings and incidents were originally separate and therefore should be studied as separate units . . . .
>
> Most of the incidents and stories were repeated without reference to time and place. They were not told as part of a biography, but as illustrations of what Jesus of Nazareth had done to warrant the Christian faith in him.
>
> Because of this situation it is impossible to write a life of Jesus. Books may bear that title, but it is a

task which is impossible to fulfill because of the nature of our tradition.

When Mark wrote his gospel, he did not know an exact sequence of events. He strung together his selection of the oral tradition for the one purpose of preaching the gospel message which centered in the death and resurrection of the Christ.

We do not know who finally placed the *pericopes* of *Matthew* 12:9-14, *Mark* 3:1-6, *Luke* 6:6-11, and *John* 11:47-51 in their present locations in our printed New Testaments, or when, or why they do not appear earlier or later. Happenstance probably dictated their positions since they play no great role in the *gospel* message. We can, however, be sure that all writers knew a tradition of Jesus facing at least two trials in the Jewish courts. They thought the tradition important enough to mention, more or less in passing; they omitted the details either because they did not know them, or thought them irrelevant to their *kerygma* (preaching) message.

Matthew, Mark and *Luke* give us the formal charge in the first Jewish trial: Sabbath-breaking.

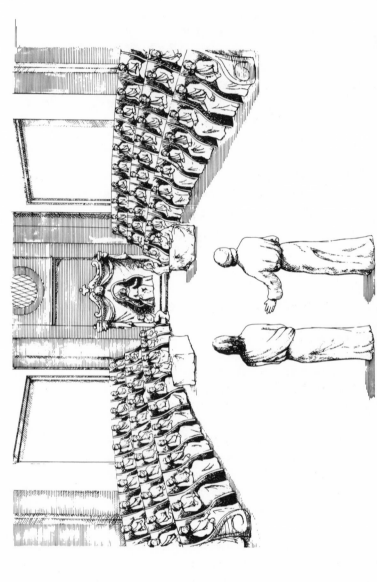

The Great Sanhedrin (Court of the Seventy-One) in the ornate basilica of the Hall of the Hewn Stone "where the Law could go out to all Israel." This Court supervised Israel's sophisticated legal system which evolved over the centuries from Moses' Covenant Constitution in 1250 B.C. at Mt. Sinai. It heard the charges of false prophecy against Jesus, and voted an acquittal.

Chapter 10

THE SMALL SANHEDRIN OF THE TEMPLE MOUNT

The *talmud's* 781-page, 490-000-word tractate *Sanhedrin* leads us through the Jewish trials,[1] with as much detail as present-day legal writers use to describe the Judeo-Anglo-American Common Law system.

The formal etiquette of the opening ceremonies of the Court of the Temple Mount (*bet din*) moved quickly, as soon as the judges could reach their places after the morning sacrifice:

> When the Nasi (*"The Prince "* = President of the Sanhedrin) enters, all the people rise and do not resume their seats until he requests them to sit. When the *Ab-bet-din* ("Father of the Court" = Vice President) enters, one row rises on one side, and another row on the other; and they remain standing until he has sat down in his place. When the *Hakam* (*"Sage "* = learned legal scholar) enters, every one whom he passes rises and sits down (as soon as he passed), until the *Sage* has sat down in his place.
> *Talmud: Horayoth* 13b

This court (also called Small Sanhedrin and Court of the Twenty-Three) sat in an open cloister inside the City Wall,[2] its roof the broad walkway atop the Wall. Only the unfettered Corinthian columns prominent throughout the Temple Mount separated the judicial area from the Court of the Gentiles, just north of the Shushan Gate, the easternmost entrance to the

Mount itself:

> THREE COURTS WERE THERE IN
> JERUSALEM: ONE SITUATE AT THE
> ENTRANCE TO THE MOUNT (on the east gate
> of the Women's Court); ANOTHER AT THE
> DOOR OF THE TEMPLE COURT (the entrance
> of the Court of the Israelites); AND THE THIRD
> IN THE HALL OF HEWN STONES (this was
> partly within and partly without the Temple).
> *Talmud, Sanhedrin* 86b

> CASES CONCERNING OFFENSES PUNISH-
> ABLE BY DEATH ARE DECIDED BY THREE
> AND TWENTY JUDGES . . . .
> *Talmud, Sanhedrin* 1:4

The precedents of a thousand years, spelled out in *torah*, dictated the court's location:[3]

> Judges and officers shalt thou make thee in all thy
> gates . . . and they shall judge the people with
> Judgment:

Clusters of Temple Police patrolled the Mount area, alert for threats to the public peace which could erupt at any time, although the Jesus case did not appear much different from many others: None called him a Zealot, only a powerful preacher from the Galilee; still, no one could take lightly a death penalty case such as Sabbath-breaking,[4] even though they recognized death by stoning[5] as one of God's useful tools to teach others not to break God's Law.

BAVA BEN BUTA (ab-bet-din = Father of the Court): My Lord, I am ready to read the charges.

GAMALIEL BEN SIMEON (*ha nasi* = *The Prince: President of the Court*): You may proceed.

BAVA BEN BUTA: Hear now the averments of the complaining witnesses, Hyman ben Boethus and Abel ben Karah... "That on the third Sabbath just past, in the synagogue of the city of

Capernaum, province of the Lower Galilee, Jesus ben Joseph, a resident of that city, did desecrate the Sabbath in violation of God's holy ordinances, by healing the right arm of one Manasses ben Jotham, whose life was not then in danger."[6]

Ben Buta performed his task of helping the *ha-nasi* move the case along, capsule its issues, call the witnesses in the proper order, and keep watch over the "due process" framework evolved over a millennium.

GAMALIEL BEN SIMEON: The witnesses are all here? We are now ready?

The Jewish system did not allow lawyers[7] to represent "sides" because of the statutes in *Numbers* (35:30) and *Deuteronomy* (17:7;19:15).

> Who so killeth any person, the murderer shall be slain at the mouth of witnesses;

> At the mouth of two witnesses, or at the mouth of three witnesses shall a matter be established.

The judges, over the centuries, held these to mean that the witnesses must tell their stories in their own words, and not through the mouths of lawyers, leaving the judges to assume the roles of questioners, some at first aligning themselves with the prosecuting witnesses, others with the accused; but this only to dig out the facts. At decision time, each judge threw off the cloak of advocate to search faithfully for God's verdict, as demanded by God's Law.

BAVA BEN BUTA: My Holy Master,[8] the witnesses are now ready.

Ben Buta used the normal term of address for those with the Pharisee "characteristics of righteousness": Love of *torah*; piety; kindness; fear of God the Father; and love of fellow man.[9]

GAMALIEL BEN SIMEON: Before I adjure the witnesses, I admonish us all in the Name of Almighty God, for whom we act, to be fearful of the fact that this charge carries the death penalty.

BAVA BEN BUTA: My Lord, the Prince, none in this court makes light of this charge. The need to cause the death of any son of God benumbs us all.

Jesus ben Joseph stood in the well of the court, the witnesses to his right, looking up at the judges:

THE SANHEDRIN SAT IN THE FORM OF A SEMI-CIRCULAR THRESHING FLOOR, SO THAT THEY MIGHT SEE ONE ANOTHER, AND TWO JUDGES' CLERKS STOOD BEFORE THEM, ONE TO THE RIGHT, THE OTHER TO THE LEFT, AND WROTE DOWN THE ARGUMENTS OF THOSE WHO WOULD AC-QUIT AND THOSE WHO WOULD CONDEMN.
Talmud: Sanhedrin 36b

The more senior the judge, the closer he sat to the President.

GAMALIEL BEN SIMON: I shall now inspire the witnesses with awe.[10]

He used a technical phrase required in the *hakirah*[11] (examination covering time and place):

HOW WERE THE WITNESSES INSPIRED WITH AWE? THE WITNESSES IN CAPITAL CHARGES WERE BROUGHT IN AND IN-TIMIDATED THUS:
Talmud: Sanhedrin 37a

GAMALIEL BEN SIMON: Perhaps what you say is based only on conjecture; and by conjecture, I mean circumstantial evidence. Or what you will say is based upon hearsay, a general rumor or secondhand reports. Or you may say to yourselves, "We heard it from a man who is trustworthy." Perhaps you are unaware that ultimately we shall scrutinize your evidence by cross-examination and inquiry . . . .

The disciples-probationers listened intently:

AND THREE ROWS OF SCHOLARS (23 in each row) SAT IN FRONT OF THEM (also in semi-circular form, but on the floor); EACH KNOWING HIS OWN PLACE (the disciples were seated according to rank).
Talmud: Sanhedrin 37a

The *intimidation*[12] dragged on, but all listeners, including the curious watchers, did not become restless: They believed it part of God's plan to sanctify their pursuit of divine justice.

GAMALIEL BEN SIMEON: . . . Perhaps you will say: "Why should we be at these pains? If the moral responsibility is so great, why should we give evidence at all? Quite unintentionally, we may cause a perversion of justice." I remind you that it was long ago written in Leviticus that "if anyone sins in that he hears a public adjuration to testify and yet does not speak, he shall bear his iniquity." So if perchance you say, "Why should we be guilty of the blood of this man?" I remind you that it was also written in the Book of Proverbs "when the wicked perish, there is rejoicing." By this, God's Law means that you have a solemn duty to Almighty God, to this man standing before the bar of this Court, and to all Israel, not to bear false witness; but the public good requires that you tell us what you know of this case.

The entire assembly sagged physically as the first phase of the trial ended.

Temple guards led away all the witnesses but Manassas ben Jothan out of earshot so they could not hear the other witnesses testify.

The rule for segregation of witnesses[13] first appeared in the case of Susanna 200 years earlier. Two "elders" accused her of adultery after she rebutted their sexual advances. A judge named Daniel doubted her guilt and cross-examined the accusers separately about the tree under which the alleged sex acts took place. Their stories did not agree, which meant they become *zomen* (false witnesses): Any case tainted by *zomen* required automatic dismissal.

GAMALIEL BEN SIMEON: (*looking directly at the accused*): I shall now proceed with the *reassurance*.[14] Jesus ben Joseph, even were I not personally so inclined, the Law requires me to *reassure* you that if you are innocent, you have nothing to fear. It was long ago decided that "He who judges his neighbor in the scale of merit is himself judged favorably."[15] God's Law entreats this to mean that we must seek "a favorable interpretation of a man's actions, even when they look suspicious."[16] You are presumed innocent of any charge until believable witnesses convince us otherwise. It has also been held that "The judge is to be concerned only with what he actually sees with his own eyes."[17] The Law cautions us that our decision must be based only upon the testimony we hear this day in this place;[18] and we must follow the admonition of God to Moses when He said, "You shall not be partial in judgment; you shall hear the small and the great alike; you shall not be afraid of the face of man, for the judgment is God's."[19]

Procedurally, they moved into the *derishah*,[20] the direct examination of who acted in what way, how and perhaps why, ready to explore whether the "healing" in the synagogue in Capernaum amounted to the grave "sin" of Sabbath-breaking.

The *theocracy*[21] of the Jews (Greek = God rule; government by a group of priests claiming divine authority; *Josephus* coined the word) did not distinguish things sacred from things secular, everything considered sacred. The Hebrew language, therefore, did not know the words "crime" or "offense." Murder, rape, incest, robbery — all told, thirty-six acts which carried the death penalty — bore the label "sins" (*het'; pesha'; avon*[22]), since they breached God's divine Law.

The purpose of it all rang clear: God's Law and God's judgments must be guaranteed by able and dedicated judges, for "A judge who delivers a judgment in perfect truth causes the *shechinah* (Holy Spirit; God's Presence) to dwell in Israel ... And he who does not deliver judgments in perfect truth causes the *shechinah* to depart from the midst of Israel."[23]

This spirit enveloped the Small Sanhedrin of the Temple Mount as Jesus bar Joseph's trial for Sabbath-breaking moved into it substantive phase.

Papyrus 2 from the Pacific School of Religion. Left: John 6:17-22. Right: John 6:8-12. (Approximately actual size. With permission of Palestine Instituture, Pacific School of Religion, Berkeley).

Chapter 11

DIRECT EXAMINATION: THE HEALING ACT

GAMALIEL BEN SIMEON: Manasses ben Jotham, the law demands that you identify the accused.[1] I adjure you by the living God, do you recognize the man standing next to your left?
MANASSES BEN JOTHAM: I do, my Lord.

The answer came slowly and with embarrassment, until Jesus' nod and smile licensed Manasses to answer the jurist's questions fully, hold back nothing.

GAMALIEL BEN SIMEON: Is he the same Jesus ben Joseph who spoke to you in the synagogue at Capernaum three Sabbaths just past?
MANASSES BEN JOTHAM: He is, my Lord.
GAMALIEL BEN SIMEON: You have no doubt?
MANASSES BEN JOTHAM: No doubt at all, my Lord, the nasi. Could I ever mistake this one?
GAMALIEL BEN SIMEON: Are we sure of the identification?

Ben Simeon looked first to his left, then to the right, the nods of his fellow judges telling him to spend no more time on the identification.

GAMALIEL BEN SIMEON: Manasses ben Jotham, I must next proceed to the seven "searching inquiries,"[2] and I caution you in advance that if your answer to any of these be in error, all that you say goes out. In what Sabbath-of-years did your meeting with

Jesus ben Joseph take place?

After their settlement in Canaan, the Jews used Sabbath-of-years in their reckoning of time, counting six years as work years, when they tilled the soil; but the seventh became the *sabbatical year* when the land lay fallow to regain its strength. They called these seven consecutive years a Sabbath-of-years, and seven Sabbath-of-years became a Jubilee: 7 x 7 + 1 = 50.

Gamaliel ben Simeon continued with the "searching inquiries":

In what year?

In what month?

On what day of the month?

On what day of the week?

In what hour?

All moved as part of a careful design to see if the witness' story should be believed.

GAMALIEL BEN SIMEON: Exactly where did this meeting with the accused take place?

MANASSES BEN JOTHAM: In the synagogue in Capernaum.[3]

That ended the "searching inquiries," save one.

BAVA BEN BUTA: My Lord, the Prince, I doubt the need to hear him relate the entire worship service.

Sitting to Gamaliel ben Simeon's immediate right where he performed his duties as *ab-bet-din*, his words came out precise, yet courteous.

JOSE BEN HISDA: Ah, most Holy Master, we must hear it all, else how can we judge the healing Act.

Ben Hisda spoke as one of the seventeen Pharisee judges who dominated the Court.[4] Whether Pharisee or Sadducee, all rated the respected title of scribe (*scribe* = legal scholar; sage; doctor of law; one learned in the Law), "rabbi" just coming into use as a synonym for "scribe."[5]

Gamaliel ben Simeon quickly sensed his associates' agreement with ben Hisda.

GAMALIEL BEN SIMEON: We must hear it all; and I remind the witness that he will be cross-examined in detail when he finishes his direct testimony.

MANASSES BEN JOTHAM: Yes, my Lord.

Manasses ben Jotham bowed his respect.

GAMALIEL BEN SIMEON: Had you known the accused before?

MANASSES BEN JOTHAM: I have heard him preach many times, not only in our synagogue, but in Nazareth and around the Lake. I have spoken to him, but only to say "shalom" in friendly greeting.

GAMALIEL BEN SIMEON: And he returned your greetings?

MANASSES BEN JOTHAM: Yes, my Lord.

GAMALIEL BEN SIMEON: How many times before the synagogue service three Sabbaths ago had you spoken to him?

MANASSES BEN JOTHAM: Perhaps half-a-dozen, my Lord.

GAMALIEL BEN SIMEON: Tell us what happened.

Manasses ben Jotham looked again to Jesus ben Joseph standing not over two feet to his left; and Jesus once more reassured him. He continued his report of the service: Song, responsive readings, prayers, readings from *torah* and the prophets, then Jesus' sermon.

GAMALIEL BEN SIMEON (*prodding patiently*): Was that the end of the sermon? Tell us what happened next?

MANASSES BEN JOTHAM: I will try, my Lord. Jesus ben Joseph started down the steps from the pulpit; and I can remember thinking that I wished he would never stop speaking. I did not see how I could ever be as close to Heaven than I was then, standing there — looking up at him — listening to his words.

BAVA BEN BUTA (*firmly*): I interrupt the witness with great regret; but I have a legal duty to *warn* him that he may be edging close to the sin of blasphemy if he continues this line of speaking.

MANASSES BEN JOTHAM: Yes, my Lord. I did not intend . . .

GAMALIEL BEN SIMEON (*interrupting again*): Please continue, and for your sake and for the rest of us, I also admonish you to heed the *warning* of the *ab-bet-din*.

MANASSES BEN JOTHAM: I will try, my Lord; and thank you — I remember thinking "I have been forgiven, I am restored . . . . "

BAVA BEN BUTA (*sternly*): . . . You ignore my warning! I admonish you once more in the Name of the Living God, that you move close to the sin of blasphemy.

MANASSES BEN JOTHAM: I mean no sin, Most Holy Master; but my Lord, the President, asked me to tell what happened next. That is all I mean to do.

GAMALIEL BEN SIMEON: Yes, please get on with it.

MANASSES BEN JOTHAM: I felt a shudder start at the top of my head and move down through my neck, and shoulders, and back, and legs, all the way to the tile floor which I felt through my sandals. I stood stunned — in a trance — as something pulled me toward Jesus ben Joseph. I took one step, then another, just to be near him. I knew I could not speak. He did not see me at first — I do not think he did; or if he did, he gave me no sign. Then, of a sudden, I stood in front of him, maybe two steps away — Half-a-dozen men between us stepped backward, as if they felt something unusual. If there were other sounds, I did not hear them, but heard only my pounding heart.

Ben Jotham stopped talking, his voice choked with emotion.

GAMALIEL BEN SIMEON: Please go on! We must have it all.

MANASSES BEN JOTHAM: I felt like a feather, expecting any puff of wind to swirl me around and raise me up. Then I knew he was about to speak to me — to me and to nobody else; and I looked straight in his eyes. I could not pull my eyes away from his. He looked in me — and at me — and all the way through me: but somehow, he stayed right inside me. Every humor of my body felt him. Then his smile came, first the sunlight dancing from his eyes;

and next, the curling of his mouth, and the dimpling of his checks; and he said "Stretch out your hand!"

BAVA BEN BUTA (*impatiently*): Did he touch you? Was he close enough to reach you with his hands?

GAMALIEL BEN SIMEON: My Lord, the *ab-bet-din*, I suggest that we let the witness finish before we begin our cross-examination.

BAVA BEN BUTA: Yes, my Lord, *ha-nasi*. Forgive my eagerness to learn the facts.

GAMALIEL BEN SIMEON: Please continue.

MANASSES BEN JOTHAM: I guess there is not much left to tell. I stretched out my right hand, and it moved. No matter what he would have told me to do, I would have done it, and could have done it! He made me want to do something for him. There was no way I could keep my right arm against my side when he told me to stretch it out. I . . .

BAVA BEN BUTA (*interrupting*): Was it a loud shout, an order, a command, or what?

Gamaliel ben Simeon did not interfere, the question totally relevant, Manasses obviously finished with his direct testimony. He needed help, to let them probe further the details of Jesus ben Joseph's healing technique.

MANASSES BEN JOTHAM: My Lord, I cannot tell you what it was. All I know is that what he said, I knew I must do; and I knew I *could* do whatever he told me. I remember looking down at my right arm, the one I held flush against my side for three long years — a lifetime — and saw it pointed toward Jesus ben Joseph. I saw first the back of my hand, and turned it over slowly until I could see the pale softness of my palm. I opened my fingers; and as they closed again, I remember thinking that, yes, they could grip my stonemason's hammer once more.

I began to move the arm from the shoulder and found I could raise it over my head, and then let it down, and move it across my chest.

I no longer felt afraid, whatever sin I committed to wither my arm forgiven. I could not control myself. I began to jump and dance, shout and cry, and laugh like a wild man: My right arm as whole as my left! The God of our fathers be praised! I would be able to work again. I could care for my wife and son.

Manasses' voice choked, tears of joy flowing down his cheeks. He swiped at his dripping nose with the wide sleeve of his coarse robe, almost ready to jump and shout again.

GAMALIEL BEN SIMEON (*helpfully*): Is that all?

MANASSES BEN JOTHAM: I guess it is, my Lord; except that when I looked for Jesus ben Joseph to thank him, he was not there. I guess he slipped out the south door of the synagogue, while everyone else watched me.

Chapter 12

CROSS-EXAMINATION: THE WARNING

JOSE BEN HISDA: Did you, or anyone in your presence, *warn*[1] Jesus ben Joseph that he would be guilty of the sin of Sabbath-breaking if he made any attempt to heal your "withered arm?"
MANASSES BEN JOTHAM: No, my Lord. How could we? I did not know what he meant to do: and how could anyone else know either?

Ben Hisda moved quickly to open the cross-examination (*bedikoth*),[2] aligning himself as champion of Jesus ben Joseph, in effect, performing the role of modern "lawyer."

In his seat five places to the President's right, I see his rank of seniority midway between the highest and the lowest of the twenty-three judges. At age fifty, he could be a graduate of either *bet Hillel* or bet *Shammai* Academy[3] nine years earlier, ordained by the Great Sanhedrin and sent to the *bet din* (Small Sanhedrin; Court of the Twenty-Three) in Joppa, on the Mediterranean coast west of Jerusalem. After apprenticeship in Joppa, he would be promoted to the *bet din* of the Temple Mount to sit as a disciple-probationer for two years, waiting to attain full judge status.[4]

We can imagine his change coming in a run-of-the-mill murder case (if any case which takes human life can be run-of-the-mill) when he identified himself with the accused and asked to speak in his defense, so impressing the twenty-three judges with his advocacy, oratory, knowledge of the law, and sensitivity that the Great Sanhedrin in the Hall of the Hewn Stone made him a full-fledged judge of the Court of the Temple Mount.[5]

Now, in his first question in the *bedikoth*, ben Hisda pricked open the key legal issue of the *warning*.

JOSE BEN HISDA (*evenly but persistently*): My Lord, *ha-nasi*, we must settle the question of the *warning* now; else, if we find later that this witness' testimony is inadmissible and the whole case falls, we will have harassed the accused without just cause.

GAMALIEL BEN SIMEON: Very well; we'll hear you on the *warning*.

JOSE BEN HISDA: Sabbath-breaking is clearly a sin which requires prior *warning*. I submit that the best statement of the rule on *warning* in general is *Tractate Sanhedrin*, 8b:[6] "For it has been taught: All those under sentence of death according to the *torah* are to be executed only by the decree of a Court of twenty-three, after proper evidence and *warning*, and provided the warners have let them know that they are liable to a death sentence at the hand of the Court.... The warners must also inform them of the kind of death they would suffer; and failing that, they are not to be executed."

RAMI BEN EZEKIEL (*testily and with some arrogance*): May we be spared the lecture of our Brother on the basic rule itself which, pray Heaven, we must all surely know by this time. If he has help to give, let it be on the reason behind the rule: How does its rationale affect the question of whether this particular witness must join in the *warning* of the accused before this witness's testimony is admissible.

Ben Ezekiel would perhaps be a graduate of the Shammai Academy (*bet Shammai*), the more conservative school, and a Sadducee.

JOSE BEN HISDA (*calmly, though fighting to maintain composure*): My Brethren well know there is no single rationale for the rule, but several. If it pleases ben Ezekiel, I will state them all, though I consider this more an intellectual insult to our learned Brethren than the one ben Ezekiel implies to me.

BAVA BEN BUTA (*losing patience*): May we get on with the argument, and be spared the endless squabbles between *bet Hillel* and *bet Shammai*.

JOSE BEN HISDA: The cases cited in *Tractates Sanhedrin* and *Makkoth* ("beatings"; "stripes"), state the reason for the rule: Ignorance of the Law *is* a valid defense to any sin triable before this Court. No person is punishable for a transgression committed in the mistaken belief that his act was lawful: It is the burden of the prosecuting witnesses to prove that at least two competent witnesses expressly *warned* him immediately before he acted that his act would be sinful. The *warning* must be clear: The accused must be told that if he commits the act, he will be liable to the penalty provided by God's Law, and the penalty must be named: Stripes, or death by stoning, burning, beheading or strangling.

RAMI BEN EZEKIEL (*haughtily*): Our Brother shows his shallowness by merely offering us the same explanation in a different suit of clothes.

JOSE BEN HISDA: I do not wish to insult the intelligence of my Brethren by suggesting that they are less learned than I; and I do so only at the urging of our Brother ben Ezekiel himself.

GAMALIEL BEN SIMEON (*patiently*): Pray be on with it.

JOSE BEN HISDA (*confidently, but without haughtiness*): There is a further reason: The antecedent *warning* lets the Court distinguish between the intentional (*mezid*) and the unintentional (*shogeg*) sinner; and this, in turn, helps the Law better decide how each shall be punished.[7]

RAMI BEN EZEKIEL (*interrupting*): I prefer to believe that the true reason behind the rule of pre-admonition is the misguided effort of certain jurists, particularly those of *bet Hillel*, to make the Law lax, and force us away from the death penalty in cases where death is the only effective deterrent. I quote *Makkoth, 7a*, which says, "A Sanhedrin that effects an execution once in seven years, is branded a destructive tribunal; other judges say once in seventy years." May I suggest that if our interpretations of the rule of antecedent *warning* become any more rigid, we will soon reach a point where we cannot convict any transgressor. The Law, upon which Judaism itself rests, can then become only a mockery, the judges a laughingstock. When we cannot preserve public order, the protection of personal liberties will become a sham.

JOSE BEN HISDA: Not so, my Brothers! The rule of preadmonition serves us well, since it is a humane rule. It has, indeed, developed technically; but need I remind this Court that personal liberty rests only on legal technicalities? Vague generalities do not preserve your rights and mine. It is only the ability of the accused to claim a legal technicality which this Court will enforce, that protects him from the arbitrary whim of his ruler, be they Roman, or Jewish, or others.

ISAAC BEN JOHAI: I suggest that both my Brethren miss the key question. No one doubts that Sabbath-breaking requires a prior *warning* since this sin does not fall within any of the exceptions,[8] such as false witness, idolatry, burglary in the nighttime, or the sins for which the punishment is *karet* (excision).[9] So let us all admit that the fundamental rule of preadmonition must be met; otherwise, the accused, Jesus ben Joseph, will go free. I suggest that the real question is whether *each* witness who testifies must begin his evidence by stating that he, personally *warned* the accused of the sin, and its punishment. I do not believe that the Law makes any such demand, else as has been suggested by our Brother ben Ezekiel, we could place ourselves in the awkward position of not being able to convict any transgressor. I assert, therefore, that the evidence of the witness, Manassas ben Jotham, can be used, even though he personally did not give the *warning*, if we hear evidence later that some other witnesses *warned* the accused.

GAMALIEL BEN SIMEON: Can you cite support for your position?

ISAAC BEN JOHAI (*confidently*): Gladly, my Lord, *ha-nasi*. We must never overlook fundamentals. Our ordinance base is Deuteronomy which provides, "On the evidence of two witnesses or of three witnesses he that is to die shall be put to death; a person shall not be put to death on the evidence of one witness." This is the springboard for our case law on all testimonies. It has produced many highlight decisions. For example, in *Tractate Sanhedrin 6b*, we find, "Ye shall not hold back your words because of anyone . . . "

RAMI BEN EZEKIEL (*interrupting, and enjoying the sound of his own voice*): My Brethren, while the concept of pre-warning goes all the way back to Noah, as spelled out in *Tractate Sanhedrin*

56b, I challenge any of you to show that either we or the Great Sanhedrin have ever held that each and every witness must give the accused a detailed *warning* before we can accept his testimony. Such a rule simply would not work; we could convict absolutely no one; our legal system would fall apart.

JOSE BEN HISDA: I accept my Brother's challenge, and cite *Sanhedrin 5:1*: "They used to prove witnesses with seven inquiries." Since one of the inquiries is still "Did ye *warn* him?", this must mean that the witness cannot be "proved" without the *warning;* and if he cannot be "proved," how can he be a valid witness?

ISAAC BEN JOHAI: May I speak without being interrupted! My Brother misses the point completely. I gladly admit that at least two witnesses must *warn* the accused . . . .

JOSE BEN HISDA (*interrupting again*): May I cite but two more cases, *Makkoth 1:8*, which states, "As the evidence of two witnesses is void if one of them is found to be a kinsman or ineligible, so the evidence of three is void if one of them is found to be a kinsman or ineligible . . ." Another case extends this rule to mean "The witness must have warned the transgressor, otherwise he is not a valid witness."[10]

RAMI BEN EZEKIEL (*arrogantly*): I know both cases; and you misconstrue them. Obviously, the opinions are poorly argued, else there would be no ambiguity. I suggest that you all overlook a graver problem. If Manasses ben Jotham is to be included in the "set" or "group" of prosecuting witnesses, the testimony of the entire "set" collapses[11] if any individual witness becomes ineligible. Let me cite the rule from *Tractate Makkoth 6b*: "If two persons see the malefactor from one window and two other persons see him from another window and one standing midway utters the pre-admonition to him, then, if some on one side and some on the other side can see one another, they constitute together one body of evidence; but if they cannot partially see one another, they are two bodies of evidence . . . A malefactor is never put to death unless two witnesses had duly pre-admonished him, as Holy Writ prescribes."

ISAAC BEN JOHAI (*warming to the contest*): There is another consideration: Manasses ben Jotham is still a valid witness under the rule of "disjointed testimony."[12] Under that rule, the witnesses who see the transgression, but who do not see each other, cannot be conjoined into one "set" or "group"; so if any two witnesses present in the Capernaum synagogue did give the pre-*warning* requirement, we can still receive Manasses ben Jotham's evidence, even though he personally did not conjoin them in giving the pre-*warning*.

JOSE BEN HISDA: Do we not face a different, perhaps even graver problem, with this man's testimony? He is also the "victim."[13] He has been called as a witness, and we have heard his direct testimony. How can we not consider him a member of the "set" or "group" of witnesses for the prosecuting side?[14] I urge that before the Law can guarantee any protection for personal rights, we must rule that Manasses ben Jotham's testimony should go out unless he can tell us, under the fear of penalty of false witness,[15] that *before* Jesus ben Joseph healed his withered arm, he forewarned him that he was about to commit the sin of Sabbath-breaking, and told the accused further that the penalty for this sin would be death by stoning.

RAMI BEN EZEKIEL: Ridiculous! That ruling would make imbeciles of us all.

GAMALIEL BEN SIMEON (*with great dignity*): If the preservation of individual rights requires each of us to slobber at the mouth and babble like an idiot, is it not a small enough price to pay?

ISAAC BEN JOHAI: Are we not getting confused with a rule of procedure instead of one of substance? I suggest that our problem is imaginary and brought on only by the order in which the witnesses are called. If some other witness had been called before Manasses ben Jotham, and this first witness testified that he and one other legally *warned* Jesus ben Joseph before the healing, this problem would never come up at all.

I raise a further and perhaps more ambiguous question. Need a scholar (*haber*) or a learned man be pre-*warned*? Some call the accused "learned."

RAMI BEN EZEKIEL: I am familiar with the decision in *Tractate Sanhedrin 8b* that "A scholar is held responsible for his sins, even without being formally warned, as *warning* is only a means of deciding whether one has committed the crime willfully or not."

ISAAC BEN JOHAI (*gleefully*): There is a similar line of cases in *Tractate Sanhedrin 72b* that a scholar need not be *warned*, because a *warning* is necessary only to distinguish between ignorance and presumption. Hence, a scholar who knows what is forbidden need not be *warned*, even if his sin is punishable by the *bet din*.

JOSE BEN HISDA: I submit that those are not binding precedents, since an opposing and better rule is also stated in *Tractate Sanhedrin 72b*: "All transgressors, including scholars, must be formally *warned*, and the *warning* accepted . . . punishment by a *bet din* must be preceded by a *warning*." To hold that the "scholar" is exempt from the pre-*warning* means that we must not only define generally who is a "scholar," but also decide whether each accused is or is not to be rated a "scholar." This would impose a more tedious burden than we could comfortably meet. Must we stop this case to decide if this accused is correctly called "learned," or perhaps a "scholar?"

RAMI BEN EZEKIEL (*pompously*): My Lord, *ha-nasi*, I'll bring the matter to a head. I move this august Court that we receive the testimony of Manasses ben Jotham, subject to casting it out later if at least two other witnesses do not testify that they gave Jesus ben Joseph an express pre-*warning* that he was about to commit the sin of Sabbath-breaking, and that if he insisted on committing the transgression, he would be subject to trial by the *bet din*, and to the penalty of death by stoning.

And so the judges argued in the Jesus ben Joseph case in the Small Sanhedrin of the Temple Mount. As in all their courts, they loved argument for argument's sake, debate only to be debating, thrilling to the challenge of dissecting a new legal issue, splitting hairs, nit-picking, bickering, parrying, most of their comments relevant, but some too tedious to shed real light.

They came to their tasks well-prepared, knowledge of the Law only the beginning, moral qualities bearing equal billing: "These are seven in number, wisdom, modesty, fear of God, love of people, of truth, hate of greed, and respectability."[16]

Their appointments attempted to guarantee understanding and compassion: "We do not appoint as members of the Sanhedrin, an aged man, a eunuch or one who is childless, or a cruel man."[17] God's justices needed also to be full-blooded Israelites, without "blemish" or physical defect,"[18] " . . . men of stature, wisdom, good appearance, mature age [40 years], with a knowledge of sorcery (so that they could detect those who seduced and perverted by means of witchcraft), and who are conversant with all the seventy languages of mankind, in order that the Court should have no need for an interpreter."[19]

They searched for God's Law in Jesus' Sabbath-breaking trial, as they did in all others, so that the *shechinah* (Holy Spirit; God's Presence) would not depart from Israel.[20]

They found God's Law to control each step of the case, by looking back to the *precedent* of decided cases:

> MOSES RECEIVED THE TORAH (Scripture and its complementary Oral Instruction, with special reference to the latter) AT SINAI AND TRANS-MITTED IT TO JOSHUA, (The transmission and reception were done orally. All evidence goes to show that there was a continuous succession of 'schools' headed by the Elders, prophets and scribes of their respective generations, which maintained and developed the theoretical study and practical application of the Torah. The strength of the schools and their influence varied from time to time, but there is no reason for supposing that there was at any time an actual break in the continuity) . . .
>
> JOSHUA TO THE ELDERS, ("Elders" includes the "Judges"),
>
> AND THE ELDERS TO THE PROPHETS,
>
> AND THE PROPHETS TO THE MEN OF THE GREAT SYNAGOGUE (*Kenesseth ha-Gedolah*: A Body of 120 men founded by the leaders of the Jews who returned from the Babylonian Captivity.)
>
> SIMEON THE RIGHTEOUS WAS ONE OF

THE LAST OF THE MEN OF THE GREAT
SYNAGOGUE.

ANTIGONUS (the first noted Jew known to have
had a Greek name, third century B.C.E.)
RECEIVED THE ORAL TRADITION FROM
SIMEON THE RIGHTEOUS.

JOSE B. JO'EZER OF ZEREDAH, AND JOSE
B. JOHANAN OF JERUSALEM RECEIVED
THE ORAL TRADITION FROM THEM
(SIMEON THE RIGHTEOUS AND AN-
TIGONUS).

JOSHUA B. PERAHIAH AND NITTAI THE
ARBELITE RECEIVED THE ORAL TRADI-
TION FROM THEM.

JUDAH B. TABBAI AND SIMEON B. SHETAH
RECEIVED THE ORAL TRADITION FROM
THEM.

SHEMAIAH AND ABTALION RECEIVED
THE ORAL TRADITION FROM THEM.

HILLEL AND SHAMMAI RECEIVED THE
ORAL TRADITION FROM THEM.
Talmud: Aboth 1:1-16

Precedent spelled it all out, if they but searched diligently to
find it, from Moses to Joshua, through Hillel and Shammai, to
Hillel's heir, the *ha-nasi* of the *bet din* of the Temple Mount that
tried Jesus ben Joseph for Sabbath-breaking.

Did they suddenly cast it all aside for that one brief moment
after Jesus' arrest in Gethsamene, and railroad him to his death
in a rump trial "in the house of the High Priest?"

Hardly!

Papyrus Bodmer II, Page 1: John 1:14. (Actual size. With permission of Bibliotheca Bodmeriana, Cologny, Geneva).

Chapter 13

CROSS-EXAMINATION: SABBATH BREAKING

GAMALIEL BEN SIMEON: Hyman ben Boethus, you were admonished at the beginning of your direct testimony that you would be tested by cross-examination. Let me reassure you that if your evidence is truthful and accurate, you have nothing to fear; but if it proves to be contradictory and unreliable, we must declare you *zomen*[1] (false witness) which makes you subject to the Law of Retaliation (*lex talionis*) as stated in *Deuteronomy*:[2] "If the witness is a false witness and has accused his brother falsely, then you shall do to him as he had meant to do to his brother; so you shall purge the evil from the midst of you. And the rest shall hear, and fear, and shall never again commit any such evil among you. Your eye shall have not pity; it shall be life for life, eye for eye, tooth for tooth, hand for hand, foot for foot." I am under a legal duty to attempt to embarrass and confuse you,[3] so that the truth may be known. Do you understand?

HYMAN BEN BOETHUS: I do, my Lord the Prince, and stand ready for your *bedikoth*.

Ben Boethus, sent by the Committee of Ten to spy on Jesus and now one of the complaining witnesses to the healing at Capernaum, a Sadducee and member of one of the four great families, perhaps flashed a cocky smile. His reports of the basic facts came out simple enough; he feared only being tripped up on minute details.

GIDEON BEN TARFON (*aligning himself for the accused*): You

witnessed the healing of the so-called "withered arm" at the close
of the regular Sabbath service in the synagogue in Capernaum?[4]

HYMAN BEN BOETHUS: Yes, most honored Master.

GIDEON BEN TARFON: And others witnessed it also?

HYMAN BEN BOETHUS: I speak only for myself with certainty;
but is it not reasonable to expect that others in the nave of the
synagogue saw it also?

GIDEON BEN TARFON: And as Jesus ben Joseph walked down
the steps toward the victim, Manassas ben Jotham . . . tell me
exactly what color of robe the accused wore?

The sudden shift of subject matter momentarily confused
ben Boethus, exactly as ben Tarfon intended. Ben Boethus stood
mute.

GIDEON BEN TARFON: Can you not answer?

HYMAN BEN BOETHUS (*hesitant, almost hostile*): I — well — I
think — is it really necessary that I remember the color of his robe?

GIDEON BEN TARFON: My Lord, *ha-nasi*, I submit that the
question is relevant, and cite *Tractate Sanhedrin 41a* as the rule:
"If one witness says, He slew him with a sword, and the other says,
with a dagger; or if one says, His clothes were black, and the other,
They were white, the evidence is not certain: This means that it
is inadmissible since the evidence must tally, even in respect of
matters which have no direct bearing on the act." I am permitted
the question to test his recollection.

Gamaliel ben Simeon nodded ben Tarfon to continue.

GIDEON BEN TARFON: I ask again, can you answer?

HYMAN BEN BOETHUS: If it was not the same robe he now
wears, it was one just like it.

GIDEON BEN TARFON: And his sandals? What color were
they?

HYMAN BEN BOETHUS: I cannot say my Lord, for I do not
remember that I looked at them.

On it went, everything coned down to the central thrust of

uncovering the truth, to keep an accused from being convicted on the evidence of *zomen* (false witness), the safety factor the *lex talionis* (Law of Retaliation) which an exposed *zomen* would face.

The judges probed deeply into the Law of Sabbath-breaking, important enough to be repeated nine separate times in the *torah's* Primitive Codes, the Priestly Codes, the Holiness Code, the Supplemental Priestly Codes, and detailed fully in *Deuteronomy* 5:12-15:

> Observe the sabbath day, to keep it holy, as the Lord your God commanded you.
>
> Six days you shall labor, and do all your work;
>
> but the seventh day is a sabbath to the Lord your God; in it you shall not do any work, you, or your son, or your daughter, or your manservant, or your maidservant, or your ox, or your ass, or any of your cattle, or the sojourner who is within your gates, that your manservant and your maidservant may rest as well as you.
>
> You shall remember that you were a servant in the land of Egypt, and the Lord your God brought you out thence with a mighty hand and an outstretched arm; therefore the Lord your God commanded you to keep the sabbath day.

Ezekiel, the brilliant writer of the Babylonia Exile, told them why they fell from God's grace and ended in captivity (*Ezekiel* 20:12-13):

> Moreover I gave them my sabbaths, as a sign between me and them, that they might know that I the Lord sanctify them.
>
> But the house of Israel rebelled against me in the wilderness; they did not walk in my statutes but rejected my ordinances, by whose observance man shall live; and my sabbaths they greatly profaned.

He told them during the captivity that God would relent and give them a second chance, provided the people would (*Ezekiel* 20:21):

> . . . hallow my sabbaths that they may be a sign between me and you, that you may know that I the Lord am your God.

The second chance came with the Return; but the Returnees and their children ignored the lessons of their horrors in Babylon. Within a century (around 400 B.C.), Ezra and Nehemiah felt the need to call the people of Jerusalem to the Great Synagogue, to read the Law and again warn them (*Nehemiah* 13:15-18):

> In those days I saw in Judah men treading wine presses on the sabbath, and bringing in heaps of grain and loading them on asses; and also wine, grapes, figs and all kinds of burdens, which they brought into Jerusalem on the sabbath day; and I warned them on the day when they sold food.

> Then I remonstrated with the nobles of Judah and said to them, "What is this evil thing which you are doing, profaning the sabbath day?

> "Did not your fathers act in this way, and did not our God bring all this evil on us and on this city? Yet you bring more wrath upon Israel by profaning the sabbath."

Over the centuries, in an effort to protect them against God's wrath and another Exile, the judges built a "fence" around the Sabbath Commandment, to guarantee its safety, and evolved 39 separate types of prohibited work:

> THE PRIMARY LABOURS ARE FORTY LESS ONE, (viz.:) SOWING, PLOUGHING, REAPING, BINDING SHEAVES, THRESHING, WINNOW-ING, SELECTING (sorting unfit food from the fit), GRINDING, SIFTING, KNEADING, BAKING, SHEARING WOOL, BLEACHING,

HACKLING (grading or separating flax or hemp), DYEING, SPINNING, STRETCHING THE THREADS (on a loom), DIVIDING TWO THREADS (the end of the web), TYING (knotting) AND UNTYING, SEWING TWO STITCHES, TEARING IN ORDER TO SEW TWO STITCHES, CAPTURING A DEER, SLAUGHTERING, OR FLAYING, OR SALTING IT, CURING ITS HIDE, SCRAPING IT (of its hair), CUTTING IT UP, WRITING TWO LETTERS, ERASING IN ORDER TO WRITE TWO LETTERS (over the erasure), BUILDING, PULLING DOWN, EXTINGUISHING, KINDLING, STRIKING WITH A HAMMER (giving the finishing blow), (and) CARRYING OUT FROM ONE DOMAIN TO ANOTHER: THESE ARE THE FORTY PRIMARY LABOURS, LESS ONE.

Talmud: Shabbath 73a

The thirty-nine "Fathers of Work" produced "offspring," as case after case came before the judges, many involving questions of "healing":

IF ONE HAS PAIN IN HIS THROAT, HE MAY POUR MEDICINE IN HIS MOUTH ON THE SABBATH, BECAUSE IT (the pain) IS A POSSIBILITY OF DANGER TO HUMAN LIFE: AND EVERY DANGER TO HUMAN LIFE SUSPENDS THE LAWS OF THE SABBATH.

Talmud: Yoma 83a

But then that line of precedent went mushy as they searched for rules of what constituted a "healing" and a "danger to human life":

WE MAY NOT EAT GREEK HYSSOP (aromatic, pungent plant) BECAUSE IT IS NOT THE FOOD OF HEALTHY PEOPLE (this makes it obviously a medicine):

Talmud: Sabbath 109a

Taking an obvious medicine automatically converted the act into a healing intention; and they would then need to prove "danger to human life" to exempt it from the Sabbath laws:

> IF ONE'S TEETH PAIN HIM, HE MUST NOT SIP VINEGAR THROUGH THEM (this is healing, forbidden on the Sabbath), BUT HE MAY DIP HIS BREAD IN VINEGAR IN THE USUAL MANNER (and eat the vinegar-soaked bread), AND IF HE IS CURED, HE IS CURED!

> IF ONE'S LOINS PAIN HIM, HE MUST NOT RUB THEM WITH WINE OR VINEGAR, BUT MAY ANOINT THEM WITH OIL (since this is done without intention of healing); BUT NOT WITH ROSE OIL (which ordinary people use only as a remedy).

They feared indulgence, the condoning of "work" that would violate God's holy Laws, and cause them another horrible punishment:

> WE MAY DELIVER A WOMAN ON THE SABBATH, SUMMON A MIDWIFE FOR HER FROM PLACE TO PLACE, DESECRATE THE SABBATH ON HER ACCOUNT, AND TIE UP THE NAVEL-STRING . . .

> If a woman is in confinement, as long as the uterus is open, whether she states, 'I need oil,' or 'I do not need it,' we must desecrate the Sabbath on her account.

> If the uterus is closed, whether she says 'I need it' or 'I do not need it,' we may not desecrate the Sabbath for her as there is no danger to life . . .
> *Talmud: Shabbath* 128a-129b

"The Judges forbad the crushing of medical ingredients . . . save where life is in danger."[5]

But what of the whole gambit of remedies around which human life turned:

" . . . the placing of a hot cup upon the navel to alleviate stomach ache is permitted."[6]

" . . . one may go out on the Sabbath with a hargol's egg which is carried for earache . . . "[7]

" . . . he who spreads a poultice evenly over a sore on the Sabbath is culpable on the grounds of scraping (one of the forbidden categories of 'work') . . . "[8]

" . . . one may not use a chip on the Sabbath as a suppository in the same way as one uses it on weekdays . . . "[9]

"If one knocks his hand or foot, he may reduce the swelling with wine (and have no fear of Sabbath-breaking) . . . but not with vinegar (its purpose is too obviously medicinal)."[10]

" . . . Scurvy [a generalized weakness due to Vitamin C deficiency] can be cured by taking stones of olives which have not become ripe, burn them in fire upon a new rake, and stick them into the inside of the gums . . . . Why is it permitted to do this on the Sabbath? . . . whereas scurvy starts in the mouth, it ends in the intestines (so it is life-threatening) . . . "[11]

" . . . vomiting cannot be induced with a drug, but it may be done by hand (by thrusting the finger down the throat)."[12]

"A woman may go out with a preserving stone on the Sabbath (as a safeguard against abortion) . . . "[13]

Talmud: Shabbath 147a stated the controlling *precedents* in Jesus' trial:

> YOU MUST NOT STRAIGHTEN AN INFANT'S
> LIMBS (by manipulation), OR SET A BROKEN
> BONE. IF ONE'S HAND OR FOOT IS DISLO-
> CATED, HE MUST NOT AGITATE IT
> VIOLENTLY IN COLD WATER BUT MAY
> BATHE IT IN THE USUAL WAY, AND IF IT
> HEALS, IT HEALS.

If Jesus spoke at all at his trial (he could not be forced to incriminate himself), he perhaps repeated his earlier-stated approach to the Sabbath Laws: "The Sabbath was made for man, and not man for the Sabbath!"[14]

After the taking of evidence ended, the arguments of the judges began:

> CAPITAL CHARGES MUST BE OPENED (judi-
> cial debate on the matter) FOR ACQUITTAL,
> BUT NOT FOR CONDEMNATION.

> ... IN CAPITAL CHARGES, WE COMMENCE
> WITH THE OPINION OF THOSE ON THE
> SIDE BENCHES (the most junior judges).
> *Talmud: Sanhedrin* 32a

This order of speaking prevented the seniority of the older judges from cowing the younger men.

Neither *John* nor *Matthew* tell us how long the trial lasted; but we know the rule for any trial running past the time of the afternoon sacrifice:

> CAPITAL CHARGES MAY BE CONCLUDED
> ON THE SAME DAY WITH A FAVORABLE
> VERDICT (acquittal), BUT ONLY ON THE
> MORROW WITH AN UNFAVORABLE VER-
> DICT.

> THEREFORE TRIALS ARE NOT HELD ON
> THE EVE OF A SABBATH OR FESTIVAL ....

> *Talmud: Sanhedrin* 32a

"Due process" required that they recess for at least one night before voting to take a man's life; but they must continue to bear the burden of the case during the recess:

IF THEY FIND HIM NOT GUILTY, HE IS DISCHARGED; IF NOT, IT [THE TRIAL] IS ADJOURNED TILL THE FOLLOWING DAY, WHILST THEY [THE JUDGES] GO ABOUT IN PAIRS, PRACTICE MODERATION IN FOOD, DRINK NO WINE THE WHOLE DAY, AND DISCUSS THE CASE THROUGHOUT THE NIGHT.

EARLY NEXT MORNING THEY REAS-SEMBLE IN COURT. HE WHO IS IN FAVOR OF ACQUITTAL STATES 'I DECLARED HIM INNOCENT AND STAND BY MY OPINION,' WHILE HE WHO IS IN FAVOR OF CONDEM-NATION SHALL SAY: 'I DECLARED HIM GUILTY AND STAND BY MY OPINION.'

ONE WHO [PREVIOUSLY] ARGUED FOR CONVICTION MAY NOW ARGUE FOR AC-QUITTAL, BUT NOT VICE VERSA. IF THEY HAVE MADE A MISTAKE, THE TWO JUDGES' CLERKS ARE TO REMIND THEM THEREOF.

Talmud: Sanhedrin 40a

John's pericope (11:54) reports only Jesus' "favorable ver-dict"[15] (acquittal), but leaves us to speculate on its reasons. My best analysis is that the judges found that he did, indeed, break the Sabbath Law by the healing, since there is no showing of any threat to the life of the man with the withered arm; but since the prosecuting witnesses could not prove the fact of pre-*warning*, an "unfavorable verdict" could not stand.

All knew that the rule against double jeopardy meant that Jesus could never be tried again for the healing act in the Caper-naum synagogue:

> IN MONETARY CASES, THE DECISION MAY
> BE REVERSED BOTH FOR ACQUITTAL
> AND FOR CONDEMNATION: WHILST IN
> CAPITAL CHARGES, THE VERDICT MAY
> BE REVERSED FOR ACQUITTAL ONLY,
> BUT NOT FOR CONDEMNATION.
>
> And whence do we infer that if the accused leaves
> the *bet-din* not guilty, and someone says: 'I have
> something to state against him,' he may not be
> brought back? From the verse, *And the righteous*
> (found righteous by the court, though not necessari-
> ly innocent), *slay thou not!* (Exodus 23:7).
>
> *Talmud: Sanhedrin* 32a, 33b

John's pericope (11:49-52) also leaves us in the dark on Caiaphas' statements. Caiaphas stood before the court in the role of private citizen (*hedyot* = commoner; layman), nothing more, nothing less: "The High Priest may judge and be judged, testify and be testified against (*Talmud: Sanhedrin* 18b)," subject to the same Law as all of Israel, God's Law. I suggest *John* knew a tradition that went something like this:

JOSEPH CAIAPHAS (*in the well of the Court of the Temple Mount after the clerk announced the "favorable verdict" for Jesus ben Joseph*): "You know nothing at all; you do not understand that it is expedient for you that one man should die for the people, and that the whole nation should not perish!"

GAMALIEL BEN SIMEON: And you, Sir, know nothing at all of the Law of our people; you are ignorant of the traditions of the nation you rule. We know no such Law as you ask us to invoke. All our Laws scream just the opposite![16]

JOSEPH CAIAPHAS (*defiant*): Why is it not right to offer one for the many? You know as well as I that the Romans are eager to destroy our Temple and our nation.[17]

GAMALIEL BEN SIMEON: The High Priest makes the demand for *masar*[18] (surrender; betrayal; to give up). Long ago our fathers ruled:

> IF GENTILES SAY TO WOMEN: 'GIVE US

ONE OF YOU THAT WE MAY DEFILE HER
(by forcibly cohabiting with her), AND IF NOT,
WE WILL DEFILE YOU ALL,' THEN LET
THEM ALL BE DEFILED RATHER THAN
HAND OVER TO THEM ONE SOUL FROM
ISRAEL.

(The general principle is that no person may be
sacrificed for the saving of others. If, however, they
specify one woman in particular, then she may be
given over in order to prevent the others from
impurity);

(But if they specify any one man for slaughter, he
must not be handed over unless he had been legally
condemned to death owing to some crime . . . .)
Talmud: Terumoth 8:12

BAVA BEN BUTA: The High Priest makes even a more
diabolical travesty of our Law: He does not wait for the Romans
to ask for this man; he would volunteer him to them, now, in
advance. Since you have no respect for God's Law and would
substitute your own personal whim, I will ask you, Sir High Priest,
like Job, "Shall mortal man be more just than God?" Can your
Bureaucracy give meaning to life? Is Bureaucracy to be a substitute for God?

So ended Jesus' trial in the Small Sanhedrin of the Temple
Mount; but the Committee of Ten dared not relax their fears of
him and his growing following.

Papyrus Bodmer II, Page 2: John 1:14-21 (Actual size. With permission of Bibliotheca Bodmeriana, Cologny, Geneva.

PART 4

THE TRIAL FOR FALSE PROPHECY: WHAT DID JESUS REALLY PREACH?

"But the prophet or that dreamer of dreams shall be put to death, because he has taught rebellion against God, to make you leave the way in which the Lord your God commanded you to walk. So that you shall purge the evil from the midst of you."
Deuteronomy 13:3

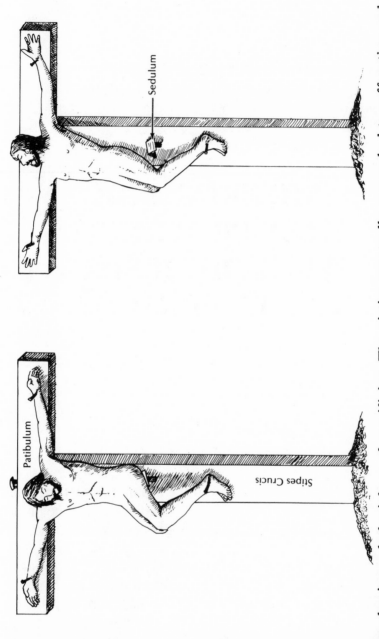

The mechanics and physiology of crucifixion. The victim eventually succumbed to suffocation and loss of heart beat, sometimes losing consciousness for a period of time before death actually came, wild dogs and vultures gnawing at his flesh while he remained alive.

Chapter 14

THE GREAT SANHEDRIN IN THE HALL OF THE HEWN STONE

The *gospel* writers play a haunting theme as they describe Jesus' preaching and death: "Destroy him! Kill him! Destroy him! Kill him!":

> " . . . and destroy Jesus."
> Matthew 27:20

> " . . . how they might destroy him."
> Matthew 12:14
> Mark 3:6

> " . . . sought how they might destroy him."
> Mark 11:18

> " . . . sought to destroy him."
> Luke 19:47

> "And therefore the Jews sought the more to kill him, because he not only had broken the Sabbath, but said also that God was his father, making himself equal to God."
> John 5:18

> " . . . because the Jews sought to kill him."
> John 7:1

> "Why go ye about to kill me?"
> John 7:19

We now know the identity of "they" and "the Jews" the writers speak of: The Committee of Ten, themselves "Jews" in name only, far more Greek than Jew, Temple Bureaucrats whose fight to retain political control over the Jewish nation made them the enemies of basic Judaism and its life in the Law, God's Law, given by God to the people through Moses at Mt. Sinai.

Still, the Committee of Ten dared not "destroy him" or "kill him" in cold blood, with hired assassins, the Law so ingrained in the genes of the people that they would rebel against such flagrant sinfulness. The Committee of Ten must get rid of Jesus under a cloak of legality; but how? The independent judges gave them pause, since the Court of the Temple Mount earlier knocked out their charge of Sabbath-breaking.

They must next try another court, with a different charge, in a different setting, with new witnesses.

Matthew (26:57, 59-63) and *Mark* (14:53, 55-61) give us *pericopes* of a second Jewish trial, this one before the Great Sanhedrin in the Hall of the Hewn Stone in the Temple.

All four *gospel* writers also leave us separate *pericopes* describing Peter's denial. The nameless editor who later arranged the location of the *pericopes* misled us grievously by intermingling the *pericopes* of the second Jewish trial with the *pericopes* of Peter's denial. This thoughtless positioning makes it look like this second trial took place immediately after Jesus' arrest in Gethsemane, at night, in the houses of the High Priests, something that could not happen.

Because of our problems with time and chronology, we do not know exactly when this second trial occurred, but can be sure that it did not happen at the time and places the mixed-up *pericopes* imply (*Talmud: Sanhedrin* 32a):

CAPITAL CHARGES MUST BE TRIED BY DAY AND CONCLUDED BY DAY . . . . CAPITAL CHARGES MAY BE CONCLUDED ON THE SAME DAY WITH A FAVORABLE VERDICT, BUT ONLY ON THE MORROW WITH AN UNFAVORABLE VERDICT. THEREFORE TRIALS ARE NOT HELD ON THE EVE OF A SABBATH OR FESTIVAL.

Since should he be found guilty, the case cannot be concluded on the morrow, execution being forbidden on Sabbaths and Festivals. (From this is seen that by "concluding" the actual carrying out of the sentence is meant, not merely the promulgation of the verdict.) Moreover, it is against the law—except in the case of a rebellious Elder (89b)—to leave judgment in suspense.

We can guess—and guess only—that this trial happened sometime after Jesus' triumphal entry into Jerusalem on what Christians now call Palm Sunday (*Mark* 11:7-11):

And they brought the colt to Jesus, and cast their garments on him; and he sat upon him. And many spread their garments in the way: and others cut down branches off the trees, and strewed them in the way.

And they that went before, and they that followed, cried, saying, Hosanna; Blessed is he that cometh in the name of the Lord: Blessed be the kingdom of our father David, that cometh in the name of the Lord: Hosanna in the highest.

And Jesus entered into Jerusalem, and into the temple: and when he had looked round about upon all things, and now the eventide was come, he went out unto Bethany with the twelve.

Some time earlier, again we do not know when, word spread about his raising his friend Lazarus from the dead (*John* 11:45):

Then many Jews which came to Mary, and had seen the things which Jesus did, believed on him.

In another episode, Jesus charged into the Temple and attacked the "bazaars of the sons of Annas," probably with a crowd of followers (*Mark* 11:15-18):

And they come to Jerusalem: and Jesus went into

the temple, and began to cast out them that sold and bought in the temple, and overthrew the tables of the moneychangers, and the seats of them that sold doves;

And would not suffer that any man should carry any vessel through the temple.

And he taught, saying unto them, Is it not written, My house shall be called of all nations the house of prayer? but ye have made it a den of thieves.

And the scribes and chief priests heard it, and sought how they might destroy him: for they feared him, because all the people was astonished at his doctrine.

He brazenly defied the Temple authorities over and over again (*Luke* 19:47-48):

And he taught daily in the temple. But the chief priests and the scribes and the chief of the people sought to destroy him.

And could not find what they might do; for all the people were very attentive to hear him.

The Committee of Ten could not let Jesus expand his following right under their noses on the Temple Mount. He proved threat enough down in the Galilee where his followers reached the thousands, some wanting to make him their king; but here in Jerusalem, on the Temple Mount!

They dared not tolerate it; but their dilemma continued: They must move against him legally, or face a rebellion against their Temple rule. But how to get around those pesky, independent judges, and their rigid "due process" rules?

When we separate the "Peter denial" *pericope* from the "trial" *pericope* in *Mark*, we get this clear report of the second Jewish trial:

And they led Jesus to the high priest; and all the chief priests and the elders and the scribes were assembled . . . .

Now the chief priests and the whole council (Sanhedrin) sought testimony against Jesus to put him to death; but they found none, for many bore false witness against him, and their witness did not agree.

And some stood up and bore false witness against him, saying, "We heard him say, 'I will destroy this temple that is made with hands, and in three days I will build another, not made with hands'."

Yet not even so did their testimony agree.

And the high priest stood up in the midst and asked Jesus, "Have you no answer to make? What is it that these men testify against you?"

The tradition from which *Matthew* and *Mark* worked described a formal, full-blown trial in the Great Sanhedrin (*bet din ha-gadol*), including the technical legal jargon of:
"sought testimony against Jesus to put him to death"
"many bore false witness against him"
"their witness did not agree"
"yet not even so did their testimony agree"
"sought false testimony"
"many false witnesses came forward"
The presiding High Priest gave Jesus a chance to defend himself, but he relied on his right to remain silent.

The scribes and the sages traced the history of the Great Sanhedrin back to the forty years in the desert, after the Jews' escape from Egypt and Moses' encounter with God at Mt. Sinai (*Numbers* 11:16-17):

And the Lord said to Moses, 'Gather for me seventy men of the elders of Israel, whom you know to be the elders of the people and officers over them; and let them take their stand there with you.

'And I will come down and talk with you there; and I will take some of the spirit which is upon you and put it upon them; and they shall bear the burden of the people with you, that you may not bear it yourself alone.'

Joseph Caiaphas, as High Priest, now sat in Moses' seat as presiding judge over the seventy justices, the historic numbers, 70 + 1, giving the Court its official name: The Court of the Seventy-One.

Except that the great bulk of its cases came to it as appeals from the lower courts throughout Israel, the Great Sanhedrin appeared but a grander, plusher, more elaborate perfection of the Court of the Temple Mount which earlier acquitted Jesus of the Sabbath-breaking charge (*Talmud Sanhedrin:* 86b):

> If there arise a matter too hard for thee in judgment . . . they (the lower Court which is in search of guidance) used to come first to the Court that was at the gate of the Temple Mount. If they had heard a tradition (a ruling handed down by their teachers bearing upon the point of Law involved in the case), they told it to them;

> otherwise they betook themselves to the Court that was at the Temple Court . . . . If they (of that Court) had heard a tradition (concerning the point of Law involved), they told it to them.

> otherwise, they both betook themselves to the Court at the Chamber of Hewn Stone, whence the Law went forth to all Israel; for it is written (*Deuteronomy* 17:10): *From that place which the Lord will choose.*

In addition to hearing appeals, the Court of the Seventy-One could also try (original trial jurisdiction) four types of cases:[1]

(1) False prophecy;

(2) The rebellious Elder;

(3) The idolatrous tribe; and

(4)   Transgressions committed by the High Priest himself.
God's High Court sat in the *lishkat ha-gazit*,[2] variously called the "Chamber," "Cell" or "Hall" of the Hewn Stone, from whence the Law could go out to all Israel.

The most elaborate of the Temple's many fine rooms, "The Cell of the Hewn Stone was built in the style of a large basilica."[3]

Its long, rectangular nave ran east and west in the southeast corner of the Temple structure proper, the sides and aisles lined with Corinthian marble columns, matching those outside, and ending in a stunning apse in the nave's easternmost side: "The Cell of the Hewn Stone was situated half on holy ground, half on non-holy ground; the Cell had two doors, one opening on holy ground and the other opening on non-holy ground."[4]

The non-holy-ground door preserved the ancient traditions of the "city Gate": Openness, access to any and all, and public involvement which made the Jewish system work, not the King's Court, nor the Bureaucrats' Court, but God's Court. No secret, rump sessions could be held, nor a single procedural step slighted that so much as hinted at non-compliance with every jot and tittle of God's own "due process" of Law.

None but the top legal scholars reached the High Court, moving up through the ranks of the lower courts, except Caiaphas whose office as High Priest made him ex officio presiding officer, regardless of his knowledge of the Law. We do not know the Pharisee-Sadducee split on the Court; but from the reign of Queen Alexandra (76-67 B.C.), the Pharisees held a majority of the seats.[5]

The judges sat at one end of the nave in three semi-circular tiers of twenty-three seats each,[6] as in an amphitheater, the High Priest, his *ab-bet-din* ("Father of the Court") and *hakam* ("learned legal scholar") on a raised dais in the center. The disciples-probationers arranged themselves behind the judges, with a large audience of legal scholars behind them.[7]

As in the Court of the Twenty-three, Jesus, the accused, stood facing the judges in the center of the well, the witnesses to his right, the clerks in their proper places,[8] an overflow crowd filling the rest of the chamber.

In an original trial as distinguished from an appeal, the

ab-bet-din gave the same *intimidation* and *reassurance* they heard in the Court of the Twenty-three, the taking of testimony ready to begin.

Chapter 15

THE CHARGE: FALSE PROPHECY

Both *Matthew* and *Mark* give us the formal charge in Jesus' Great Sanhedrin trial: *False prophecy*!

In view of the limits on the Great Court's *trial* jurisdiction (false prophecy; rebellious elder; idolatrous tribe; sins of the High Priest) the only other possible charge would be *rebellious elder*; but none of the *gospel* accounts hint that Jesus ever occupied the position of elder (judge) where he might fail to follow *precedent*, thereby committing a sin which could subject him to trial as *rebellious elder*.

From time to time in his preaching, Jesus used language to imply that he followed the prophet's format:

> They [the parables Jesus used in his preaching] are a fulfillment of Isaiah's prophecy.
> Matthew 13:14

> He that receiveth a prophet in the name of a prophet shall receive a prophet's reward.
> John 10:41

> It was indeed of you that Isaiah prophesied when he said . . . .
> Matthew 15:7

> And he said, I say unto you, No prophet is accepted in his own country.
> Luke 4:24

But Jesus said unto them, A prophet is not without honor, save in his own country, and in his own house.

Matthew 13:57

Nevertheless I must walk to day, and tomorrow, and the day following: for it cannot be that a prophet perish out of Jerusalem.

Luke 13:33

Jesus warned his own followers against false prophets who would come after him, and imitate him:

Beware of false prophets which come to you in sheep's clothing, but inwardly they are ravening wolves.

Matthew 7:15

And many false prophets shall arise, and shall deceive many.

Matthew 24:11

For false messiahs and false prophets shall make their appearance, and shall give out signs and wonders, and lead astray, if it were possible, even the elect. But you be on your guard, because I have foretold you all.

Mark 13:23-24

Woe unto you when all men shall speak well of you, for so did their fathers to the false prophets.

Luke 6:23

Many of Jesus' followers thought him a prophet:

And they glorified God, saying, that a great prophet is risen up among us; and that God hath visited His people.

Luke 7:16

Without doubt, this man is a prophet.
John 7:40

And the multitude said, This is Jesus the prophet of Nazareth of Galilee.
Matthew 21:11

The woman said unto him, Sir, I perceive that thou art a prophet.
John 4:19

They said unto the blind man again, What sayest thou of him, that he hath opened thine eyes? He said, he is a prophet.
John 9:17

But when they [chief priests and Pharisees] sought to lay hands on him, they feared the multitude, because they took him for a prophet.
Matthew 21:45-46

Soldiers everywhere know what goes on around them and include it in their barracks jokes. When the Temple Guards mocked and abused Jesus after his third and final arrest, they taunted him:

Prophesy to us, thou Christ, Who is he that smote you?

Now play the prophet for us, you Christ . . .

Now Messiah, if you are a prophet, tell us who hit you . . . .
Matthew 26:68

. . . And to say to him, Now prophesy . . .

. . . and crying, Prove that you are a prophet . . .

. . . saying, Now prophesy who hit you . . . .
Mark 14:65

... saying, Prophesy, who is it that smote you?

Prove to us that you are a prophet, by telling us ...

Now, prophet, guess who hit you that time!
Luke 22:64

Mark's language particularly implies that Jesus is prophesying when he talks of destroying the Temple, and rebuilding it.[1]

Even during the hours he hung on the cross, passers-by derided him about his prophecies for rebuilding the Temple: "Aha! You who would destroy the Temple and build it again in three days, save yourself and come down from the cross!"[2]

Finally, Jesus' laments over Jerusalem imply that he fears his fate will be the same as prophets before him: "O Jerusalem, Jerusalem, killing the prophets and stoning those who are sent to you ...."[3]

We must understand the uniqueness of prophecy and prophets in the scheme of Israel's God before we can weigh the import of Jesus' false prophecy trial. The *Encyclopaedia Judaica*[4] gives this terse account:

> *Nature of Prophecy*: The institution of prophecy is founded on the basic premise that God makes his will known to chosen individuals in successive generations.
>
> A prophet is a charismatic individual endowed with the divine gift of both receiving and imparting the message of revelation.
>
> As the spokesman for the deity, he does not choose his profession but is chosen, often against his own will, to convey the word of God to his people, regardless of whether or not they wish to hear it (*Ezek.* 3:11). A prophet does not elect to prophesy, nor does he become a prophet by dint of a native or an acquired faculty on his part. Prophecy is not a science to be learned or mastered. There is no striving to be one with God, no *unio mystica*, no

indwelling of God within the spirit of the prophet through rapture, trances, or even spiritual contemplation.

The prophet is selected by God and is irresistibly compelled to deliver His message and impart His will, even if he personally disagrees with it.

He is consecrated to be set apart from his fellowmen and is destined to bear the responsibility and burden of being chosen.

The prophet stands in the presence of God (*Jer.* 15:1, 19) and is privy to the divine council (*Isa.* 6; *Jer.* 23:18; *Amos* 3:7). He speaks when commanded, but once commanded, must speak (*Amos* 3:8) . . . .

He is God's mouthpiece (*Jer.* 15:19).

Caiaphas perhaps delegated the reading of the *specifications* against Jesus to his *ab-bet-din* or a clerk, but the "set" of "prosecuting witnesses," perhaps composed it like this:[5]

That on the second day of Nisan, within the hour following the morning sacrifice, on the east side of the Temple Mount, in the Court of the Gentiles between the Court of the Women and the Shushan Gate, Jesus Bar Joseph did commit the sin of false prophecy by saying to a group of worshipers assembled around him: "Do you see these great buildings? There will not be left one stone upon another, that will not be thrown down."

That this and his other teachings show Jesus bar Joseph to be a dreamer of dreams, who gives signs and wonders to teach rebellion against the Lord our God, and to make loyal Israelites leave the way in which the Lord our God commanded us to walk.

That this same Jesus bar Joseph presumes to speak a word in the name of Jehovah Who has not authorized him to speak; and he has committed evil in our midst which must be purged before all Israel can be restored.

The sin of false prophecy constituted one of their most heinous transgressions; but God did not define it crisply.

On one side, the true prophet *must* speak the words which God puts in his mouth: As God's direct agent, he occupied an official place in Israel's scheme of things; and he himself sinned if he did not cry out loudly and with force. By the same token, the people sinned if they did not heed the admonitions which the true prophet hurled at them on God's behalf.

On the other hand, the Law commanded them to stone and strangle the false prophets who appeared among them.

But without a safe test of true or false prophecy, how could they know whom to follow, or whom to stone?[6]

The Ancient Codes stated little more than vague generalities (*Deuteronomy* 13:1-5):

> If a prophet arises among you, or a dreamer of dreams, and gives you a sign or a wonder,

> and the sign or wonder which he tells you comes to pass, and if he says, 'Let us go after other gods,' which you have not known, and 'let us serve them,'

> you shall not listen to the words of that prophet or to that dreamer of dreams;

> But that prophet or that dreamer of dreams shall be put to death, because he has taught rebellion against the Lord your God, to make you leave the way in which the Lord your God commanded you to walk. So you shall purge the evil from the midst of you."

Even if the false prophet turned out to be a man's own brother, the son of his mother, his son, his friend, or the wife of his bosom, " . . . you shall not yield to him or listen to him, nor shall your eye pity him, nor shall you spare him, nor shall you conceal him, but you shall kill him; your hand shall be first against him to put him to death, and afterwards the hand of all the people. You shall stone him to death with stones, because he sought to draw you away from the Lord your God, who brought you out of the land of Egypt, out of the house of bondage. And all Israel shall hear, and fear, and never again do any such wickedness as this among you."[7]

The *precedent* of the decided cases showed only that each case must be tried on its own merits, to see whether the prophet spoke truly, or whether he led the people away from the Lord their God.

Even the accuracy of the prophet's predictions could not prove a practical test, especially if he did not give an early date for the happening of the event, although some judges tried to use this rule: " . . . when a prophet speaks in the name of the Lord, if the word does not come to pass or come true, that is a word which the Lord has not spoken; the prophet has spoken presumptuously, you need not be afraid of him."[8]

They dared take no shortcuts: This Court of the Seventy-One, sitting in the Hall of the Hewn Stone, must take apart Jesus bar Joseph's preachings, teachings, prayers and dictums, then measure them against the yardstick of basic Judaism, a task so formidable that God decreed centuries earlier that it must be done only in His Great Court, not in a lesser one.[9]

(The transcript format we used for a segment of Jesus' earlier Sabbath-breaking trial in the Court of the Temple Mount showed how the judges heard the evidence, argued the case and reached a verdict. We need not repeat it for the false prophecy trial before the Great Sanhedrin. Rather, this format summarizes the evidence presented by both the prosecuting and defense witnesses, bearing in mind the basic legal issue: Did Jesus preach treason against God by urging his followers to leave the paths their fathers trod?)

Chapter 16

"THE KINGDOM OF GOD"

We find no clues to let us identify the prosecuting witnesses the Committee of Ten called against Jesus at the false prophecy trial, the *gospels* content to tell us that "the Jews sought to kill him"[1] ".... So they watched him, and sent spies, who pretended to be sincere, that they might take hold of what he said .... "[2] They needed witnesses who could report Jesus' teaching verbatim, and who could withstand the rigors of the *bedikoth* (cross-examination) by some judge who would feel duty-bound to take Jesus' side during the trial.

The Committee faced a vexing paradox: The witnesses needed to be followers of the accused, not mere casual listeners; even spies and informers might not hold up; but the reports of true believers also might not add up to the sin of false prophecy, show that Jesus " ... taught rebellion against the Lord your God, to make you leave the way in which the Lord your God commanded you to walk."[3]

The detailed probe into this death-penalty charge would require time, perhaps several days, not just an hour or two with a few cursory questions.

Whoever the witnesses, we can assume that the judges would insist on hearing background data on Jesus' entire public ministry, when it began, where, to whom directed, and its main themes.

After the seven searching inquiries, they perhaps began with an event which took place at the River Jordan, two miles south of Jericho, possibly three years earlier.

John the Baptist, Jesus' cousin, drew "multitudes"[4] who came out from as far away as Jerusalem to listen to his preaching and be baptized. He flashed into the Judean "wilderness" along the western shores of the Dead Sea like a comet, his impact still felt throughout all of Judea and parts of the Galilee.

Beginning his passionate soul-saving at thirty years, the age when the Levites assumed their Temple roles,[5] he filled a segment of Judaism's spiritual void, brought on by the suffocating, bird-like minds of the Temple Bureaucrats.

Dressed in "a garment of camel's hair, a leather girdle around his waist," and "eating locust and wild honey,"[6] John "exhorted the Jews to lead righteous lives, to practice justice toward their fellows and piety toward God, and so doing, to join in baptism,"[7] his basic message similar to that of the Dead Sea Scrolls community at Qumran, six miles further south, which took its theme for existence from *Second Isaiah* (40:3-5):

> A voice cries: "In the wilderness prepare the way of the Lord, make straight in the desert a highway for our God.

> "Every valley shall be lifted up, and every mountain and hill made low; and the uneven ground shall become level, and rough places a plain.

> "And the glory of the Lord shall be revealed, and all flesh shall see it together, for the mouth of the Lord has spoken."

John's fire-and-brimstone sermons[8] attracted tens of thousands of spiritually starved people who flocked to hear him: Soldiers, the Roman legionnaires as well as their mercenaries recruited from the Mediterranean world; tax collectors; Pharisees; Sadducees; aristocrats; paupers; " . . . and there went out to him all the country of Judea, and all the people of Jerusalem; and they were baptized by him in the River Jordan, confessing their sins."[9]

"Repent, for the kingdom of heaven is at hand,"[10] John preached; and the people went down into the river so that John and his disciples could immerse them.

John's baptism took on a new thrust, considerably more than

the baptism of proselytes which the Jews practiced for at least two centuries to initiate converts into Judaism. It went further than the ceremonial rites of the closed community at Qumran (probably Essene), exhorting the penitents that "they must not employ (baptism) to gain pardon for whatever sins they committed, but as a consecration of the body implying that the soul was already thoroughly cleansed by right behaviour."[11]

John baptized Jews as well as Gentiles, using baptism to lead his followers into a direct, personal, mystical union with God, an ecstatic experience, permitting a man to become a "born again" Jew, a vibrant, rededicated "son of the living God."[12]

John baptized Jesus bar Joseph,[13] *Matthew, Mark* and *Luke* later writing that a *bat(h) kol*[14] followed the event.

The *bat kol* ("daughter of a voice"; "resonance"; "echo") always played a significant role in Israel's efforts to receive direct messages from her God. It came as "a reverberating sound, a voice descending from heaven to offer guidance in human affairs, and regarded as a lower grade of prophecy."[15]

Jehovah used a *bat kol* to prophesy Moses' death: "The end, the time of your death has come";[16] and when Moses died, a *bat kol* could be heard "over an area of twelve *mil* square, corresponding to that of the camp of Israel."[17]

A *bat kol* helped Solomon decide the true mother between the disputing women of the child whom he threatened to cut in two with his sword.[18]

"It has been taught: After the later prophets Haggai, Zachariah, and Malachi had died, the holy spirit (of prophecy) departed from Israel, but they still availed themselves of the *bat kol*."[19]

God used the device also to single out great leaders from among the people: "A *bat kol* was granted to them from heaven which announced 'There is in your midst one man who is deserving that the *Shechinah* (Holy Spirit; Divine Inspiration), should alight upon him, but his generation is unworthy of it!' They all looked at Samuel the Little; and when he died, they lamented over him."[20]

Matthew (3:16-17) reported his oral tradition of the *bat kol*: "And when Jesus was baptized, he went up immediately from the water, and behold, the heavens were opened and he saw the Spirit of God descending like a dove, and alighting on him; and lo, a voice from heaven, saying, 'This is my beloved Son, with whom I am well pleased.'"

At Jesus' trial, some judges possibly viewed the report of the *bat kol* as a claim to the role of prophet, in an era which no longer formally recognized prophecy as a vital part of Judaism.

John stirred up a great following during his short ministry, perhaps no longer than a few months; so Herod Antipas, tetrarch (ruler under the Romans) of the Galilee, ordered John's arrest, and death.[21]

After John's arrest, Jesus took over John's disciples who then numbered thousands, giving him a sizable congregation the day he launched his public ministry.[22]

The witnesses reported Jesus' main theme to be the same as John's, Jesus echoing John's exact words: "Repent, for the kingdom of heaven is at hand,"[23] Jesus always speaking fondly of John: "I tell you, among those born of women, none is greater than John."[24]

Under diligent probing by the judges, all the witnesses admitted that Jesus never defined what he meant by either "kingdom of heaven" or "kingdom of God," obviously assuming that his listeners understood the phrases. He did not give them any new meaning, no novel twist or revelation.

The prophet Amos (780-760 B.C.) laid the foundation for the "kingdom of God," although he called it the "Day of the Lord,"[25] his dream later elaborated by all three Isaiahs, by Hosea, Zaphaniah and Joel, its steady, pulsating theme logically evolving over seven hundred years, with many slants and literary flourishes.

When God created the earth and all that was therein, including man, He "saw that it was good,"[26] but somehow, man and His world got off target, good no longer reigning supreme: Men humbled and humiliated other men. The rich took from the poor. Multitudes suffered from illness, hunger, pestilence, and torture. Israel lived under a whole series of foreign oppressors, with wars and rumors of wars. Pleading widows and blighted orphans stood abandoned. Wherever man looked about him, he saw good replaced by evil.

God's covenant with Noah after the Great Flood kept Him from destroying the sinning creatures a second time; but God needed to work drastic changes to get the world back on its course of Goodness, else life would not be bearable. Many solutions appeared over the centuries. *Third Isaiah*, for example, saw God's solution as a drastic, thrilling new creation to warm the hearts of social reformers for all time to come (65:17-23):

> For behold, I create new heavens and a new earth; and the former things shall not be remembered or come into mind.

> But be glad and rejoice for ever in that which I create; for behold, I create Jerusalem a rejoicing, and her people a joy.

> I will rejoice in Jerusalem, and be glad in my people; no more shall be heard in it the sound of weeping and the cry of distress.

> No more shall there be in it an infant that lives but a few days; or an old man who does not fill out his days, for the child shall die a hundred years old, and the sinner a hundred years old shall be accursed.

> They shall build houses and inhabit them; they shall plant vineyards and eat their fruit.

> They shall not build and another inhabit; they shall not plant and another eat; for like the days of a tree shall the days of my people be, and my chosen shall long enjoy the work of their hands.

> They shall not labor in vain, or bear children for calamity; for they shall be the offspring of the blessed of the Lord, and their children with them.

They could hope for the future, all not wormwood and gall. God would restore His handwork, His own good world.

Amos saw the "Day of the Lord" arriving in a cosmic cataclysm, the land trembling (*Amos* 9:5), the sun going down at noon (8:9), the earth melting (9:5), "a judgment by fire . . . . and it devoured the great deep and was eating up the land (7:4)."

Israel's God of history would no longer act through His slow, wavering, cautious evolutions: He would intervene directly, physically, startlingly, to reestablish Goodness so that "justice" could "roll down like waters, and righteousness like an ever-flowing stream."[27]

Over the years, the prophet Amos's phrase "Day of the Lord" merged into "kingdom of God": "And the Lord will become king over all the earth,"[28] God as Israel's one and only King, Israel His "kingdom."

But the "kingdom of God" did not come! Evil persisted; suffering remained; mercy gone; injustices commonplace. The predictions of the prophets (the three Isaiahs, Hoseas, Zephaniah and Joel) evaporated; Israel's God of creation and history somehow refused to save His people.

After the last of the prophets Haggai, Zechariah and Malachi (400-350 B.C.), the hopes and yearnings of the suffering, oppressed Jews flowed in a great body of literature called "apocalyptic." It sounded a dominant, central, compelling theme from 200 B.C. on: God's need to intervene directly to bring off this new "kingdom of God";[29] and by Jesus' day, the cities, villages, countrysides and farms flamed with talk of "the last days," the "end of days," the Better Age, Golden Age, Future Age, or the Age to Come.[30]

To John, the scholars at Qumran, and thousands of others, the "age to come" became "the age that is"; and the "end of days" became the "end of *evil* days," the "kingdom" either imminent and "at hand," or already begun, depending upon a man's point of view.[31]

They did not treat this End of the World as terrifying or morbid. Quite the opposite! It promised total Goodness, after a traumatic Final Judgment in which God would dispose of the wicked and preserve the good, the good obtaining salvation through repentance and love of *torah;* and all would delight in the "Law of the Lord."

The "kingdom of God" really meant the "reign of God"[32] (*malkuth*) who would usher in total Utopia: With God Himself ruling as King, no foreign dictators, whether Persian, Greek, Roman or other would ever oppress them; and peace would envelop the earth:[33]

> He shall judge between the nations, and shall decide for many peoples; and they shall beat their swords into plowshares, and their spears into pruning hooks; nation shall not lift up sword against nation, neither shall they learn war any more.

Under this "reign of God," in His "kingdom," the land would bring forth a bountiful harvest: Hunger would fly away; mourners would be comforted; the meek could inherit the earth; spiritual and emotional thirsts would be sated; mercy and purity of heart would prevail. Tensions and disharmony would be no more, and "the wolf shall dwell with the lamb, and the leopard shall lie down with the kid, and the calf and the lion and the fatling together, and a little child shall lead them."[34]

Every redeemed man would be part of this thrilling "kingdom of God." Those dead long ago would rise from their graves, to join those living on that "great day" when God chose to act. All would "rejoice in that day, and leap for joy, for behold, your reward is great in heaven."[35]

The "kingdom of heaven" would be God's new kingdom *on earth*,[36] open to all, welcomed by all, dwelt in by all, raptured by all, Jew and Gentile alike, *provided* they repented and kept *torah*.

Whoever the witnesses in Jesus' Great Sanhedrin trial, all testified that the main thrust of Jesus' message, the "coming of the kingdom," did not differ in the slightest from the prevailing opinions of thousands of others around him.

On this point, the judges could find no ground to rule him guilty of false prophecy.[37]

Chapter 17

"HEAR, O ISRAEL, THE LORD OUR GOD...."

The judges could not avoid probing Jesus' teaching on the *shema*, the most far-reaching sentence ever written (*Deuteronomy* 6:4):

Hear, O Israel: The Lord our God is one Lord;

As the capsule of Israel's faith, it served as both her creed and doxology, the mortar that formed her into a theocracy, the umbilical cord that united all Jews with their one God, and with each other. It hailed their "acceptance of the yoke of the kingdom of heaven"[1] because of their one, unique God.

His astounding character and their union with Him, in turn, made them separate, special, and chosen apart from their neighbors who ran blindly after their own gods of sex, fertility, nature, lust, hurt, fear and power, gods who could be worshiped in the form of graven images, stones, trees, poles, mountains, men who paraded as emperors, or in hundreds of shapely idols.

The *shema* began as Israel's common shield against the temptations of competing gods; but over the years, *Deuteronomy* 6:5-9 embellished the formal statement, as well as 11:13-21; and *Numbers* 15:37-41. Still, this simple, fragile, revolutionary line shaped them into brothers with each other, all united with, to and in their wondrous God:

"Hear, O Israel: The Lord our God is one Lord!"

Anything as important as the *shema* automatically inspired uncounted Laws and technical rules[2] governing its use, its meaning stressed by the rule: "He who recites the *shema* in its proper time is greater than he who studies the *torah*."[3] On the other hand, if a man did not accept the *shema*, the *torah* could mean nothing but dross.

Workmen could speak the *shema* on the top of a tree or the top of a scaffolding; a bridegroom exempt from saying it from the wedding night until the end of the next Sabbath, "if he has not consummated the marriage";[4] women excused from specific hours because of their domestic duties; and slaves and minors not compelled to recite it at all,[5] although their masters complimented them when they did.

The judges searched for but could find no evidence that Jesus taught anything new and different about the *shema*. *Mark's* oral tradition (12:28-30) reports that Jesus preached it verbatim:

> And one of the scribes came up and heard them disputing with one another, and seeing that he answered them well, asked him, "Which commandment is the first of all?"
>
> Jesus answered, "The first is, 'Hear, O Israel: The Lord our God, the Lord is one;
>
> 'and you shall love the Lord your God with all your heart, and with all your soul, and with all your mind, and with all your strength.'"

His respectful attitude toward the *shema* could not possibly support a conviction of false prophecy.[6]

Chapter 18

THE "SON OF GOD"

The judges probed Jesus' references to himself, to see if he ever claimed to be anything other than a preacher with the message about the "kingdom of God."

They learned that others called him "son of God" (some who saw him walking on the sea;[1] the demons he cast out of those possessed;[2] and Satan when Jesus meditated for forty days in the mountains);[3] but the judges needed to know if he ever called himself "son of God" in a way that departed from their ancient traditions.[4]

God considered them all "sons of God," Jesus bar Joseph, Joseph ben Caiaphas, every justice sitting in the three banks of the Court of the Seventy-One, their disciples-probationers arranged about them in the great basilica of the Hewn Stone, the spectators, every Jew in the whole wide world; and to some of their poets, prophets and legal scholars, the peoples of the other "seventy nations" of mankind as well.

The Scriptures spelled it out too clearly for anyone to doubt: All races of mankind descended from a single ancestor called "Man" (Hebrew = *adam*) whom God created "in our image, after our likeness[5] . . . the Lord God formed man of dust from the ground, and breathed into his nostrils the breath of life; and man became a living being."[6]

Could there be a greater thrill for any of them than to know that they inhaled the breath of the Holy One, Blessed be He? Did not this, in and of itself, make man special, give them all a mystical unity, an earthly sonship with God the Father?

God created man, His sons and daughters, only a little lower than the angels: "Thou hast made him little less than God, and dost crown him with glory and honor. Thou hast given him dominion over the works of Thy hands; thou hast put all things under his feet,"[7] intelligence the great difference between man and the earth's other creatures: "He made for them tongue and eyes; He gave them ears and a mind for thinking. He filled them with knowledge and understanding, and showed them good and evil. He set His eye upon their hearts to show them the majesty of His works[8] . . . . He bestowed knowledge upon them, and allotted to them the Law of life."[9]

God thought so highly of this crown of His creation that He made man immortal: "For God created man for immortality, and made him in the image of His own eternity . . . . In the eyes of the foolish, they seemed to have died, . . . but they are at peace . . . though in the sight of men they were punished, their hope is full of immortality. Having been disciplined a little, they will receive great good, because God tested them and found them worthy of Himself; like gold in the furnace, He tried them, and like a sacrificial burnt offering, He accepted them."[10]

They knew from watching the decay process of dead bodies that the vital force that held together all of man's separate parts, that made man a living being, came as God's divine spark, flowing in on His breath: God's secret, conceived in His holy blueprint, delivered on His outstretched arm, and matured over the eons. Anonymous poets among the Dead Sea Scroll scholars at Qumran proclaimed it in their thanksgiving hymns:[11]

> I thank thee, O Lord, because thou hast done wondrously with dust; with a thing formed of clay thou hast done powerfully.

> For what is man? He is earth, a cut off bit of clay, and to dust is his return;

> but thou dost make him wise in wonders like these, and of thy true counsel thou wilt give him knowledge.

> But I am dust and ashes. What can I plan unless

thou hast desired it, and what can I think apart
from thy will?

What can I accomplish unless thou hast established
me, and how can I be wise unless thou hast planned
for me?

What shall I speak unless thou openest my mouth,
and how should I reply if thou didst not make me
wise?

Confessing, confessing, what am I? For thou hast
given me knowledge of thy true counsel and hast
made me wise by thy wondrous works.

Thou hast put praises in my mouth and on my
tongue rejoicing, and the circumcising of my lips
in a place of loud praise, that I may sing of thy
steadfast love and meditate on thy power all the
day.

Continually I will bless thy name and tell of thy
glory among the sons of man; in the abundance of
thy goodness my soul shall delight; for I know that
what thou sayest is truth, and in thy hand in
righteousness;

in thy purpose is all knowledge, and in thy strength
all power; and all glory is with thee.

In thy warmth are all judgments of affliction; in
thy goodness is abundance of pardon and mercy for
all the sons of thy good pleasure.

For thou hast given them knowledge of thy true
counsel and made them wise in thy wondrous
mysteries.

For thy glory's sake thou hast cleansed man from
transgression, to consecrate himself to thee from all
unclean abominations and guilt of unfaithfulness;
to unite himself with the sons of thy truth and to

be in the same lot with thy holy ones.

The evidence showed that Jesus never once called himself "son of God." He did not teach *anything* new and different about the nature and character of man, or about their traditional use of the term "son of God."[12]

Further, he claimed no special "sonship" relationship with God not possessed by the High Priest, the witnesses themselves, the justices or any other "son of God" sitting or standing in the Court of the Seventy-One the day of Jesus' false prophecy trial.

Chapter 19

"MY FATHER WHO IS IN HEAVEN ...."

As the judges pressed on to see if Jesus' teachings "taught rebellion against the Lord your God, to make you leave the way in which the Lord your God commanded you to walk," they needed to probe the way Jesus addressed the Holy One.

First Century Jews labeled their attitude toward God piety[1] (godliness), shown openly by bringing their one and unique God into the routines of daily living.

The testimony of the witnesses showed that Jesus addressed God by "your[2] Father in heaven," or "our Father,"[3] or "my Father in heaven,"[4] all the terms logical outgrowths of their special "sonship" with God the Father: "I will be their father and they will be My sons, and they shall all be called sons of the living God, and all angels and spirits shall know and recognize that they are My sons, and I their Father in fidelity and righteousness, and that I love them."[5]

Their pagan neighbors ridiculed this father-son relationship: "[the Israelite] boasts that God is his father. Let us see if his words are true, and let us test what will happen at the end of his life; for if the righteous man is God's son, He will help him, and will deliver him from the hand of his adversaries."[6]

The Jews sloughed off these taunts for they knew their place, living in God's divine Presence and His Grace: "Beloved are Israel in that they are called sons of God. It is a mark of super-abundant love that it was made known to them that they were called sons of the All-Present, as it is said: *Ye are sons of the Lord your God, Deut.* 14:1)."[7]

They brought the phrase "Father in heaven" into their vocabulary to permit them to separate a man's earthly, blood father, from the Almighty Father of them all.[8] Still, "heavenly Father" and "Father in heaven" did not amount to mere synonyms of "God"; rather, the words denoted their special, intimate, abiding closeness to the Ever-Present that could best be pictured by the love and concern of an earthly father for his blood son:[9] "It is like a man who was walking on the way and letting his son go on before him; came robbers in front to take the boy captive, the father put him behind him; came a wolf from behind, he put him in front; came robbers in front and wolves behind, he took him up in his arms; when he began to be troubled by the heat of the sun, the father stretched his own garment over him; was he hungry, he gave him food, thirsty, he gave him drink. Just so God did, so it is written . . . . "[9]

Even when Israel, God's "firstborn son," turned its back on the Holy Father in heaven to go whoring after other Gods, the Father could never reject His sons for long. A faithful remnant always remained to call back the whole nation to repentance, as John the Baptist stirred up a righteous rebirth of God's sons, to let God's will be done.[10]

The witnesses who traveled with Jesus testified that he always said the daily prayers and benedictions they all used, the *berachoth*[11] ("Blessings") of both the synagogue and private worship, moving in the pious Jew's perpetual state of prayer and grace, alone enough to separate him from all his neighbors. At the beginning of the day (sundown):[12]

> On going to bed one said from "*Hear, oh Israel*" to "*And it shall come to pass if ye hearken diligently*." Then he said: "Blessed is He who causes the bands of sleep to fall upon my eyes and slumber on my eyelids, and gives light to the apple of the eye.
>
> "May it be Thy will, O Lord, my God, to make me lie down in peace, and set my portion in Thy law and accustom me to the performance of religious duties, but do not accustom me to transgression; and

bring me not into sin, or into iniquity, or into temptation, or into contempt.

As the day continued, so also a man's conversations with his God:[13]

When he wakes he says: "My God, the soul which Thou has placed in me is pure. Thou hast fashioned it in me, Thou didst breathe it into me, and Thou preservest it within me and Thou wilt one day take it from me and restore it to me in the time to come.

"So long as the soul is within me I give thanks unto Thee, O Lord, my God, and the God of my fathers, Sovereign of all worlds, Lord of all souls. Blessed are Thou, O Lord, who restorest souls to dead corpses."

When he hears the cock crowing, he should say: "Blessed is He who has given to the cock understanding to distinguish between day and night."

When he opens his eyes, he should say: "Blessed is He who opens the eyes of the blind."

When he stretches himself and stirs up, he should say: "Blessed is he who looseneth the bound."

When he dresses he should say: "Blessed is He who clothes the naked."

When he draws himself up, he should say: "Blessed is He who raises the bowed."

When he steps on to the ground, he should say: "Blessed is He who spreads the earth on the waters."

When he commences to walk, he should say: "Blessed is He who makes firm the steps of man."

When he ties his shoes, he should say: "Blessed is

He who has supplied all my wants."

When he fastens his girdle, he should say: "Blessed is He who girds Israel with might."

When he spreads a kerchief over his head, he should say: "Blessed is He who crowns Israel with glory."

When he wraps himself with the fringed garment, he should say: "Blessed is He who hast sanctified us with His commandments and commanded us to enwrap ourselves in the fringed garment."

Jesus emphasized a man's right to go directly to God in his prayers, teaching his followers to address Israel's God as *abba*,[14] the Aramaic equal of the intimate "Daddy," a far cry from the Temple Bureaucrats' monopoly of "The Ineffable Name"[15] with which they enslaved the people.

He taught his followers a simple prayer[16] that swept the countryside, a prayer to let them talk personally with Israel's God: A brilliant eclectic stripping down the *kaddish*[17] (*Aramaic* = "holy"), one of the synagogue prayers, to which he added other common prayers and quotations from the *torah*:

Lord's Prayer[18]	**Other Jewish Sources**[19]
Abba, who art in heaven, Hallowed be thy name.	Exalted and hallowed be His great name in the world which he created according to His will.
Thy kingdom come, Thy will be done, On earth as it is in heaven.	May He let his kingdom rule in your days and in the lifetime of the whole house of Israel, speedily and soon.

	Do Thy will in heaven, and on earth give comfort to them that fear Thee, and do what is right in Thy sight.
Give us this day our daily bread;	Give me the bread that is needful for me. May it be Thy will, O our God, to give to every one his needs and to every being sufficient for his lack.
And forgive us our debts, As we forgive our debtors.	Forgive us our debts. Forgive thy neighbor's sin and then, when thou prayest, thy sins will be forgiven; man cherisheth anger against man, and doth he seek forgiveness from the Lord?
And lead us not into temptation, But deliver us from evil.	Lead us not into sin or iniquity or temptation.
Amen.	And to this, say: Amen.

The prosecuting witnesses could not testify to a shred of evidence that Jesus himself claimed to occupy any special, personal, unusual relationship with the Holy One which the rest of them could not also claim. He stressed his own humbleness before God, taught that his Apostles and disciples could all do the same things he did,[20] if they but recognized that all Goodness came directly from the Father in heaven. He preached God's greatness and goodness (*Matthew* 19:17: "And he said unto them, Why callest me good? There is none good but one, that is God; ... "). No matter what others said about him or called him, he made no personal claims to any exalted position above the scribes or scholars at the Temple, or the poets at Qumran, the preachers in the Galilee, or the most learned doctor of the Law in Hillel's Academy.

And how could he? No man could dare say that he sat on a pedestal of rank that even remotely equaled the Holy One, Blessed be He: Man remained man; angels, angels; God, God! All as simple as that. How could anyone merge, fudge or blur these groupings, clearly spelled out in Genesis of how God created it all. Anyone who taught otherwise would be guilty of false prophecy, possibly idolatry, of high treason against God in some form or other.

But the Great Court in Jesus' false prophecy trial never made any such finding.

Chapter 20

"THEREFORE, CHOOSE LIFE!"

The trial moved into its second full day, the judges following the *talmud's* admonition to think on the case overnight, but refrain from prejudging the accused until they heard all the evidence.

The Court reassembled after the morning sacrifice, all seventy justices, Caiaphas, the legal scholars, the clerks and the probationers, each in his own place.

The judges next probed Jesus' teachings on the nature of good and evil.[1]

No witness could remember a sermon exactly on the subject, but some repeated a few of Jesus' scattered sayings: "Every sound tree bears good fruit, but the bad tree bears evil fruit";[2] "No one can serve two masters; for either he will hate the one and love the other, or he will be devoted to the one and despise the other. You cannot serve God and mammon (evil)."[3]

At least since the *Deuteronomy* Law Code (619 B.C.), the Jews believed that man must avoid evil to live in this world and in the world to come (30:15, 19-20): "See, I have set before you this day life and good, death and evil . . . blessing and curse; therefore, choose life, that you and your descendants may live, loving the Lord your God, obeying His voice, and cleaving to Him . . . ."

This precept fixed the mold for the whole of life: God's divine blueprint laid out a promise of never-ending battle between good and evil. It explained the thrill of the contest, planned the lasting conflict.[4]

Man's option to choose between good and evil brought a

direct face-off with another solid premise: "No man bruises his finger here on earth unless it was so decreed against him in heaven, for it is written, *It is of the Lord that a man's goings are established* (*Psalm* 37:23). *How then can man look to his way?* (*Proverbs* 20:24)"[5]

Man needed the security of God's safe arms, of His protection and guidance, His pre-destination: "Never does a serpent bite unless it has been incited from Above, nor does a lion rend its prey unless it has been incited from Above, nor does a government interfere with men unless it has been incited from Above."[6]

Still, if man lived only as God's puppet, man could never develop the Attributes God meant for him to enjoy. God did not create man to be a vacant, trifling robot: God could not demean man, the crown of His creation, without demeaning Himself.

They never really tried hard to reconcile the two opposites: "Everything is foreseen (by God). God sees all. God is independent of time and space, there is with Him neither past nor future nor distance, and He sees everything at once. But the right of choice, authority over self, Free-will, is granted. And the world (even the wicked) is judged with goodness, and everything is in accordance with the preponderance of man's deeds."[7]

They boiled down the tensions between the two conflicting truths into a single sentence which they quoted often: "Everything is in the hand of heaven except the fear of heaven,"[8] God Himself bowing out of the option process, leaving man with the free choice to be God-fearing or not, a man's basic qualities fixed by nature; but his moral character and his standing before God depended upon man's own taste.

No complaining witnesses could testify that Jesus ever made the slightest attempt to explain why the Holy One, Blessed be He, created evil in the first place, or permitted it to last. He taught no new doctrines about good or evil that would lead loyal Israelites away from the paths wherein they walked for generations. As a good Jew, Jesus strayed not from the teachings of his fathers.

No false prophecy here!

Chapter 21

"THERE IS MORE JOY IN HEAVEN OVER ONE SINNER...."

The biting, dogged, stubborn questions of the judges probably dragged the case into its third day, some taking the side of the prosecuting witnesses, others probing for the accused, all trying to sort out the facts relative to the false prophecy charge.

"Did the accused ever teach anything about the nature of sin, or explain what sin was?" one of the judges perhaps asked as they continued to explore Jesus' preachings.

The prosecuting witness answered that Jesus never once defined "sin," assuming that his listeners knew what he preached against. One of the judges, after questioning several witnesses, suggested that they pull his teachings on sin out of his parables, like the parable of the "Ninety-and-Nine":[1]

And the Pharisees and the scribes murmured, saying, "This man receives sinners and eats with them."

So he told them this parable: "What man of you, having a hundred sheep, if he has lost one of them, does not leave the ninety-nine in the wilderness, and go after the one which is lost, until he finds it?

"And when he has found it, he lays it on his shoulders, rejoicing.

"And when he comes home, he calls together his

friends and his neighbors, saying to them, 'Rejoice with me, for I have found my sheep which was lost.' Just so, I tell you, there will be more joy in heaven over one sinner who repents than over ninety-nine righteous persons who need no repentance . . . . "

His listeners needed no definition of sin from Jesus, sin one of the first precepts they learned at their mothers' knees, and in the synagogue schools (*bet-ha-midrashim*). Since God gave man the unbridled option between good and evil, man's choice of the path of evil needed a label; so they called it "sin":[2]

> He created man with four attributes of the higher beings (angels) and four attributes of the lower beings (beasts) . . . .

> The Holy One, Blessed be He, said: 'If I create him of the celestial elements he will live forever and not die, and if I create him of the terrestrial elements, he will die and not live in a future life.

> 'Therefore I will create him of the upper and of the lower elements; his body of the earth and his soul of heaven: If he sins, he will die; while if he does not sin, he will live.'

Two witnesses described Jesus' hassle with some scribes over his healing technique which included the formula of "forgiving sins" (*Mark* 2:1-12):

> And when he returned to Capernaum after some days, it was reported that he was at home. And many were gathered together, so that there was no longer room for them, not even about the door; and he was preaching the word to them.

> And they came, bringing to him a paralytic carried by four men.

> And when they could not get near him because of

the crowd, they removed the roof from above him; and when they had made an opening, they let down the pallet on which the paralytic lay.

And when Jesus saw their faith, he said to the paralytic, "My son, your sins are forgiven."

Now some of the scribes were sitting there, questioning in their hearts, "Why does this man speak thus? It is blasphemy! Who can forgive sins but God alone?"

And immediately Jesus, perceiving in his spirit that they thus questioned within themselves, said to them,

"Why do you question thus in your hearts? Which is easier, to say to the paralytic, 'Your sins are forgiven', or to say, 'Rise, take up your pallet and walk?'" . . . .

He said to the paralytic, "I say to you, rise, take up your pallet and go home."

Jesus did not himself claim the power to forgive sins, which rested solely with God, his words only part of his healing formula which he clearly explained, then changed it to be sure no one mistook his intentions.

They all understood the need for the healing formula, although most of the wonder-healers of the day stayed clear of using "forgiveness" in their rituals: It bordered too close to an invasion of God's sole power. Jesus recognized the danger and quickly backed off as soon as the scribes called him on it.

Other witnesses could report nothing from any of Jesus' actions or teachings that implied a new or different twist of his attitudes toward sin, nothing from which the judges could infer any measure of false prophecy.

"Repent! Repent! Repent!" of the sins they all understood.

Chapter 22

"THOU ART A GOD
READY TO FORGIVE"

The judges questioned more witnesses about Jesus' teachings on repentance[1] and pardon for sin,[2] other key tenets of Pharisaic Judaism.[3]

The need for repentance always came back to the vexing problem of evil: Why did God create it? How could God and man handle man's yielding to evil's temptations to betray his God and harm his fellowman?

Their reasoning started with the premise that since God created evil, it must serve some useful purpose, motivating man's creativity: "*And, behold, it was very good* (Genesis 1:31).... 'good' alludes to the creation of man and the Good Inclination, 'very' alludes to the Evil Inclination. Is then the Evil Inclination '*very good*'! It is in truth to teach you that were it not for the Evil Inclination, nobody would build a house, marry and beget children; and thus Solomon says, *That it is a man's rivalry with his neighbor* (Ecclesiastes 4:4). (The ambition to excel is a motive force in keeping the world going)."[4]

Still, the Evil Impulse stalked them all: "Man's Evil Desire renews itself daily against him .... It gathers strength and seeks to slay him . . . and were it not for the Holy One, blessed be He, to help man, he would not be able to prevail against the Evil Desire, for it is said, *The Lord will not leave man in his hand* (Psalm 37:33)."[5]

Over the centuries, they developed an elaborate jargon in their troubled efforts to move some logical solution into an illogical collision: "The Evil Inclination has seven names. The

Holy One, blessed be He, called it *Evil* . . . Moses called it the *Uncircumcised* . . . David called it the *Unclean* . . . Solomon called it the *Enemy* . . . Isaiah called it the *Stumbling-Block* . . . Ezekiel called it *Stone* . . . Joel called it the *Hidden One*."[6]

From the neighboring Persians and Egyptians, they drew in other names and concepts for the archenemy of God and His goodness: Satan, Belial, Beliar, Mastema,[7] the Evil Prompter.[8] Yet, why would an All-powerful, All-good God permit Evil of any kind?

The debates raged unchecked, even to a point of injecting God's own thoughts into the riddle of evil. God finally admitted that perhaps He made a mistake: "There are four things of which the Holy One, blessed be He, repents that He had created them, and they are the following: 'The Exile' (Babylonian Captivity = 586-537 B.C.); the Chaldeans (astrologers; Babylonians); the Ishmaelites (descendants of Abraham's son by Hagar); and the Evil Inclination."[9]

Certainly, the God of the Universe would never leave man defenseless in his battle against the Evil Inclination: "Even so did the Holy One, blessed be He, speak unto Israel: 'My children! I created the Evil Desire, but I also created the *Torah*, as its antidote; if you occupy yourselves with the *Torah*, you will not be delivered into his hand . . . . But if you do not occupy yourselves with the *Torah*, ye shall be delivered into his hand, for it is written, *sin coucheth at the door* (Genesis 4:7). Moreover, he (Evil Impulse) is altogether pre-occupied with thee, to make thee sin, for it is said, *and unto thee shall be his desire* (Genesis 4:7).'"[10]

Evil hid inside a man's soul: "A man should always incite the Good Impulse in his soul to fight against the Evil Impulse . . . . (The good impulses and the evil impulses of a man are personified as two genii or spirits dwelling in his soul, the one prompting him to do good things and the other one to do wicked things.)"[11]

The clear-cut, internal struggle never let up!

Against the Hebrew view of the residing place of the Evil Impulse, they knew the Persian images: Called *Cosmic Dualism*, the Jews brought it back from the Babylonian Exile; and it blossomed under the later Hellenizers. Led by Satan, or Matsema, or Belial and Beliar, the choice of name really didn't matter, the evil forces existed in space, *outside* man's soul, fighting against the Armies of God, each man pulled and tugged, pummelled and assaulted by these contending *external* powers who battled to capture him alone, and his fellows as a group: "Satan comes down to earth and seduces, then ascends to heaven and awakens wrath; permission is granted to him and he takes away the soul.... Satan, the evil prompter, and the Angel of Death are one. He is called Satan, as it is written, *And Satan went forth from the presence of the Lord* (Job 1:12)."[12]

Judaism could not live with the Persian idea that no single All-Powerful God sat in ultimate control over these conflicting powers of light and darkness, although some sectors of Judaism (Jesus among them) accepted an Oriental angelology, demonology, spirit-invasion and demon-possession of man, all outside forces that could invade a man's soul, to help him either fight evil or destroy him.

Tones of debate over this Evil Impulse raged within all of Judaism's varied hues, among Pharisees and Sadducees, the *bet hillel* and the *bet shammai* academies, the Essenes and Qumran scholars, in the apocalyptic writings. The tightly-knit Dead Seas Scrolls community argued within its self, some urging the ancient line that the Evil Impulse lurked *within* man's soul, waging an internal struggle day in and day out; others, that the forces of Good and Evil came from *without*.

All sides agreed that there could be no doubt who would win the seventh decisive battle, after each side took three preliminary skirmishes apiece: Israel's supreme God, creator of the forces of both evil and good, would preside over the final outcome as a commanding General of the Armies. As the dualism of Qumran predicted, this would usher in the "end of days" ("final days") as pre-ordained by Israel's own all-powerful, good and complete God.

The witnesses never heard Jesus specifically discuss the question of where the Evil Impulse resided; but they did know that he cast out seven demons who hounded Mary Magdalene.[13] Obviously, he believed in these demonic forces, and knew how to get rid of them; and he talked about people with "an unclean spirit."[14] He once asked: "How can Satan cast out Satan?"[15]

Jesus preached his main message, the witnesses testified, that all men must repent to enter the "kingdom": "Unless you repent, you will all likewise perish."[16] When he sent out "The Twelve" on their practice preaching missions, he told them specifically to preach that "men should repent,"[17] repeating his first sermon after taking over John's disciples: "Repent, and believe on the gospel."[18]

Still, he never defined repentance, assuming that his listeners knew exactly what he preached about.

They did not need a definition, repentance at least their second most ancient precept: "Seven things were created before the world was created, and these are they: The *Torah*, repentance, the Garden of Eden (Paradise), Gehenna (Hell), God's Throne of Glory, (God's Celestial) Temple, and the name of the Messiah . . . . Repentance, for it is written, *Before the mountains were brought forth, Thou turnest man to contrition, and sayest, Repent, ye children of men* (Psalm 90) . . . . "

"Repent" meant "turn about," "return," "go back" to God and God's life-sustaining Law: "Scripture says: 'Let the wicked man forsake his way and the bad man his plans, and let him return to the Lord (repent), and He will have mercy upon him' (*Isaiah* 55:7). For God desires repentance; He does not desire to put any creature to death, as it is said: 'As I live saith the Lord Jehovah, I do not desire the death of the wicked man, but that the wicked man turn from his evil way and live (*Ezekiel* 3:11).'"[19]

Without repentance, the elaborate Day of Atonement rituals in the Temple would be but hollow rote: "Death and the Day of Atonement effect atonement if there is repentance. Repentance effects atonement for lesser transgressions against both positive and negative commands in the Law; while for graver transgressions, it suspends punishment until the Day of Atonement comes and effects atonement."[20]

The Jews' literature throughout the ages stressed God's goodness in building repentance into His divine blueprint for their hopes and progress: "Thou, O Lord, according to they great goodness hast promised repentance and forgiveness to those who have sinned against thee; and in the multitude of thy mercies thou hast appointed repentance for sinners, that they may be saved....["21]

God's great scheme also required confession of sins, else it would not work. As far back as their 40 years in the desert, God told Moses: "Say to the people of Israel, When a man or woman commits any of the sins that men commit by breaking faith with the Lord, and that person is guilty, he shall confess his sin which he has committed; and he shall make full restitution for his wrong, and giving it to him he did the wrong."[22]

They worked out supplication formulas for their personal and group confessions: "Then I turned my face to the Lord God, seeking Him by prayer and supplications with fasting and sackcloth and ashes. I prayed to the Lord my God and made confession, saying, 'O Lord, the great and terrible God who keepest covenant and steadfast love with those who love Him and keep His commandments, we have sinned and done wrong and acted wickedly and rebelled, turning aside from Thy commandments and ordinances; we have not listened to Thy servants the prophets, who spoke in Thy name to our kings, our princes, and our fathers, and to all the people of the land .... All Israel has transgressed Thy law and turned aside, refusing to obey Thy voice .... O my God, incline Thy ear and hear; open Thy eyes and behold our desolation ... for we do not present our supplications before Thee on the ground of our righteousness, but on the ground of Thy great mercy. O Lord, hear; O Lord, forgive."[23]

If a man, or the nation, showed genuine grief for his sins, like Reuben who mourned for seven years over his grave iniquity of lying with his father's concubine,[24] God's contractual obligation forced Him to forgive them: "For I the Lord do not change; therefore you, O sons of Jacob, are not consumed. From the days of your fathers you have turned aside from My statutes and have not kept them. Return to Me, and I will return to you, says the Lord of hosts ... put Me to the test ...."[25]

Contract obligation or no, God's sense of justice, His mercy, the God of history who walked with their fathers, Abraham, Isaac and Jacob, and above all, God's Goodness, made Him eager to forgive: "When you are in tribulation, and all these things come upon you in the latter days, you will return to the Lord your God and obey His voice, for the Lord your God is a merciful God; He will not fail you or destroy you or forget the covenant with your fathers which He swore to them."[26]

God's forgiveness became a matter of right, not God's discretion, provided man repented, confessed his wrongdoing, became genuinely sorry for his sins.

Salvation followed four basic steps: Repentance, sorrowful regret, forgiveness and restoration, the steps orderly, logical, simple and without confusion.

As the judges debated the Jesus case in the great basilica of the Hewn Stone, it became clear that the accused never taught any new matter on the subject of repentance, the confession of sins, the need for grief over past sins, or the sinner's restoration to the Ever-Present's Grace after forgiveness. His teachings followed solid, orthodox, Pharisee doctrine, and did not present the slightest threat of leading loyal Israelites from the paths their fathers walked throughout the generations.

It became increasingly clear to seasoned court observers that Jesus' conviction on the false prophecy charge would be nigh to impossible.

Chapter 23

"DO THIS, AND YOU WILL LIVE . . . "

Under the questioning of the judges, the witnesses testified to Jesus' teachings on the Golden Rule. After calling the *shema* the "great and first commandment," Jesus added: "The second is this, You shall love your neighbor as yourself. There is no other commandment greater than these. On these two commandments depend all the Law and the prophets. Do this and you will live."[1]

The judges knew this "second commandment" as a direct quote from *Leviticus* (19:17-18): "You shall not hate your brother in your heart, but you shall reason with your neighbor, lest you bear sin because of him. You shall not take vengeance or bear any grudge against the sons of your people, but you shall love your neighbor as yourself."[2]

The great *Hillel*, an older contemporary of Jesus, also taught on this "second commandment" (*talmud, Shabbath* 31a):

> On another occasion it happened that a certain heathen came before *Shammai* and said to him, "Make me a proselyte (convert to Judaism), on condition that you teach me the whole *Torah* while I stand on one foot." Thereupon he repulsed him with a builder's cubit (ruler) which was in his hand.
>
> When he went before *Hillel,* he said to him, "What is hateful to you, do not to your neighbor (the Golden Rule): that is the whole *Torah,* while the rest is commentary thereof; go and learn it."

It all turned on brotherhood,[3] this emphasis which the basic

Judaism of Jesus' time placed on morals and ethics: "May it be Thy will, O Lord our God, to cause to dwell in our lot love and brotherhood and peace and friendship,"[4] all men brothers as sons of God.

When God created the Evil Impulse, he denied man the hope of earthly perfection,[5] so He spelled out a down-to-earth attitude for daily living in the *torah*; and His children, the Jews, practiced His rules of "morals" and "ethics," as well as Law.

In their unique Father-son, family-sibling arrangement, a man could not achieve piety in his "Fatherhood of God"[6] unless he lived in an aura of "Brotherhood of man"[7] as he moved among his fellows.

They developed no crisp distinctions between morals and ethics, perhaps using "morals" (*musar*) for the general rules of good and bad, right not wrong, righteous not evil, just not unjust: "Let justice roll down like waters, and righteousness like an ever-flowing stream[8] . . . . He has showed thee, O man, what is good; and what does the Lord require of you but to do justice, and to love mercy, and to walk humbly with your God."[9]

Jeremiah described the moral man who gloried in the Lord: "Thus says the Lord: 'Let not the wise man glory in his wisdom, let not the strong man glory in his strength, let not the rich man glory in his riches. Only in this should one glory: In his devotion to Me."[10]

They considered morals and piety a state of mind, one merged into the other: An early Psalmist shared the Prophet's view of the moral man, even though no one gave specific definitions: "Blessed is the man who walketh not in the counsel of the ungodly, nor standeth in the way of sinners, nor sitteth in the seat of the scornful. But his delight is in the Law of the Lord; and in His Law doth he meditate day and night."[11]

The moral man walked in God's goodness, shunning evil, as he moved among his fellows day in and day out, abiding not only the Laws of the torah which carried penalties, but those rules that let a civilized society exist, even though they did not spell out sanctions: "Ethics" became the half-way ground between "morals" and "Law," standards of conduct enforced by the social and economic pressures of the people themselves in their contacts of daily living, without resort to the courts as the compliance tool.

Subjective morals left too much to the selfish man's own conscience; so they thrashed out specific ethics. The prophet Ezekiel, for example, started to describe the moral, righteous man, but found that he could not do it without specifics: "If a man is righteous and does what is lawful and right — if he does not eat upon the mountains or lift up his eyes to the idols of the house of Israel, does not defile his neighbor's wife or approach a woman in her time of impurity, does not oppress any one, but restores to the debtor his pledge, commits no robbery, gives his bread to the hungry and covers the naked with a garment, does not lend at interest or take any increase, withholds his hand from iniquity, executes true justice between man and man, walks in My statutes, and is careful to observe My ordinances, he is righteous, he shall surely live, says the Lord God."[12]

The moral man became also an ethical man who practiced far more than legality as he moved among his fellowman: "*But thou shalt love thy neighbor as thyself* is even a greater principle. Hence, you must not say, Since I have been put to shame, let my neighbor be put to shame. If you do so, know whom you put to shame, for *In the likeness of God made He him*."[13]

Judaism's unique concern over a man's neighbor became the base of its ethics: "He who oppresses a poor man insults his Maker, but he who is kind to the needy honors Him . . . . "[14]

They all took pride in the system of ethics the Lord their God gave them, Judaism's label, "ethical religion," setting it apart from the pagan cults around her.[15]

Jesus, both the prosecuting and accused's witnesses reported, preached the *shema* and the Golden Rule commandment of Leviticus with vigor, adding nothing and taking nothing away, forever using his dramatic parables to show how the two articles of faith worked in daily life.

He neither urged nor suggested any basic changes, teaching with pride, the traditions of Abraham, Isaac and Jacob, never once offering a new rule of either morals or ethics. The "kingdom" he and John preached called the people back to repentance, and to their precepts of the "Fatherhood of God" and the "Brotherhood of man," his message far removed from anything close to false prophecy.

Chapter 24

"GIVE TO HIM WHO BEGS FROM YOU . . . . "

The judges' questions on Jesus' teachings on the "Brother-hood of man" led them to examine his precepts on "loving-kind-ness." Here again, they found that he taught traditional doctrine, once giving a one-sentence summary of the case Law on the subject (*Matthew* 5:42): "Give to him who begs from you, and do not refuse him who would borrow from you."

The Jews called charity by many names: "Righteousness," "blessing," "kindness," "loving-kindness," "alms-giving" and "jus-tice,"[1] one of the clearest commands in *Deuteronomy* (15:7-8): "If there is among you a poor man, one of your brethren, in any of the towns within your land which the Lord your God gives you, you shall not harden your heart or shut your hand against your brother, but you shall open your hand to him, and lend him sufficient for his need, whatever it may be."

Loving-kindness sustained the world: "Simon the Just was one of the remnant of the Great Synagogue (established by Ezra around 400 B.C.). He used to say: By three things is the world sustained: By the Law (study of *torah*), by the Temple Service (worship), and by deeds of loving-kindness (charity)."[2]

The theme of charity flowed through all of *Deuteronomy*: "For the poor will never cease out of the land; therefore, I command you, You shall open wide your hand to your brother, to the needy and to the poor in the land."[3]

Over the centuries, the call for charity became a rushing river through the whole Bible: "He who despises his neighbor is a sinner, but happy is he who is kind to the poor[4] . . . . All day long the wicked covets, but the righteous gives and does not hold back[5] .... He who gives to the poor will not want, but he who covers his eyes will get many a curse."[6]

Their non-biblical writings stated and restated this basic tenet of their rules (*Ecclesiaticus, or the Wisdom of Jesus, Son of Sirach* 29:14): "My son, deprive not the poor of his living, and do not keep needy eyes waiting. Do not grieve the one who is hungry, nor anger a man in want. Do not add to the troubles of an angry mind, nor delay your gift to a beggar. Do not reject an afflicted suppliant, nor turn your face away from the poor[7] .... He that shows mercy will lend to his neighbor, and he that strengthens him with his hand keeps the commandments. Lend to your neighbor in time of his need; and in turn, repay your neighbor promptly .... A good man will be surety for his neighbor, but a man who has lost his sense of shame will fail him."[8]

Charity helped man triumph over death: "Great is charity, in that it brings the redemption nearer: Ten strong things have been created in the world. The rock is hard, but the iron cleaves it. The iron is hard, but the fire softens it. The fire is hard, but the water quenches it. The water is strong, but fright crushes it. Fright is strong, but wine banishes it. Wine is strong, but sleep works it off. Death is stronger than all, but charity saves from death, as it is written, *Righteousness (charity) delivereth from death* (Proverbs 10:2)."[9]

Charity to the poor equated lending to God Himself: "What is the meaning of the verse, *He that hath pity on the poor lendeth unto the Lord* (Proverbs 19:17). Were it not written in the Scripture, one would not dare say it: As it were, *the borrower is servant to the lender* (Proverbs 22:7)."[10]

The witnesses reported Jesus' many teachings on the need to practice charity, unselfishly, person-to-person, one-on-one, instead of leaving it to the charity wardens of the city or village. He taught: "When you give a dinner or a banquet, do not invite your friends or your brothers or your kinsmen or rich neighbors, lest they also invite you in return, and you be repaid. But when you give a feast, invite the poor, the maimed, the lame, the blind, and you will be blessed, because they cannot repay you. You will be repaid at the resurrection of the just .... [11]When you give alms, sound not a trumpet before you, as the hypocrites do in the synagogues and in the streets, that they may be praised by men. Truly I say to you, they have their reward. But when you give alms, do not let your left hand know what your right hand is doing, so that your alms may be in secret; and your Father who sees in secret will reward you."[12]

Jesus' main teaching on charity rested on the Golden Rule in *Leviticus*.

Living on charity, unable to work for the good of the community, made a man a social cripple, reducing him from a "son of God" to something just above an animal, a numbed actor without dignity, bereft of the creative breath of God the Father which made different every man born of woman.

The judges' decisions over the centuries recognized different styles of relief, eight in fact, each more virtuous than the other: "To give (1) but sadly; (2) less than is fitting, but in good humor; (3) only after being asked; (4) before being asked; (5) in such a manner that the donor does not know who the recipient is; (6) in such a manner that the recipient does not know who the donor is; (7) in such a way that neither the donor nor the recipient knows the identity of the other; and (8) the highest form of charity is not to give alms but to help the poor to rehabilitate themselves by lending them money, taking them into partnership, employing them, or giving them work, for in this way the end is achieved without any loss of self respect."[13]

The rulings described the required one-to-one duties clearly: "He who lends money is greater than he who performs charity (because the poor man is not ashamed to borrow; also perhaps because one generally lends a larger sum than he would give as charity, and that may suffice to make the poor man independent); and he who forms a partnership is greater than all."[14]

To make the poor man independent: That the divine goal, the Holy One's master blueprint!

The witnesses reported Jesus abhorrence of the relief programs of the Temple: They debased not only the person who received relief, but also the one granting it. The rulers became swallowed up in technical rules to let them improve their roles as Bureaucrats, not rendering to the poor and defenseless to help them find a new way of life. The Temple Bureaucrats did not want any great number of the poor to find a way off relief, which would cause their roles as Bureaucrats to cease. They lived off the backs of their brothers whom they claimed they served. If they did not hold them down, they themselves would be thrown down.

One of Jesus' greatest parables stressed the required one-to-one approach to charity, not by chance that he made a lowly Samaritan the hero, since the Jews looked down on their Samaritan neighbors, considering them racial and religious misfits:[15]

> And behold, a lawyer stood up to put him to the test, saying, "Teacher, what shall I do to inherit eternal life?"
>
> He said to him, "What is written in the Law? How do you read?"
>
> And he answered, "You shall love the Lord your God with all your heart, and with all your soul, and with all your strength, and with all your mind; and your neighbor as yourself."
>
> And he said to him, "You have answered right; do this, and you will live."
>
> But he, desiring to justify himself, said to Jesus, "And who is my neighbor?"
>
> Jesus replied, "A man was going down from Jerusalem to Jericho, and he fell among robbers, who stripped him and beat him, and departed, leaving him half dead.
>
> "Now, by chance a priest was going down that road; and when he saw him he passed by on the other side.
>
> "So likewise a Levite; when he came to the place and saw him, passed by on the other side.

"But a Samaritan, as he journeyed, came to where he was; and when he saw him, he had compassion, and went to him and bound up his wounds, pouring on oil and wine; then he set him on his own beast and brought him to an inn, and took care of him.

"And the next day he took our two denarii and gave them to the innkeeper, saying, 'Take care of him; and whatever more you spend, I will repay you when I come back.'

"Which of these three, do you think, proved neighbor to the man who fell among the robbers? He said, "The one who showed mercy on him."

And Jesus said to him, "Go and do likewise."

The parable stressed good, sound, Pharisee doctrine, while damning the arrogant Temple Bureaucrats. Jesus' teachings on "loving-kindness" cut through the rubbish of the Bureaucracy, calling the people back to Judaism's simple theme: Three things sustain the world: (1) the Law, (2) the worship services, and (3) charity.

Chapter 25

"I HAVE GIVEN TO
ALL ABLE MEN ABILITY . . . ."

The case dragged on, approaching the noon hour, making them wonder if they would finish by the time of the afternoon sacrifice, or if they would take another overnight recess.

Teaching on charity required instruction on work, a subject vital to all Jews; so the judges questioned the witnesses on Jesus' preachings on work.

One witness reported Jesus' Parable of the Talents:[1]

> For it will be as when a man going on a journey called his servants and entrusted to them his property; to one he gave five talents, to another two, to another one, to each according to his ability. Then he went away.

> He who had received the five talents went at once and traded with them; and he made five talents more. So also, he who had the two talents made two talents more. But he who had received the one talent went and dug in the ground and hid his master's money.

> Now after a long time the master of those servants came and settled accounts with them.

> And he who had received the five talents came forward, bringing five talents more, saying, 'Master, you delivered to me five talents; here I have made five talents more.' His master said to him, 'Well

done, good and faithful servant; you have been
faithful over a little, I will set you over much; enter
into the joy of your master.'

And he also who had the two talents came forward,
saying, 'Master, you delivered to me two talents;
here I have made two talents more.' His master said
to him, 'Well done, good and faithful servant; you
have been faithful over a little, I will set you over
much; enter into the joy of your master.'

He also who had received the one talent came
forward, saying, 'Master, I knew you to be a hard
man, reaping where you did not sow, and gathering
where you did not winnow; so I was afraid, and I
went and hid your talent in the ground. Here you
have what is yours.' But his master answered him
'You wicked and slothful servant! You knew that
I reap where I have not sowed, and gather where
I have not winnowed? Then you ought to have
invested my money with the bankers, and at my
coming I should have received what was my own
with interest.

'So take the talent from him, and give it to him
who has the ten talents. For to everyone who has
will more be given, and he will have abundance;
but from him who has not, even what he has will
be taken away. And cast the worthless servant into
the outer darkness; there men will weep and gnash
their teeth.'

The Jews honored labor as far back as man's creation since
God conferred upon Adam the duty to maintain the Garden of
Eden: "The Lord God took the man and put him in the garden
of Eden to till it and keep it."[2]

God worked with His own hands to form the earth: "When I
look at Thy heavens, the work of Thy fingers, the moon and the
stars which Thou hast established, what is man that Thou art
mindful of him, and the son of man that thou dost care for him
.... [3] Of old, Thou didst lay the foundation of the earth, and the

heavens are the work of Thy hands."[4]

It followed, then, that man as an extension of the breath and hands of God, should do God's work with his hands, in honor, reverence, pride, diligence and delight: "A man who lives from the labour of his hands is greater than the one who fears heaven (but for his living relies upon the support of other people)."[5]

If labor lifted man up, idleness pressed him down: "Idleness leads to unchastity . . . idleness leads to idiocy."[6]

Even the sages made their living with their hands so that their lofty studies of *torah* could carry a practical balance: "Excellent is the study of the *torah* together with a worldly occupation, for the energy taken up by both of them keeps sin out of one's mind; and as for all study of the *torah* where there is no worldly occupation, the end thereof is that it comes to nought and brings sin in its train."[7]

If God created all forms of labor, all must be good: "Do not hate toilsome labor, or farm work, which were created by the Most High."[8]

No kind of honest work degraded: "At all times, shall one rather hire himself out to work which is strange to him than be in need of the help of his fellow creatures . . . . Flay a carcass in the street and earn a wage, and say not, 'I am a great man and the work is degrading to me.' (The greatest man on earth is not degraded by honest work)."[9]

Accepting honest work kept a man off Temple relief and saved him from faking the need for organized charity: "It is only thanks to the rogues who claim charity under false pretenses that we have an excuse for not responding to every appeal . . . . Our Rabbis taught: If a man pretends to have a blind eye, a swollen belly or a shrunken leg, he will not pass out from this world before actually coming into such a condition. If a man accepts charity and is not in need of it, his end will be that he will not pass out of the world before he comes to such a condition."[10]

It followed that a man should teach his sons the glories of work, God's divine scheme for the world: "The father is bound to respect his son, to circumcise him, redeem the firstborn, teach him *Torah*, take a wife for him, and teach him a craft. Some say, to teach him to swim too. He who does not teach his son a craft, teaches him brigandage (robbery)."[11]

As the judges heard the evidence on Jesus' approach to work, it became clear that he taught nothing new on it, proud of the fact that he knew the carpentry trade taught him by Joseph, his father. In all respects, he agreed with the great ode to the workers, composed by *Jesus, Son of Sirach*, around 180 B.C.[12]

> He sets his heart on plowing furrows, and he is careful about fodder for the heifers.

> So too is every craftsman and master workman who labors by night as well as by day; those who cut the signets of seals, each is diligent in making a great variety; he sets his heart on painting a lifelike image, and he is careful to finish his work.

> So too is the smith sitting by the anvil, intent upon his handiwork in iron; the breath of the fire melts his flesh, and he wastes away in the heat of the furnace; he inclines his ear to the sound of the hammer, and his eyes are on the pattern of the object. He sets his heart on finishing his handiwork, and he is careful to complete its decoration.

> So too is the potter sitting at his work and turning the wheel with his feet; he is always deeply concerned over his work, and all his output is by number. He mounds the clay with his arm and makes it pliable with his feet; he sets his heart to finish the glazing, and he is careful to clean the furnace.

> All these rely upon their hands, and each is skilful in his own work.

> Without them a city cannot be established, and men can neither sojourn nor live there.

> Yet they are not sought out for the council of the people, nor do they attain eminence in the public assembly. They do not sit in the judge's seat, nor

do they understand the sentence of judgment; they cannot expound discipline or judgment, and they are not found using proverbs.

But they keep stable the fabric of the world, and their prayer is in the practice of their trade.

Chapter 26

"BESIDE ME THERE IS NO SAVIOR"

The taking of testimony began to wind down; but the judges dared not leave dangling the matter of salvation,[1] a basic tenet of Judaism.

Except for man's inborn yearning for "life everlasting," there would be no need for "salvation"; but the creative breath of God gave man his craving to live forever, this longing so deep-seated that no man could see himself completely dead, in a state where he could not feel, think, hear, see and react. The doctrine of salvation for the Jews took a long time to develop; but though it came late, it helped give Judaism its lasting power.

As all men, before and since, they watched death's traumas firsthand. When God's breath (soul) left their fellow, they placed his lifeless body in a cave, or a tomb cut in rock, anointed it with spices, and wrapped it in burial strips to make the decaying process more bearable for the survivors: But what of the soul that did not putrify or return to "dust?"

From all time past, down through the years of the Babylonian Captivity, they believed that the dead went to *sheol*, a netherland under the earth, a place their poets called "perdition" (*abaddon*), "death" (*mawet*), "pit" (*bor shahat*) and "darkness" (*salmut*),[2] a continuous tomb where the "*shades*" ("shadows") and "impotents" = (*refa'im*) roamed aimlessly in a dazed, drugged state, without feeling or contact with the world of the living: "I am consigned to the gates of Sheol for the rest of my years."[3]

Every man and woman went to this gloomy abode on God's appointed day, the good and the evil alike, the great and the small, the righteous and the wicked: "The wicked cease from troubling, and there the weary are at rest."[4]

The dead held no hope of ever leading any other form of life: "If a man die, shall he live again? . . . So man lies down and rises not again; till the heavens are no more, he will not wake."[5]

No exceptions! The just and the unjust, the moral man and the pagan, the believer and the scoffer, the pious and the self-centered, all suffered the same fate of eternal arrest behind the barred gates of *sheol*!

Toward the end of the Exile (538 B.C.), God, speaking through Ezekiel, gave them a spark on which to build a structure of personal salvation; and Judaism pursued the doctrine of personal hope that let it soar above its neighbors and rivals: "But if a wicked man turns away from all his sins which he has committed and keeps all my statutes and does what is lawful and right, he shall surely live; he shall not die. None of the transgressions which he has committed shall be remembered against him; for the righteousness which he has done, he shall live . . . . Therefore, I will judge you, O house of Israel, every one according to his ways, says the Lord God. Repent and turn from your transgressions, lest iniquity be your ruin . . . . Get yourselves a new heart and a new spirit! Why will you die, O house of Israel? For I have no pleasure in the death of any one, says the Lord God; so turn, and live."[6]

They turned and lived, developing a practical tenet of personal immortality (salvation), whose beauty and simplicity flowed up past the Gates of Heaven, reaching the Throne of God: "Return O my soul, to your rest; for the Lord has dealt bountifully with you. For thou hast delivered my soul from death, my eyes from tears, my feet from stumbling; I walk before the Lord in the land of the living . . . . Precious in the sight of the Lord is the death of His saints."[7]

Personal and national salvation extended God's own logic, His fairness with His people; but claiming it required special doing: God must mete out just rewards and punishments spelled out in the *torah* at Mt. Sinai, the detailed system of blessings and curses growing into the great Law Codes over the centuries, with their moral and ethical demands.

Describing a Great Judgment, a "final forensic act," for those alive at the "end of days" or the "final days," this Golden Age on earth that John the Baptist and Jesus bar Joseph preached, took no great imagination: "And therefore will the Lord wait, that He may be gracious unto you, and therefore will He be exalted, that He may have mercy upon you: For the Lord is a God of judgment: Blessed are they that wait for Him."[8]

But what of those who died long ago, especially the martyrs who fell defending the faith of their fathers against pagan and heathen, tyrant and oppressor? How could they share in the Golden Age, in the "kingdom" of the "Reign of God?"[9]

Greek king Antiochus IV Epiphanes (175-164 B.C.) tried hard to wipe out Judaism; and his harsh persecutions made thousands of martyrs. It also produced the Pharisees who worked out the doctrine of resurrection of the dead, so that all could be part of God's glorious plan for man's salvation: "In those days, the earth will restore what has been delivered to it, and Sheol what it has received, and hell will deliver up hers. He [God] shall select the righteous and holy from among them; for the day of their salvation has approached . . . . In those days the mountains shall skip like rams, and the hills leap like young sheep satiated with milk; and all the righteous shall become angels in heaven. Their countenance shall be bright with joy; for in those days shall the Elect One be exalted. The earth shall rejoice; the righteous shall inhabit it, and the elect possess it."[10]

How far back would this retroactive resurrection go? As far as the great patriarchs: "Then you will see Enoch, Noah and Shem, and Abraham, Isaac, and Jacob rising up on the right hand in exultation. Then shall we also rise, each over his tribe, worshipping the King of heaven."[11]

The witnesses testified that Jesus preached "salvation" through his parable format, but never once defined it. This meant, of course, that he used the term in its usual sense, so his listeners could understand.

One of the witnesses reported Jesus' Parable of the Rich Young Man:[12]

> And as he was setting out on his journey, a man ran up and knelt before him, and asked him, "Good Teacher, what must I do to inherit eternal life?"

And Jesus said to him, "Why do you call me good? No one is good but God alone. You know the commandments: 'Do not kill, Do not commit adultery, Do not steal, Do not bear false witness, Do not defraud, Honor your father and mother.'"

And he said to him, "Teacher, all these I have observed from my youth."

And Jesus looking upon him loved him, and said to him, "You lack one thing; go, sell what you have, and give to the poor, and you will have treasure in heaven; and come, follow me."

At that saying his countenance fell, and he went away sorrowful; for he had great possessions.

And Jesus looked around and said to his disciples, "How hard it will be for those who have riches to enter the kingdom of God!" And the disciples were amazed at his words. But Jesus said to them again, "Children, how hard it is to enter the kingdom of God! It is easier for a camel to go through the eye of a needle than for a rich man to enter the kingdom of God."

And they were exceedingly astonished, and said to him, "Then who can be saved?"

Jesus looked at them and said, "With men it is impossible, but not with God; for all things are possible with God."

Who shall be saved?
Who shall inherit eternal life?
As far back as memory could go, these became man's most pressing questions: "When Rabbi Eleazer fell ill, his disciples went in to visit him. They said to him: Master, teach us the paths of life so that we may through them win the life of the future world. He said to them: Be solicitous for the honour of your colleagues, and keep your children from childish talk, and set

them between the knees of scholars; and when you pray, know before whom you are standing; and in this way you will win the future world."[13]

Their neighbors around them in the Greek, Mesopotamian and Egyptian worlds also asked the same question: How can man be saved to inherit eternal life? They answered the question through a dozen mystery cults, each with its own *soter* (*Greek* = "savior"), plus warring idols, multiple Gods and pagan rituals, each God making its own demands, extracting its special sacrifices.

Endemic to the era and area, the pagans all handled it the same way, with Savior-gods called *Adonis* in Syria; *Attis* (*Atys*) in Phrygia; *Dionysus* throughout Greek soil; *Melkart* (*Melqart*) in Phoenicia; *Mithra* in Persia; *Osiris* in Egypt; *Tammuz* and *Marduk* in Mesopotamia; and dozens of others.[14]

The Mystery Cults made no moral or ethical demands on their initiates, promising salvation and immortality to all who gained cult membership. Joining up was enough, although reinitiation took place every so often in some. Nor did these Mystery Religions demand exclusiveness: A man could be initiated, but continue to worship his other gods openly and without limitation.

Under cross-examination, the witnesses denied that Jesus ever taught the doctrine of personal salvation patterned after the *soters* of the heathen nations around Israel. Any good Jew would consider such beliefs heresy, high treason against Israel's God, dangerous false prophecy. Jesus believed firmly, the witnesses testified, in Isaiah's ringing doxology of Israel's salvation: "For I am the Lord your God, the Holy One of Israel, your Savior .... Because you are precious in my eyes, and honored, and I love you, I give men in return for you, peoples in exchange for your life .... I, I am the Lord, and besides me there is no savior."[15]

After hours of argument and tedious debate, following their rigorous rules of technical procedure spelled out in thousands of decisions stretching back over the centuries to Mt. Sinai, the judges ruled that Jesus preached the "kingdom of God" as part of the Holy One's divine plan of salvation; that it would dawn soon; that the people must repent to be saved, just as the Holy One,

Blessed be He, worked out the way of salvation for them all, before the creation of the world.

And these teachings did not come close to the sin of false prophecy.

Chapter 27

" . . . AND THEIR WITNESS DID NOT AGREE"

Mark (14:55-59) does his best to tell us of Jesus' acquittal in this trial before the Great Sanhedrin, flashing us not one message in legal jargon, but *five*:

(1) "Now the chief priests . . . sought *testimony* against Jesus to put him to death; but *they found none*."

(2) "For many bore *false witness* against him . . . . "

(3) " . . . . and their witness *did not agree*."

(4) "And some stood up and bore *false witness* against him . . . . "

(5) "Yet *not* even so did their *testimony agree*."

None of the *gospel* writers hints that he understood anything at all about the Jewish legal system, which makes *Mark's* message even more compelling: He knew a tradition that at this trial in the Hall of the Hewn Stone, the Committee of Ten felt compelled to use *false witness* against Jesus; but they could not find witnesses whose stories held up; so they lost in their second attempt to put him to death "legally."

Or maybe *Mark* did understand the nature of the "due process" demands of the Jewish system and assumed that readers would conclude from his reports of "false witness," lack of evidence, and disagreement of the witnesses, that the accused received a "favorable verdict" in this trial.

We cannot now probe *Mark's* thinking processes, nor do we know exactly how the testimony of the witnesses failed to agree. No point is served in forcing the issue, although we could show the conflicts in the different *gospel* accounts of what Jesus prophesied about the destruction of the Temple:

> And Jesus said to him, "Do you see these great buildings? There will not be left here one stone upon another, that will not be thrown down."
> *Mark* 13:2

> "We heard him say, 'I will destroy this temple that is made with hands, and in three days I will build another, not made with hands.'"
> *Mark* 14:58

> "This fellow said, 'I am able to destroy the temple of God, and to build it in three days.'"
> *Matthew* 26:61

> And as he spoke of the temple, how it was adorned with noble stones and offerings, he said, "As for these things which you see, the days will come when there shall not be left here one stone upon another that will not be thrown down."
> *Luke* 21:5

We will not argue the exact details. Our prime interest is in the final result, and our effort to mesh *Mark's* legal flashes with our other sources.

The judges of the Court of the Seventy-One faced the same problem that plagued all fact-finders from the days of recorded legal systems, and before:[1] Moses (1250 B.C.); the Middle Assyrian Laws (1450 B.C.); Hammurabi (1700 B.C.); the Lipit-Ishtar Law Code (1950 B.C.); the Laws of Eshnunna (2000 B.C.); and those whose broken shards of ordinances still lie below ground, awaiting the archaeologists' pick and shovel.

Because of the frailties of human reporting, no past event can ever be restored completely, be it a battle, a fall down a flight of steps, a sermon, a dispute between two neighbors over a common fence, a political debate, an agreement to plant a vineyard, the identity of a robber or murderer, a bullock cart accident, a fight between friends, an historic trial, a contract to divide up an inheritance, or the healing of a sick man. The exact words a person spoke, especially their meaning, are always in doubt.[2]

"Fact" and "truth" become subjective illusions,[3] the positive assertion of a witness often ending as the judge's negative rejection; and the witness who parades his truthfulness on his sleeve is usually the one least reliable.

Every legal system is forced to develop rules to help it sort out man's testimonial weaknesses; and all begin with a condemnation of the witness who *deliberately* reports falsely: "The judges shall inquire diligently, and if the witness is a false witness and has accused his brother falsely, then you shall do to him as he had meant to do to his brother; so you shall purge this evil from the midst of you."[4]

The rules against false witness (*zomen*) in Israel's earliest Codes led not only to the application of the Law of Retaliation against the witness, it meant the automatic release of the accused the witness testified against.

But how to tell the false witness from the truthful one, sort the willful perjurer from the one who makes an innocent mistake? Does the trial stop when a conflict between witnesses develops, the fact-finder deciding then and there who states the "truth," who does not report the "facts?" Or does the judge go on to decide the original case and later probe the problem of false witness?

Over the centuries, long before Jesus' trials, the Jewish system plowed that ground from one end to another, in case after decided case.

Zomen (false witness) developed into a broader meaning than mere perjury, almost reaching the rule of "inadmissible" or "excluded" testimony, its biblical foundation resting firmly on the requirement that an accused could not be convicted on the testimony of a single witness: "At the mouth of two witnesses, or at the mouth of three witnesses shall a matter be established."

The "mouth of two witnesses" clearly implied "the mouth of two witnesses *who spoke the truth*" as best they saw it, any accused, therefore, entitled to his automatic release if *any* of the witnesses in the "set" against him proved false.[5]

But the judges and scholars, over the centuries, did not stop with the false witness alone. They reasoned, logically enough, that the basic Law also required at least two witnesses *to agree* in their reports of the past sinful event; and the witnesses called by each side (prosecuting and defense) became the "set," each side with its own "set of witnesses."

But how much agreement should be required? Too little, and they ran the risk of convicting an innocent man; too much and they would bog down the system, make it helpless to pronounce the guilt of any accused.

The rules became severe:[6] If the "set" included an incompetent witness (kinsman; minor; gambler with dice; usurer; pigeon trainer; shepherd; woman; slave; demented person; deaf or mute; blind; person convicted of irreligion or immorality; publican (tax collector); illiterate or immodest person; person directly interested in the case), the incompetent witness disqualified the entire "set," though it contained 100 witnesses.[7] Without witnesses, that side lost its case, be it plaintiff or defendant in a civil action, or the accused or complaining witnesses in a "sin" trial.

The problem of "agreeing" reports from different witnesses within the same "set," however, proved more vexing: Total agreement among the "set" on every trivial detail could be achieved only through collusion and rehearsal. The judges' compromises came down in hundreds of decided cases with elaborate rules of "disproval," "confutation," and "impeachment,"[8] all designed to help recapture the "truth" and "facts" of the past event before the court.

Mark tells us that the judges of the Great Sanhedrin solved the problem of the conflicting testimony in Jesus' false prophecy trial routinely: They found some of the witnesses *zomen*, the conflict within the prosecuting "set" produced by the Committee of Ten too serious to ignore ("their witness did not agree"; "Yet not even so did their testimony agree").[9]

The judges further found no evidence of false prophecy "against Jesus to put him to death."[10]

The verdict: Acquittal!

We owe *Mark* a resounding apology, individually and collectively over the last 1900 years, for failing to read correctly his clear, clarion, legal signals about what really happened in Jesus' false prophecy trial before the Great Sanhedrin, his second trial in the Jewish courts.

PART 5

IN THE HOUSES OF THE HIGH PRIESTS

So the band of soldiers and
their captain and the
officers of the Jews
seized Jesus and bound him.
First, they led him to Annas;
for he was the father-in-law
of Caiaphas,
Annas then sent him bound to
Caiaphas . . . .
John 18:13,24

Chapter 28

THIRD ARREST: GETHSEMANE

Over 1900 years, almost everyone believes that Jesus' one, brief, compact "trial" began with his arrest in the Garden of Gethsemane on the night before Passover, after he ate the "Last Supper" with his disciples somewhere in Jerusalem, this story line almost an article of Christian faith.

Not a Sunday goes by in a Christian pulpit somewhere without a minister preaching on Jesus' "agony" in Gethsemane (*Matthew* 26:36-39):

> Then Jesus went with them to a place called Gethsemane, and he said to his disciples, "Sit here, while I go yonder and pray."

> And taking with him Peter and the two sons of Zebedee, he began to be sorrowful and troubled. Then he said to them, "My soul is very sorrowful, even to death; remain here, and watch with me."

> And going a little farther, he fell on his face and prayed, "My father, if it is possible, let this cup pass from me; nevertheless, not as I will, but as thou wilt."

What should he do?

Jesus knew The Committee of Ten would be more determined than ever to destroy him after their second defeat in the Jewish courts. His following would surely grow. He would become a far greater threat to the Committee and their flunkies than before.

He faced certain death if he remained in Jerusalem; but as he told his disciples earlier, prophets must perish in Jerusalem.

Need he perish?

Would it not be better to live?

Should he attempt to reach the comparative safety of the Galilee, where The Committee of Ten would find it harder to take him?

Might not this be easier for his disciples, and sounder for his fight against the Bureaucrats who perverted the Temple?

Worn out in mind and body, he left it all in the hands of Israel's God, their *abba* in heaven, the Holy One, Blessed be He, Who willed the fate of all His children, as Jesus told them before (*Luke* 12:6-7):

> Are not five sparrows sold for two farthings, and not one of them is forgotten before God?
>
> But even the hairs of your head are numbered. Fear not therefore: ye are of more value than many sparrows.

It makes no great difference which *gospel* account we use of this third and final arrest. *John* (18:1-14, 19-24, 28) gives more dramatic details, and shows clearly that he does *not* report a "trial" at all. Rather, he describes a desperate action by the Committee of Ten to build evidence against Jesus which they would need the next morning when they took him to Pilate, this nighttime arrest only a preliminary step to the final Roman trial before the Provincial Governor. It did not involve a Small Sanhedrin, the Great Sanhedrin or any other Jewish court; it could not:

> When Jesus had spoken these words, he went forth with his disciples across the Kidron valley, where there was a garden, which he and his disciples entered. Now Judas, who betrayed him, also knew the place; for Jesus often met there with his disciples.
>
> So Judas, procuring a band of soldiers and some officers from the chief priests and the Pharisees,

went there with lanterns and torches and weapons.

Then Jesus, knowing all that was to befall him, came forward and said to them, "Whom do you seek?" They answered him, "Jesus of Nazareth." Jesus said to them, "I am he."

Judas, who had betrayed him, was standing with them. When he said to them, "I am he," they drew back and fell to the ground. Again he asked them, "Whom do you seek?" And they said, "Jesus of Nazareth."

Jesus answered, "I told you that I am he; so, if you seek me, let these men go."

This was to fulfill the word which he had spoken, "Of those whom thou gavest me I lost not one."

Then Simon Peter, having a sword, drew it and struck the high priest's slave and cut off his right ear. The slave's name was Malchus. Jesus said to Peter, "Put your sword in its sheath; shall I not drink the cup which the Father has given me?"

So the band of soldiers and their captain and the officers of the Jews seized Jesus and bound him.

First they led him to Annas; for he was the father-in-law of Caiaphas, who was high priest that year. It was Caiaphas who had given counsel to the Jews that it was expedient that one man should die for the people . . . .

The high priest then questioned Jesus about his disciples and his teaching.

Jesus answered them, "I have spoken openly to the world; I have always taught in synagogues and in the temple, where all Jews come together; I have said nothing secretly. Why do you ask me? Ask those who have heard me, what I said to them; they

200

know what I said."

When he had said this, one of the officers standing
by struck Jesus with his hand, saying, "Is that how
you answer the high priest?"

Jesus answered him, "If I have spoken wrongly, bear
witness to the wrong; but if I have spoken rightly,
why do you strike me?" Annas then sent him bound
to Caiaphas the high priest . . . .

Then they led Jesus from the house of Caiaphas to
the praetorium. It was early.

Desperation caused the Committee of Ten to make this final
move against Jesus, his actions in Jerusalem gaining alarming
momentum. *John* (12:12-14, 17, 19) describes the crowd that went
from Jerusalem to Bethany, only two miles to the east, in more
detail than we heard before:

The next day a great crowd who had come to the
feast heard that Jesus was coming to Jerusalem. So
they took branches of palm trees and went out to
meet him, crying, "Hosanna! Blessed is he who
comes in the name of the Lord, even the King of
Israel . . . . "

The crowd that had been with him when he called
Lazarus out of the tomb and raised him from the
dead bore witness.

The reason why the crowd went to meet him was
that they heard he had done this sign.

The Pharisees then said to one another, "You see
that you can do nothing; look, the world has gone
after him."

John (12:9-11) also relates the terror of the Committee of
Ten by telling us that they planned to kill Lazarus to take some
of the steam out of this most spectacular of all of Jesus' miracles:

When the great crowd of the Jews learned that he was there, they came, not only on account of Jesus but also to see Lazarus, whom he had raised from the dead.

So the chief priests planned to put Lazarus also to death, because on account of him many of the Jews were going away and believing in Jesus.

We can safely believe that Annas, Caiaphas or one of their aides went to Pilate before the Gethsemane arrest, to get his agreement to hear the Jesus case early the next morning at the praetorium, and to send a mess-unit[1] of eight Legionnaires to accompany the Temple Guard[2] who would actually make the arrest later that evening. Neither Pilate nor the Committee wanted any breach of the peace, what with the hundreds of thousands already in Jerusalem for the Passover Festival: Rome feared crowds, all crowds! Riots and rebellion came from crowds!

For the two hours required to make the arrest and bring the prisoner to the High Priest's palace, the Committee of Ten debated their tactics: They knew they needed an admission from Jesus' own mouth to help them draft the formal accusation (*information = accusatio nominis delatio*)[3] which Pilate would demand in his own trial.

John is the only writer who mentions that they took Jesus first to Annas' house,[4] and then to Caiaphas' palace. It makes no difference whether the interrogations took place in one or the other house, or in both, or what happened where, or in what order. We must, however, turn to either *Matthew, Mark,* or *Luke* to see what went on, *Luke* my personal preference (22:66-71):

> . . . and they led him away to their council, and they said, "If you are the Christ, tell us."

> But he said to them, "If I tell you, you will not believe; and if I ask you, you will not answer. But from now on the Son of Man shall be seated at the right hand of the power of God."

> And they all said, "Are you the Son of God, then?"

And he said to them, "You say that I am."

And they said, "What further testimony do we need? We have heard it ourselves from his own lips."

Ambiguous though it is, it became the admission they thought Pilate would require! As *Luke* tells us, why did they need to go further?

Matthew[5] and *Mark*[6] add an embellishment:

> Then the high priest tore his robes, and said, "He has uttered blasphemy. Why do we still need witnesses? You have now heard his blasphemy. What is your judgment?"
>
> They answered, "He deserves death."

The mention of blasphemy once more shows *Matthew's* and *Mark's* lack of knowledge of the Jewish legal system (*talmud: Sanhedrin* 55b-56a):

> THE BLASPHEMER IS PUNISHED ONLY IF HE UTTERS [THE DIVINE] NAME . . . . THE WITNESSES ARE EXAMINED BY MEANS OF A SUBSTITUTE FOR THE DIVINE NAME. THUS, 'MAY JOSE SMITE JOSE' . . . .
>
> The witnesses, in giving testimony, do not state that they heard the accused say, 'May he slay himself,' uttering the actual divine name, but use the word 'Jose' as a substitute for the divine name. 'Jose' is chosen as a substitute, because it has four letters, like the actual Tetragrammaton, which must have been used by the blasphemer for him to be punished. Moreover, the numerical value of 'Jose' is the same as *Elohim* (God).
>
> WHEN THE TRIAL WAS FINISHED, THE ACCUSED WAS NOT EXECUTED ON THIS EVIDENCE, BUT ALL PERSONS WERE REMOVED [FROM COURT], AND THE

CHIEF WITNESS WAS TOLD, 'STATE WHAT
YOU HEARD.' THEREFORE HE DID SO
[USING THE DIVINE NAME].

That's all the *gospel* writers tell us of Jesus' "secret," "single," "nighttime" "trial."

From what we know of the Jewish legal system, how dare anyone say that the Committee's interrogations even vaguely resembled a court "trial" of any kind!

Chapter 29

"ARE YOU THE CHRIST?"

Caiaphas' palace stood some fifty yards to the south of Herod's great ediface on Mt. Zion, David's own hill, the High Priest's building smaller than Herod's, but no less ornate.

From *Josephus'* description of Herod's palace,[1] we can assume similar features for the place where the Committee of Ten interrogated Jesus: Tessellated floor; multi-colored squares producing an illusion of roundness in the flat ceiling; gold-leaf trim in raised floral design separating the two-storied, vertical panels of the walls; formal desks, benches and seats that gave cold comfort to those who awaited audience with the rulers of the Temple-State; carved, roaring lions of pink Galilean marble guarding the door to the great chamber; black and white mosaic tiles, some inlaid with gold, composing the giant zodiac wheel in the floor on which the Committee of Ten stood awaiting Jesus' arrival.

It and they oozed opulence, arrogance, wealth and privilege — this crude, insensitive, Bureaucratic Temple clique that evolved as a different species from the orthodox Jews they commanded, virtually enslaved.

In addition to Annas, Caiaphas and the other Committee of Ten members, perhaps dozens of minions stood sandal-clad on the marble tiles, leaning against the two-storied Corinthian columns that supported the gaudy ceiling: Shouting, swearing, gesturing, pointing, accusing, shoving, jostling. Other hangers-on probably milled about outside, around the lighted fountains in the courtyard.

These, the petty Bureaucrats most threatened by this heretic from the Galilee: As Jesus preached it, they interposed a stifling barrier between man and his God. Unless they mended their ways, no place for them in the "kingdom of Heaven" about to dawn: "Have you not read in the Law how on the Sabbath the priests in the temple profane the Sabbath, and are guiltless? I tell you, something greater than the temple is here."[2]

We can be positive who did *not* appear: No member of the Great Sanhedrin, of the Small Sanhedrins, of the Courts of Three, or any other judge in the land, their job to judge impartially, not participate in the investigations of any case which might reach them later (*Talmud, Sanhedrin* 34b-35a):

> . . . a witness cannot act as judge (when they hear a bequest at night, they can obviously do so only as witnesses, since a court cannot function at night; consequently, they cannot subsequently constitute themselves a court for they have the status of witnesses).

Even if a murder took place before the eyes of a sitting court, the judges could not try the case (*Talmud, Makkoth* 12a):

> Whence may it be shown that, if a Sanhedrin had been an eye-witness to an act of murder, they cannot themselves have him put to death until he stand for trial before another tribunal?

> From the instructive text, *the manslayer die not until he stand before the congregation [of judges]* for judgment, [which means, not] until he stood [for trial] before *another* tribunal.

> (The reason being that it is as much the duty of judges to save as to condemn (Numbers 35:24-25), and, judges having witnessed the act themselves, their minds are already made up before the trial commences); therefore, there is really no trial.

The Committee of Ten earlier decided the goal of this midnight meeting: Roman law *did* admit confessions extracted from the mouth of an accused as evidence of guilt;[3] so at some point,

Caiaphas asked Jesus: "Are you the Christ?"

Caiaphas' Hellenistic attitudes caused him to interchange the Greek "*Christos*" with the Hebrew *mashiah*; but it did not matter: Both terms transliterated to "the Anointed," sometimes, "Anointed One." By this time, though, *mashiah*[4] (Messiah) stood as a technical term.

From her earliest days as a nation, (1250 B.C. or thereabouts at Mt. Sinai), Israel "anointed" her High Priests: "Then Moses took the anointing oil . . . and he poured some on Aaron's head, and anointed him to consecrate him."[5]

In the first monarchy that began with Saul (1050 B.C.), they consecrated their kings with the "anointing" ritual. The tradition separated one man from his fellows, raising him up to perform a special task of leadership.[6]

The prophets, from Amos (760 B.C.) through Malachi (400 B.C.), believed themselves elevated to their special station of "God's mouthpiece" by a direct call from God Himself. God personally, not man in a formal ceremony, "anointed" them for their special mission of "spokesman for God,"[7] the prophets evolving what became known as the "Messianic Idea" ("Messianic Expectation"), the "great deliverance".

But over the centuries, too may hands stroked the canvas to produce a neat, seasoned, well-formed, logical structure. The Messianic Idea sprang directly from the needs of the people of each historical era, their preachers and writers embellishing it with literary twists, which grew from the political and spiritual crises they passed through.

The Messianic Idea asserted nothing more or less than an elaborate, piecemeal formula for delivering the people (giving them "salvation") from their oppressive burdens: Spiritual, social, economic and political. When the stresses and strains became most severe, when despair and hopelessness bore down upon them like thick smoke, their need for the Messianic Expectation deepened.

As the prophets and later writers worked on the subject over the centuries, in varying periods of stress, the Messianic Idea for Israel's redemption took on a formality which led to the Messianic Chain:[8]

(1) The signs of the Messiah;

(2) The birth pangs of the Messiah;

(3) The coming of the prophet Elijah;

(4) The trumpet of Messiah;

(5) The ingathering of the exiles;

(6) The reception of proselytes;

(7) The war with Gog and Magog;

(8) The days of the Messiah (to last 40, 70, 400 or 1,000 years);

(9) The resurrection of the dead;

(10) The day of Judgment (the Day of the Lord);

(11) The renovation of the world; and

(12) The World to Come (Kingdom of God).

The "signs of the Messiah" and "Days of the Messiah" served as important links in the Chain, but links only, parts of a much larger, more complex system to usher in the Kingdom of God (Heaven) which John the Baptist and Jesus bar Joseph preached.

Only a small handful of the people understood all the components leading to the World to Come (Kingdom of God), the details wearisome; and probably none of the Bureaucrats in the High Priest's audience hall in the first hours of that Friday (maybe) morning knew all the parts.

None of the books of the Old Testament or the *apocrypha* ever used the word "Messiah" to designate a specific redeemer, the original idea meaning *kingship* and *priesthood*, not the "anointing" of any lesser figure.

The fuzzy meaning of the technical term *christos-mashiah* confused most of those present when Caiaphus put his question to Jesus bar Joseph, the term holding no legal import in Jewish Law, totally meaningless in any of the Sanhedrins. For the courts of Rome, however (including the provinces), interested only in doing the will of the Emperor, an affirmative reply could be urged as a declaration of rival kingship: *Sedition against Rome!* The desperate Bureaucrats lived by building mountains from molehills.

Caiaphus perhaps asked more than once: "Are you the Christ?"

And Jesus responded: "If I tell you, you will not believe; and if I ask you, you will not answer,"[9] a "What's the use?" answer of a man worn out by the Bureaucracy. Debate with them would be futile; and for a fleeting moment, he perhaps dreamed mistily of the forensic arguments of his youth, of his first visit to the Temple of Jerusalem at age twelve when he debated the Pharisees and the Hellenists, of his later trips to the Temple for the Pilgrimage festivals.

By comparison with the true scholars, these men he now faced seemed a sorry lot, barely Jews, and that in name only, they the real *am-ha-arez*, the religiously ignorant, not his friends and neighbors back in Nazareth, Capernaum and throughout the Galilee.

Slowly, uncertainly he perhaps wondered, as when he prayed in the Garden of Gethsemane before his arrest, if his real mission might be that of God's carefully chosen vehicle to cut through the Bureaucratic sham and get them back to Judaism's prime theme of *God is Good*!

Perhaps he should avoid death, at least for a while, to rally the people against Annas and the Committee of Ten, against the Hellenizers who placed their faith in *soters*, living and dead? He stood for God, Judaism's one, true and always Jehovah, who "has showed you, O man, what is good; and what does the Lord require of you but to do justice, and to love mercy, and to walk humbly with your God?"[10]

He would do whatever Israel's God, his *abba* in Heaven, willed!

Chapter 30

THE SON OF MAN

Only a handful of the Bureaucrats heard the rest of Jesus' one-sentence answer: "But I tell you hereafter you will see the Son of man at the right hand of Power, and coming on the clouds of heaven."[1]

The tradition *Matthew, Mark* and *Luke* (*John* does not include it) relied on may or may not be a verbatim report of Jesus' words. Some scholars find it garbled; but the use of the term "son of man" shows the compelling need of the questioners to wring incriminating statements from Jesus' lips.

For centuries, the scribes and scholars debated its meaning!

It appeared first in the book of Ezekiel where the prophet used it over 80 times as a literary term of address for himself: "The word of the Lord came to me again: "son of man, mark two ways for the sword of Babylon.... [2] And you, son of man, prophesy and say, Thus says the Lord God concerning the Ammonites .... [3] Moreover the word of the Lord came to me, saying, 'And you, son of man, will you judge, will you judge the bloody city?'"[4]

The term held no mysterious meaning, nothing more than a part of Ezekiel's literary style.

A century apart, Daniel (around 165 B.C.) and Enoch later introduced "son of man" into the Hebrew vocabulary as another synonym for "Messiah," although it did not receive widespread use, nothing like the older, more glamorous "son of David."

During Jesus' preaching days, he always spoke of the "son of man" in the third person, as someone other than himself; and nothing in his reply to Caiaphus showed any change in his third-party use of the term.[5]

Matthew,[6] *Mark* and *Luke* insert the *pericope* of the blasphemy accusation, with the high priest tearing his robes, to give them a base on which to report the cry of the audience: "He deserves death!"[7]

The long night merged into morning.

The Committee of Ten followed Annas and Caiaphas from the audience chamber, confused, exhausted, insecure and fearful.

The Captain of the Temple turned Jesus over to the Temple police: "Now the men who were holding Jesus mocked him and beat him; they also blindfolded him and asked him, 'Prophesy! Who is it that struck you?' And they spoke other words against him, reviling him . . . . And some began to spit in his face, and struck him, and some slapped him."[8]

Now, it all depended on whether the Committee of Ten could persuade Pilate to order Jesus' death later in the morning.

PART 6

THE ROMAN PRESENCE IN JUDEA

Now Cyrenius, a Roman senator ...
came at this time into
Syria .... being sent by Caesar
to be a judge of that nation.

Coponius also, a man of
equestrian order, was sent
together with him, to have
the supreme power over the
Jews.
Josephus: Antiquities
of the Jews: Book
XVIII, Chapter 1,
Paragraph 1

Chapter 31

HEROD: "FORCED JEW" — "HALF JEW"

Rome formally entered Judea in 63 B.C., to settle a dispute over succession between contending heirs of the Jewish Hasmonean (Maccabees) Royal House. Rome settled it by settling in, for the duration of the Empire.

The best way to understand Rome's presence is to let Josephus tell us about Herod. By knowing Herod, we know the details of the Rome-Judea axis at the time of Jesus' life and trials.

Each time a High Priest performed at one of the great Pilgrimage Festivals in the Temple, he competed with the shouts which arose from the hippodrome[1] only 300 feet south of the Hulda Gate, a chorus from the past echoing, "Herod! Herod! Herod!".[2]

> On this account it was that Herod revolted from the laws of his country, and corrupted their ancient constitution, by the introduction of foreign practices:
>
> . . . . For, in the first place, he appointed solemn games to be celebrated every fifth year, in honour of Caesar, and built a theater at Jerusalem, as also a great amphitheater in the plain . . . . "
>
> Herod . . . called men together out of every nation. The wrestlers, and the rest of those that strove for

the prizes in such games, were invited . . . .

. . . . So the principal persons . . . were gotten together, not only those that performed their exercises naked, but to those that played the musicians also . . . .

At first, the Jews felt hot blushes of shame at the nakedness of the athletes; but this changed to wonderment as they saw young Jews among them after cosmetic surgery to hide the "flaw" of earlier circumcision. Not many spectators recognized the games as one of Herod's many subtleties to blot out their Jewishness by his substitutions of Greek culture:[3]

. . . . Inscriptions also of the great actions of Caesar, and trophies of those nations which he had con- quered in his wars, and all made of the purest gold and silver, encompassed the theater itself:

Nor was there anything that could be subservient to his design whether it were precious garments, or precious stones set in order, which was not also exposed to sight in these games.

Herod[4] strove to be more Roman than Rome, more pagan than the entire pantheon of Greek gods, more vulgar than those rightfully born to kingship:[5]

. . . . He had also made a great preparation of wild beasts, and of lions themselves in great abundance, and of such other beasts as were either of uncom- mon strength, or of such a sort as were rarely seen.

They were prepared either to fight one with another, or that men who were condemned to death were to fight with them.

When High Priests stood before the altar in the Temple to preside over the sacrifice and heard the roar of the crowd mingle with their own chants, they knew that the blood which flowed from the cut throat of their sacrificial rams looked for all the world like the spurting blood of the gladiators and lions in the hippodrome, only a stone's throw down the hill from the Temple:[6]

.... And truly foreigners were greatly surprised and delighted at the vastness of the expenses here exhibited, and at the great dangers that were here seen;

but to natural Jews, this was no better than a dissolution of those customs for which they had so great a veneration.

It appeared also no better than an instance of barefaced impiety to throw men to the wild beasts, and it appeared an instance of no less impiety to change their own laws for such foreign exercises.

In his groveling effort to please the Caesars at Rome, Herod became the world's greatest Hellenizer (*Hellas* = the ancient name of Greece), determined by every means at this command to make the Jews Greek in language, customs, character and ideals. To reach this goal, he saturated Judaism with Hellenism:[7]

... but, above all the rest, the trophies gave most distaste to the Jews;

for, as they imagined them to be images, included within the armour that hung round about them, they were sorely displeased at them, because it was not the custom of their country to pay honors to such images.

Pious Jews honored God's Second Commandment of the *torah*:

Thou shalt not make unto thee any graven image, or any likeness of anything that is in heaven above, or that is in the earth beneath, or that is in the water under the earth.

Exodus 20:4

An attack upon any of the Ten Commandments, especially the Second, assaulted God Himself: Herod, therefore, threatened God; but later, if Annas and his Committee of Ten appreciated this blot of Hellenization, they buried it in their minds, not letting it become a burden.

Scholars fit Herod's reign into three distinct periods:[8]

40-25 B.C. = the struggle for power and empire;
25-15 B.C. = the builder and Hellenizer; and
13-4 B.C. = domestic nightmare, madness and death. (Jesus' birth: 4 B.C.)

Being born a "private man"[9] in 73 B.C. proved but one of Herod's many burdens. His birth took place in Idumea,[10] that rugged, rural province between Judea and Egypt, running from the Dead Sea on its east to the Mediterranean on the west.

As Semites[11] ("desert-living people") residing in that wide sweep of sand and forest, rocky hill and lush valley that comprised Palestine and Arabia, the Idumeans did not become Jews until a scant thirty years before Herod's birth, when a Jewish king forced circumcision and baptism upon them;[12] and all his life, friend and foe alike taunted Herod with the cries of "forced Jew," or "half Jew," his mother an Arabian.[13]

Herod's ambitious father (family name Antipater or Antipas)[14] served as Governor of Idumea before the Romans took over in 63 B.C., an era of power struggles both inside and out of Rome itself. The Republic[15] (509-31 B.C.) died; the First Triumvirate[16] of Julius Caesar, Pompey and Crassus appointed Herod's father chief minister in Jerusalem;[17] the father, in turn, made Herod Governor of the Galilee at age twenty-five.[18]

Herod launched an aggressive program as soon as he reached his post:[19]

> . . . . But as he was a youth of great mind, he presently met with an opportunity of signalizing his courage; for, finding one Hezekias, a captain of a band of robbers, who overran the neighboring ports of Syria, he seized him and slew him, as well as a great number of the other robbers that were with

him; for which action he was greatly beloved by the Syrians; . . . .

For all of Herod's great heroism to the Syrians and Romans, the Galileans hated him bitterly: His treatment of Hezekias and the robbers violated the Jews' "due process of law":[20]

> . . . for Antipater and his sons . . . are evidently absolute lords; for Herod . . . hath slain Hezekiah and those that were with him, and hath thereby transgressed our law, which hath forbidden to slay any man, even though he were a wicked man, unless he had been first condemned to suffer death by the Sanhedrin . . . .

The Sanhedrin summoned Herod to Jerusalem; and even he and his father dared not ignore its order, so great its standing in the Jewish tradition:[21]

> Accordingly he came; but his father had persuaded him to come not like a private man, but with a guard, for the security of his person . . .

Antipater and Herod knew the Sanhedrin's reputation for independent action: They needed political intervention:[22]

> However, Sextus Caesar, president of Syria, wrote to Hyrcanus (High Priest), and desired him to clear Herod, and dismiss him at his trial, and threatened him before hand if he did not do it . . . .

This threat of political interference of the judicial function of the Sanhedrin almost worked:[23]

> but when Herod stood before the Sanhedrin, with his body of men about him, he affrighted them all, and no one of his former accusers durst bring any charge against him; but there was a deep silence, and nobody knew what was to be done . . . .

One forthright man rose to urge the integrity of the

Sanhedrin:[24]

> When affairs stood thus, one whose name was
> Sameas rose up and said, 'O you that are assessors
> with me, I have (never) known such a case, . . . this
> admirable man Herod, who is accused of murder,
> and called to answer so heavy an accusation, stands
> here clothed in purple, and with the hair of his
> head finely trimmed; and with his armed men about
> him, that if we shall condemn him by our law, he
> may slay us, and by overbearing justice may himself
> escape death; . . . .

Sameas' oratory convinced and persuaded, in the tradition of
men stirred by crises throughout Israel's history:[25]

> ' . . . yet do not I make this complaint against Herod
> himself: but my complaint is against yourselves and
> your king, who give him a license so to do. However,
> take you notice, that God is great, and that this
> very man, whom you are going to absolve and
> dismiss, for the sake of Hyrcanus, will one day
> punish both you and your king himself also . . . . '

Sameas thwarted the political and military corruption of the
Great Court:[26]

> But when Hyracanus (the High Priest) saw that the
> members of the Sanhedrin were ready to pronounce
> the sentence of death upon Herod, he put off the
> trial to another day, and sent privately to Herod,
> and advised him to fly out of the city; that by this
> means he might escape . . . .

This postponed a head-butting, saber-rattling show-down
between Herod and the Sanhedrin, a victory for the Rule of Law
when one of the most powerful princes in all the Roman Empire
dared not overwhelm the Jewish Court by murder and assassination: Herod's youth warped his judgment as he prepared to
slaughter the judges who stood ready to force his trial:[27]

but his father Antipater, and his brother (Phasaelus) met him, and hindered him from assaulting Jerusalem; they also pacified his vehement temper, and persuaded him to do no overt action . . . .

Herod remained a fugitive for a dozen years,[28] so great the tradition of "due process of law"[29] and the Sanhedrin's right to enforce it that even this Governor of the Galilee, the son of the chief Roman minister in Jerusalem and grandson of the former Governor of Idumea, dared not confound it.

His flight took him to Damascus and Arabia, Rhinocorura and Alexandria in Egypt, and finally to Rome.[30] For a great part of the time, he served as paid mercenary for the Romans,[31] showing a remarkable ability to shift loyalties at the right moment, from Julius Caesar to Crassus to Cassius to Marc Antony, and finally to Octavian, later to become Augustus Caesar.[32]

At last, in 40 B.C., the Roman Senate surprised Herod by decreeing him king:[33]

> . . . and Antony informed them further that it was for their advantage in the Parthian War that Herod should be king. This seemed good to all the senators; and so they made a decree accordingly . . . .

Herod then shifted his loyalties to Rome's Gods:[34]

> . . . . But when the Senate was dissolved, Antony and Caesar went out of the Senate-house with Herod between them, and with the consuls and other magistrates before them, in order to offer sacrifices, and to lay up their decrees in the capital.

> Antony also feasted Herod the first day of his reign. And thus did this man receive the kingdom, having obtained it on the hundred and eighty-fourth Olympiad . . . .

Even though Herod owned the title "king," it took him three more years to possess his kingdom,[35] never forgetting that two Pharisees, Pollio and Shemaiah, opened the gates of the city of

Jerusalem for Herod's armies during his final siege:[36] Throughout the remainder of his life, the Pharisees occupied a special place with Herod, as did another important sect, the Essenes.[37]

But the Sanhedrin could not escape Herod's wrath forever. The minute he thought it personally and politically safe, Herod ordered the murder of forty-five members of the Great Court,[38] the courageous ones who rallied to Sameas' exhortation to moral strength, those judges ready to convict Herod of the murder of Hezekias and his men; but strangely enough, Herod spared Sameas whose courage he admired.[39]

These forty-five murders totally decimated any political and executive role of the Sanhedrin, Herod setting up a Greek- style council of elders, a *gerousia*,[40] in its stead, a body in name only, for Herod now ruled as dictator;[41] but this *gerousia* eventually evolved into The Committee of Ten which ruled at Jesus' time.

Even so, Herod dared not strip the Sanhedrin of its jurisdiction to try criminal and civil cases, its historic right to administer the sophisticated Jewish legal system evolved over a thousand years.

To consolidate his power, which meant to prevent the Temple from becoming too dangerous a threat, Herod downgraded the office of High Priest.[42] Up to this point, Judaism maintained at least the fiction that each High Priest could trace his priestly lineage back to Aaron,[43] the "anointing" as High Priest heredity, the appointment for life.[44]

Now, Herod abandoned even the fiction of the *torah's* qualification for office, naming the High Priest at will from any rank of priesthood, and removing him at his own personal whim.[45] All told, he appointed seven different High Priests to the office, and then demoted them, creating the awkward problem of protocol of more than one "High Priest" alive and present at the same time.

Herod married Doris as the bride of his youth, but sent her away before his kingship, probably because of her lowly Idumean birth.[46] With Jerusalem in his hands, he thought himself ready to wed Mariamne,[47] the second of his ten wives, a princess of the Royal Hasmonean House, so beautiful that Josephus would not attempt to describe her.[48]

Although safely married to the Royal Princess Mariamne, Herod could not feel secure so long as a single heir of the Hasmonean House lived.

The Hasmoneans[49] (also known as Maccabees), a Jewish family in a small town west of Jerusalem, began as religious "freedom fighters" against the Greeks in 166 B.C., and wrested a precarious independence for the Jews by 142 B.C.[50] Within a generation, however, their religious fervor gave way to a secular greed; their rulers combined the titles of "High Priest" and "King,"[51] monarchy merging into theocracy, or vice versa, their internecine family squabbles opening the door for the Roman occupation in 63 B.C.[52]

Now, Herod's final fight for his kingdom in Jerusalem turned against Antigonus, Mariamne's uncle, Marc Antony's friendship for Herod strong enough to let Herod order Antigonus' assassination:[53]

> . . . . As he [Antigonus] was of the royal blood, and Herod but a private man, therefore [the kingdom] belonged to [Antigonus'] son in case [Herod] offended the Romans. Out of Herod's fear of this, he endeavored to have Antigonus slain which, if it were once done, he should be free from that fear. And thus did the government of the Hasmoneans cease, a hundred and twenty-five years after it was first set up . . . .

But the royal family, even after the arrival of the Romans, continued to draw nostalgic support from the Jews:[54]

> This family was a splendid and illustrious one, both on account of the nobility of their stock, and of the dignity of the High Priesthood, as also for the glorious actions their ancestors had performed for our nation: But these men lost the government by their dissensions, one with another; and it came to Herod, the son of Antipater, who was of no more than a vulgar family, and of no eminent extraction, but one that was subject to other kings . . . .

Herod next moved against Mariamne's brother, Aristobulus, whom he appointed High Priest, at age sixteen,[55] the minimum ritual requirement for High Priesthood being twenty. Herod viewed Aristobulus' death as a chance to both eliminate a potential royal rival and to denigrate the High Priesthood still further:[56]

> When the festival was over, and [Herod] was feasting in Jericho, he was then very pleasant with the young man [Aristobulus], and drew him into a lonely place, and at the same time played with him in a juvenile and ludicrous manner . . . .
>
> and as they stood by the fish pond, they went to cool themselves [by bathing,] . . . .
>
> but after a while, the young man, at the instigation of Herod, went into the water among them, while such of Herod's acquaintance as he had appointed to do it, dipped him as he was swimming, and plunged him under water, in the dark of the evening, as if it had been done in sport only; but did not they desist until he was sufficiently suffocated.
>
> And thus was Aristobulus murdered, being not eighteen years old, and having kept the High Priesthood one year only . . . .

Mariamne and her mother complained to Cleopatra, then in Arabia; and Cleopatra induced Marc Antony to summon Herod to an accounting. It came to naught, Herod smart enough to repulse Cleopatra's efforts to seduce him:[57]

> When she was there, and was very often with Herod, she endeavored to have criminal conversation with the king: Nor did she effect secrecy in the indulgence of such sort of pleasures; and perhaps she had in some measure a passion of love for him, or rather, what is most probable, she laid a treacherous snare for him, by aiming to obtain such adulterous conversation from him . . . .

Who knows what the history of Egypt, the Roman empire, or the Jews and western civilization might be today if Herod's scheme to murder Cleopatra had succeeded:[58]

> However, [Herod] refused to comply with her proposals, and called a council of his friends to consult with them whether he should not kill her, now he had her in his power; but that he should thereby deliver all those from a multitude of evils to whom she was already becoming irksome;
>
> and that this very thing would be much for the advantage of Antony himself, since she would certainly not be faithful to him . . . .
>
> But when [Herod] thought to follow this advice, his friends would not let him; and told him, that, in the first place, it was not right to attempt so great a thing, and run himself thereby in the utmost danger . . . .

Upon his return to Jerusalem, Herod's marriage to Mariamne fell apart: She taunted him sexually:[59]

> However, these misfortunes, which had been kept under some decency for a great while, burst out all at once upon such an occasion as was now offered;
>
> for as the king was one day about noon lain down on his bed to rest him, he called for Mariamne, out of the great affection he had always for her. She came in accordingly, but would not lie down by him; and when he was very desirous of her company, she showed her contempt for him . . . .

For all her beauty, she went too far in slurring Herod's "common" birth, until he arranged her death:[60]

> And thus died Mariamne, a women of an excellent character, both for chastity and greatness of soul;

but she wanted [in] moderation, and had too much
of contention in her nature; yet had she all that can
be said in the beauty of her body, and her majestic
appearance and conversation;

for while she was most indulgently used by the
king, out of his fondness for her, and did not expect
that he could do anything hard to her, she took too
unbounded a liberty . . . .

From Mariamne's death on, Herod's psychosis worsened. In
his youth, he attempted suicide;[61] and his life-long changes of
mood paint a clear picture of the manic-depressive personality,
with paranoia and schizophrenia thrown in for good measure:[62]

But when she was once dead, the king's affections
for her were kindled in a more outrageous manner
than before, for his love to her was not of a calm
nature; nor was it, by their long cohabitation and
free conversation together, brought under his power
to manage;

but [after her death] his love to Mariamne seemed
to seize him in such a peculiar manner, as looked
like divine vengeance upon him for taking away
her life . . . .

Those around Herod watched in horror as his mental confusion deepened:[63]

For he would frequently call for her, and lament
for her, in a most indecent manner.

Moreover, he bethought him of everything he could
make use of to divert his mind from thinking of
her, and contrived feasts and assemblies for that
purpose, but nothing would suffice;

he therefore laid aside the administration of public
affairs, and was so far conquered by his passion,
that he would order his servants to call for

Mariamne, as if she were still alive, and could still hear them . . . .

Grief overwhelmed him, his complaints taking the form of "distemper" and headache, with horrendous feelings of guilt:[64]

All the physicians also that were about him . . . left little hopes of his recovery. And thus did his distemper go on while he was at Samaria, now called Sebaste . . . .

Herod partially recovered, to launch the building and Hellenizing phase of his reign.[65]

He molded a tiny coastal town into a great city on the Mediterranean, creating an artificial harbor, and calling it Caesarea[66] to honor his emperor, Caesar Augustus. He restored the ancient city of Samaria,[67] renaming it Sebaste (Greek = *Sebastos* = "Augustus"), also for his emperor. He built dozens of Greek city-states, in Palestine and throughout the empire, with gymnasia, public baths, colonnaded streets, theaters, stadiums, hippodromes, market places with elegant statues, and countless pagan temples.[68] He developed a new irrigation system that breathed life into the parched Jordan river valley.[69]

Everywhere, he copied the grand Hellenistic style for his buildings, cities and government Bureaucracy, showing uncanny genius as planner and organizer.[70]

He hired an army of mercenaries, settling them around the northern and eastern borders of his nation, and built a tight line of impregnable fortresses,[71] some as palaces for his own large family.[72]

To the Romans, he became *rex socius et amicus populi Romani*[73] ("a king who was an ally and friend of the Roman people"). Rome let him handle the internal affairs of his nation more or less at will; in foreign affairs, he followed Rome's orders, protecting her eastern borders from armed invaders.[74]

For the most part, it became a time of peace for the entire Jewish nation; but peace at a horrible price![75]

Herod next entered a final stage of pathetic physical and mental decline.

The predictable fights for succession among his fifteen children and nine living wives became exaggerated by the presence of his two sons by Mariamne, Alexander and Aristobulus,[76] their veins coursing with Mariamne's royal Hasmonean blood which Herod could never tolerate:[77]

> Alexander and Aristobulus were brought to Sebaste, by their father's command, and there strangled; but their dead bodies were in the nighttime carried to Alexandrium, where their uncle, by the mother's side, and the greatest part of their ancestors, had been deposited . . .

Finally, five days before his own death, Herod ordered the murder of Antipater,[78] his eldest son, the child by Idumean first-wife Doris.

Augustus Caesar earlier observed: "I would rather be Herod's pig than his sons!"[79]

Herod proved as dramatic in death as in life:[80]

> But now Herod's distemper greatly increased upon him after a severe manner, and this by God's judgment upon him for his sins:
>
> For a fire glowed in him slowly, which did not so much appear to the touch outwardly, as it augmented his pains inwardly;
>
> for it brought upon him a vehement appetite to eating, which he could not avoid to supply with one sort of food or other.
>
> His entrails were also exulcerated, and the chief violence of his pain lay on his colon;
>
> an aqueous and transparent liquor also had settled itself about his feet, and the like matter afflicted him at the bottom of his belly.
>
> Nay, further, his privy-member was putrefied, and produced worms;

and when he sat upright he had difficulty breathing, which was very loathsome, on account of the stench of his breath and the quickness of its returns;

He had also convulsions in all parts of his body, which increased his strength to an insufferable degree.

It was said by those who pretended to divine, and who were endued with wisdom to foretell such things, that God inflicted this punishment on the king on account of his great impiety; yet was he still in hopes of recovering, though his afflictions seemed greater than any one could bear . . . .

Josephus' description of Herod's illness is a classic case of uncontrolled diabetes mellitus,[81] a disease in which the body's use (metabolism) of sugars falls because of faulty secretion of insulin by the pancreas. This causes uncontrollable appetite and thirst, since the "flesh is melted down into urine."[82] The victim does not heal his wounds properly, which leads to ulceration and gangrene. He pants rapidly as the body attempts to rid itself of excessive amounts of fatty acids which lower the pH factor; the breath becomes putrid, due to ketone bodies (chemical compounds of the carbonyl group). He may continue to keto-acidosis, with convulsions and coma, and suffer from diarrhea and colitis. Frequently, bleeding hemorrhoids produce excruciating pain.[83]

Herod entered the final stages of congestive heart failure,[84] the heart unable to maintain sufficient blood pressure to empty the veins, which become distended. Pressure in the veins rises, and the tissues swell (edema)[85] in various parts of the body, notably the feet and ankles, as fluids and minerals seep through the enlarged capillaries. The lungs become so engorged with blood that they lose their ability to take in and exchange oxygen. Unless treatment reverses the condition, the person literally suffocates in his own blood.[86]

When Herod finally admitted his approaching death, he summoned 150 of the leading citizens of the Jewish nation to Jericho, imprisoning them in the hippodrome, instructing his captain of guards to kill them all the moment Herod's own death took place:[87] He wanted a period of national mourning, but knew the Jews would be more inclined to rejoicing if he died alone![88]

Herod convulsed and reshaped the Jewish nation: It reeled under his imprint for the remainder of its days.

He created a new nobility, an aristocratic hierarchy that purchased its rank by money and personal service to Herod,[89] these new "nobles" crude and uneducated, lacking the poise and culture of their predecessors, ignorant of the Jews' religious traditions.[90]

After stripping the Sanhedrin of any political role, Herod's Greek-style *genousia* (the Committee of Ten by Jesus' time) developed into an inflexible, self-centered Bureaucracy,[91] anchored in the Temple, interested only in itself, never in the people it should be serving.

Although Herod built the Jews a Temple, the Second Temple, the most lavish religious complex of all time, he never really understood the Jewish religion, never once venturing inside the Temple, though a place for the king in the Temple rituals existed since Solomon.[92]

Judaism survived Herod, his Temple, and the Temple's Bureaucracy only because of its synagogues;[93] but Herod never understood what they did or why!

Chapter 32

PONTIUS PILATE

Herod's will named Archelaus "king" of Judea; but Emperor Augustus would not confirm it, instead making Archelaus *ethnarch* (governor) until he could prove himself capable of ruling as "king." He never did; so Augustus banished him in 6 A.D., placing Judea under the governorship of Syria, and naming an on-site Judean governor called a *praefectus*. Until 1961, everyone knew this sub-ruler as "procurator," but then an archeologist found "The Pilate Stone" in Caesarea: (PON)TIUS PILATE (PRAE)FECTUS JUDAE(AE).[1]

The *praefectus* came from the equestrian class[2] (*equites* = "knight"; "business man"; "middle class"), Pontius Pilate, probably the protege of Lucius Aelius Sejanus,[3] getting the job in Judea in 26 A.D.

Both men reached their posts by entering military service at age sixteen, since no one could hold public office until he served ten years in the army.[4]

Even more important, a man's political career thereafter remained tied to his "Century" (regiment).[5] After Emperor Augustus (31 B.C.-14 A.D.) formed the Praetorian Guard of 9 cohorts of 1,000 men each (*praetorium* = "headquarters of the commander-in-chief"), stationing them at the Viminal Gate in Rome to give him unquestioned control over the army,[6] the route to most political appointments passed through this elite corps. Will Durant states that on them, in the final analysis, rested the so-called Roman "constitution."[7]

Sejanus rose faster and higher than most. After Tiberius succeeded Augustus in 14 A.D., Sejanus hitched his consuming ambition to the new Emperor's passion for seclusion, self-imposed exile to the Isle of Capri, and introspection,[8] Sejanus ending up not only in control of the Praetorian Guard, but access to the Emperor and the City of Rome as well. While Tiberius kept an active interest in the affairs of the provinces, his Guard Commander became dictator over everything else that went on; and Sejanus almost pulled off the considerable feat of becoming Emperor himself.[9]

Emperor Augustus had changed his Judean governors every three years with three men in the post between 7 and 14 A.D.; but Tiberius brought in a more realistic view, keenly aware of the graft on which the Empire rested. He chose to leave the governors at their posts for longer periods of time on the theory that their pillages from their subjects might be less:[10]

> For it was a law of nature that governors are prone to engage in extortion.
>
> When appointments were not permanent, but were for short terms, or likely to be cancelled without notice, the spur of peculation was even greater.
>
> If, on the contrary, those appointed kept their posts longer, they would be gorged with their robberies and would, by the very bulk of them, be more sluggish in pursuit of further gain.

As an old battle commander, Tiberius liked the fable of the wounded man and the flies:[11]

> Once a man lay wounded, and a swarm of flies hovered about his wounds.
>
> A passerby took pity on his evil plight and, in the belief that he did not raise a hand because he could not, was about to up and shoo them off.
>
> The wounded man, however, begged him to think no more of doing anything about it . . . .

'Why,' said he, 'you would put me in a worse position if you drove the flies off. For since the flies have already had their fill of blood, they no longer feel such a pressing need to annoy me, but are in some measure slack. But if other flies were to come with a fresh appetite, they would take over my now weakened body, and that would indeed be the death of me.'

Valerius Gratus held the Judean governorship for eleven years, from 15 A.D.;[12] but Sejanus, who sold offices to the highest bidder to advance his own personal fortunes, wanted a new man and a more profitable financial deal.[13] His new man turned out to be Pontius Pilate.

Upon his arrival in Judea, Pilate installed himself in the Roman governor's ornate palace in Caesarea, another of Herod's legacies: Herod! Herod! Herod!

Shortly afterward, Pilate decided to show Sejanus and Tiberius his firm anti-Jewish posture; but Josephus reports its backfire:[14]

Now Pilate, the procurator of Judea, when he brought his army from Caesarea and removed it to winter quarters in Jerusalem, took a bold step in subversion of the Jewish practices, by introducing into the city the busts of the emperor that were attached to the military standards, for our law (The Second Commandment) forbids the making of images.

It was for this reason that the previous procurators, when they entered the city, used standards that had no such ornaments.

Pilate was the first to bring the images into Jerusalem and set them up, doing it without the knowledge of the people, for he entered at night.

But when the people discovered it, they went in a throng to Caesarea, and for many days, entreated him to take away the images.

He refused to yield, since to do so would be an outrage to the emperor; however, since they did not cease entreating him, on the sixth day he secretly armed and placed his troops in position, while he himself came to the speaker's stand. This had been constructed in the stadium, which provided concealment for the army that lay in wait.

When the Jews again engaged in supplication, at a pre-arranged signal he surrounded them with his soldiers and threatened to punish them at once with death if they did not put an end to their tumult and return to their own places.

But they, casting themselves prostrate and baring their throats, declared that they had gladly welcomed death rather than make bold to transgress the wise provisions of the laws.

Pilate, astonished at the strength of their devotion to the laws, straightway removed the images from Jerusalem and brought them back to Caesarea.

Pilate could never find out exactly how it happened; but some Jews sneaked letters of complaint to Tiberius on Capri, by-passing Sejanus in Rome:[15]

When he [Tiberius] had read them through, what language he used about Pilate, what threats he made! The violence of his anger, though he was not easily roused to anger, it is needless to describe since the facts speak for themselves. For at once, he wrote to Pilate with a host of reproaches and rebukes . . . .

Within a matter of months, Pilate caused another face-off, even more disastrous than the first:[16]

Pilate spent money from the sacred [Temple] treasury in the construction of an aqueduct to bring water into Jerusalem, intercepting the source of the stream at a distance of 200 furlongs (23 miles).

The Jews did not acquiesce in the operations that this involved; and tens of thousands of men assembled and cried out against him, bidding him relinquish his promotion of such designs.

Some too even hurled insults and abuse of the sort that a throng will commonly engage in.

He thereupon ordered a large number of soldiers to be dressed in Jewish garments, under which they carried clubs; and he sent them off this way and that, thus surrounding the Jews, whom he ordered to withdraw.

When the Jews were in full torrent of abuse he gave his soldiers the prearranged signal. They, however, inflicted much harder blows than Pilate had ordered, punishing alike both those who were rioting and those who did not.

But the Jews showed no faintheartedness; and so, caught unarmed, as they were, by men delivering a prepared attack, many of them actually were slain on the spot, while some withdrew disabled by blows.

Pilate's anti-Jewish reputation now became prime conversation among Jews throughout the Empire, their numbers estimated at five million.[17] No matter where they lived, Jerusalem still pulled them; and all actions of the Roman governor "back home" concerned them deeply.

Philo wrote from Alexandria to brand Pilate's conduct as:[18]

. . . full of briberies, insults, robberies, outrages and wanton liberties, the executions without trial constantly repeated, the ceaseless and supremely grievous cruelty . . . his vindictiveness and furious temper. He was naturally inflexible, a blend of self-will and relentlessness.

The probabilities are that Pilate loathed and feared Jerusalem and all Judea: It meant crowds, crowds of swarming Jews; screaming mobs against the governor; strikes against the Legion's standards; complaints of his use of Temple funds for public works; guerrillas in the form of *Zealots*; a whining High Priest too incompetent to solve trivial religious questions which could not possibly concern Rome. He moved from Caesarea to Jerusalem for all their great Festivals, to be sure that no serious breach of the peace took place; or if it did, he would be there to quell it.

Then came the most damaging blow of all: Tiberius permitted Sejanus to be named co-consul in 31 A.D.[19] Almost immediately, Sejanus plotted to make himself Emperor, either at Tiberius' natural death, or before. Through the aid of Marco, Sejanus' successor as commander of the Praetorian Guard, Tiberius smuggled a letter from his headquarters on Capri to the Senate in Rome, denouncing Sejanus and calling for his death. In Roman fashion, without a trial and before the day ended, Sejanus' strangled body lay near the Tiber, covered with spittle and other signs of shame: He rose that morning the second most powerful man in the Empire, and before the sun set, he became its most disgraced, solid proof that Rome's "constitution" indeed rested upon the whim of whomever commanded the Praetorians.[19]

Pilate waited in Caesarea; but instead of a summons to return to Rome for reprimand, exile, even execution (since Roman courts could not protect the individual against the changing whims of the ruler), the Roman "Pony Express" brought Tiberius' orders of his new, contradictory, confusing "Jewish policy":[20]

> For Tiberius knew the truth: He knew at once after Sejanus' death that the accusations made against the Jewish inhabitants of Rome were false slanders, invented by Sejanus because he wished to make away with the Jewish nation, knowing that it would take the sole or the principal part in opposing Sejanus' unholy plots and actions, and would defend the emperor when in danger of becoming the victim of treachery.

And Tiberius charged his procurators in every place to which they were appointed to speak comfortably to the members of [the Jewish] nation in the different cities, assuring them that the penal measures did not extend to all, but only to the guilty, who were few;

and to disturb none of the established customs;

but even to regard them as a trust committed to their [Procurators'] care, the people as naturally peaceable, and the institutions as an influence promoting orderly conduct.

Sejanus, Pilate's long-time friend, sponsor, buffer, advocate and protector in Rome lay dead, in treasonable disgrace. Guard Commander Marco carefully avoided declaring himself on any subject whatsoever. Emperor Tiberius, now sick, melancholic, and psychotic, aged 73, waged a vicious purge against his enemies, real or imagined; and Pilate knew well the danger of being the former protege of Lucius Sejanus: How should he interpret the Emperor's new Pro-Jewish program, operating in Rome and the provinces? How should he apply it in the seat of all the Jewish problems: Jerusalem?

That Friday (?) morning, Pilate seethed as he awaited the arrival of the High Priest and his party, not wanting to displease Rome, careful to do nothing that could stir up the crowds on the Temple Mount already arrived for the Passover celebrations.

Crowds! Crowds! Crowds! The cause of riots; breaches of the peace; reports to Rome; reprimands for commanders; calls home in disgrace.

PART 7

THE IMPERIAL ROMAN LEGAL SYSTEM

senatus-consultum ultimum
" . . . that the consuls should
see to it that no harm should
come to the state."
Will Durant: *Caesar and Christ*, pgs. 27-28

Chapter 33

THE JUDGMENT SEAT

All four *gospels* cover the Roman trial in far greater detail than their cursory references to the first two Jewish trials, for the simple reason that Jesus' appearance before Pilate caused his death, his two acquittals in the Jewish courts not particularly relevant to the writers' theological thrusts.

Even so, *Mark*, whom many scholars consider the most "factual," warns us right off that he gives only a quick summary (15:3):

> "And the chief priests accused him of many things."

What "many things?"
Acts of kingship?
Statements amounting to sedition?
It needed to be a crime against Rome, not just a breach of Jewish Law.

We already know that "chief priests and elders of the people" really means the Committee of Ten (*Matthew* 27:1-2):

> When morning came, all the chief priests and the elders of the people took counsel against Jesus to put him to death; and they bound him and led him away and delivered him to Pilate, the governor.

As Pilate moved onto the portico of the Antonia,[1] his adjutant saluted, bowed, then made a brisk about-face, while the six lictors[2] snapped to attention. Marching in precise two-step and carrying the bundles of rods with the protruding axe-heads, the symbols of the Emperor's power of life and death over his subjects, they escorted Pilate to the front of the porch, their leader chanting the call for the court: "Hear and give ear! Hear and give ear! Hear and give ear! The court of his imperial majesty, our Lord and Savior Tiberius Claudius Nero Caesar Augustus,[3] is hereby convened, his imperial surrogate Pontius Pilate, Praefectus of Judea, Samaria and Idumea, presiding. Let all who have business before the Emperor's most-wise and all-powerful court bend the knee and step forth, so that the Emperor's sovereignty can forever be acknowledged, and the peace of the Empire continue unbroken. Hear and give ear! Hear and give ear! Hear and give ear!"

Caiaphas and his coterie of minions struggled from bent knees to stand as the Praefectus settled himself upon the *bema*, the formal judgment seat.[4]

Taking the form of a curule chair with purple fringed bottom, the campstool without back, its legs of ornate olive wood, could be opened and folded at will for easy moving. The judgment seat signaled the physical location of the court which could sit anywhere, at any time, day or night, open or in secret, the Roman court and court site personal to the whim and body of the Emperor and his magistrates. In criminal cases, no fixed rules of practice and procedure bound them, as did those of the Jewish system which, for example, required the Great Sanhedrin to sit physically in the Hall of Hewn Stone, openly and in the daytime, before any of its decrees could claim legality.

Pilate perhaps primped at his toga, trying to expose as much of its wide, purple stripes as possible, far more than he would dare show in Rome. His own position on the portico, some six feet above the courtyard, exalted him over the petitioners. He alone enjoyed the comfort of the shade while the hot sun beat down upon all those standing below.

As an old battle commander, he looked first to his camp security, and smiled with confidence.

In building the elaborate Temple Mount structures, Herod separated the Antonia from the Court of the Gentiles by its own forbidding wall, and a series of covered porticoes:[5]

The tower of Antonia lay at the angle where the

two porticoes, the western and the northern, of the first court of the temple met;

it was built upon a rock fifty cubits [seventy-five feet] high, and on all sides precipitous.

It was the work of King Herod and a crowning exhibition of the innate grandeur of his genius. For, to begin with, the rock was covered from its base upwards with smooth flagstones, both for ornament and in order that anyone attempting to ascend or descend it might slip off.

Next, in front of the actual edifice, there was a wall three cubits high; and behind this, the tower of Antonia rose majestically to an altitude of forty cubits [sixty feet].

The interior resembled a palace in its spaciousness and appointments, being divided into apartments of every description and for every purpose, including cloisters, baths, and broad courtyards for the accommodation of troops; so that from its possession of all conveniences, it seemed a town; from its magnificence, a palace.

Pilate stayed overly solicitous of the Antonia's internal security, permitting no one to enter it except those directly connected with the cohorts (auxiliary personnel, concubines and purveyors), these "guests" passed through the gates by guards monitored by a veteran officer of the day.

Shifting his weight on the judgment seat, Pilate knew that the crowd of Jews supporting Caiaphas and his Committee of Ten all served as Bureaucratic flunkies, vouched for by Jonathan ben Annas' Temple Guards, who helped Pilate's own guards screen each man as he moved into the Antonia and onto the Praetorium, from the Court of the Gentiles. This meant that no single follower of Jesus bar Joseph stood among them, no *Zealot* revolutionary to start a riot or other trouble, not a single non-Bureaucrat among them.

The orthodox, practicing Jews of both Palestine and the Diaspora ("scattering," "dispersion") went about their own tasks of the Day of Preparation outside the Antonia's walls, making ready for the slaughtering of the ten thousand sacrificial animals by the Temple priests which would commence at noon. No other person outside the Antonia, on the Temple Mount or elsewhere in city, knew that a trial of any kind began before Rome's imperial representative inside the great fortress high above them, the military post which dominated them all, resident and non-resident alike, in its hovering, threatening, terrifying beauty.

Pilate's military eye read his troop deployments at a glance: The First Century (originally 100 men, but now 80) of the Fifth Maniple (2 Centuries)^6 rimmed the courtyard, discreetly back near the walls so that their presence would not suffocate, yet close enough to sop up any disturbance that might arise, the rest of the cohort hidden at battle readiness inside the fortress.

Pilate smiled, knowing that a single, eight-man mess-unit would suffice, every Jew standing below him a trusted Temple Bureaucrat, specially sorted out by the Committee of Ten to parrot their statements, yell out their commands, march in lock step to their orders, all equally interested in preserving Bureaucracy's status quo at any price, forfeiting or warping "outsider" lives when necessary.

Finally, and almost as an afterthought, Pilate found the prisoner: Hair stained with matted blood, a mouse puffing the space under his left eye, the skin abraded off both cheek bones, his blood-soaked robe solid evidence of his raw back.

Jesus bar Joseph stood between two Roman legionnaires, the matter now entirely committed to Roman hands. Except for the accusatory roles played by Caiaphas and his Bureaucratic confederates, no Jew would be an official part of the trial, or ever again be involved with the Jesus case.

Chapter 34

THE ACCUSERS

"Who are the accusers?" Pilate no doubt asked in a voice more suitable to the drill field than Senate or assembly, appropriate since he sat as a one-man military court.

When Augustus (then called Octavian) became supreme ruler of Rome and its "Republic" in 27 B.C., he retained some of the provinces under his personal control as *imperator*[1] ("commander of the army"), assigning others to loyal cronies in the Senate. Syria remained a military (imperial) province; and to it, he attached Judea, Samaria and Idumea in 6 A.D., when he deposed Herod Archelaus, and chose to rule it directly.

Tiberius left the structure alone, which continued throughout the entire reign (14-37 A.D.): Judea an imperial province under the governor in Syria, the Praefectus of Judea and the Praefectus of Syria both army commanders, responsible directly to the Emperor, along with their legions. Because of the area's strategic position as a land bridge[2] between Egypt and the two-score kingdoms in and around Asia Minor (present-day Turkey), these two vice-rulers of this shaky edge of the Empire supported each other with troops and whatever else they needed, to (1) keep the Emperor's peace, and (2) to keep his tax revenues flowing to Rome. They shared the same goals of the Temple Bureaucrats: Preserve the status quo so that no one in power gets jostled about.

A Roman maxim summed it up beautifully: *senatus-consultum ultimum*: " . . . that the consuls should see to it that no harm should come to the state,"[3] the ancient formula for invoking martial law when needed, to give the consuls of the Republic absolute control over all persons and property.[4]

. . . "no harm should come to the state!"

It became Rome's corporate way of life that lasted throughout its history, during the monarchy, the period of "democracy" and the *principate* (rule by emperor),[5] the "state" being the clique in power, the current "establishment." Since Roman criminal law rested upon the army, more specifically, the commander of the Praetorian Guard, the presiding judge (whether back in Rome or out in the provinces) could decide any criminal case (*delict*) on little more than whim, no practical legal appeal existing for even the Roman citizen, none for the non-citizen.

The Romans opted years earlier for criminal laws based upon the raw, physical, grasping power of men,[6] not the justice and mercy of an interested, personal God, the Roman judge sitting supreme,[7] not bound by silly, restrictive concepts of *precedent* or individual rights, such as Moses and his worthy successors evolved for the Hebrews.

The Romans saw no need to record the testimony of the witnesses or make a formal transcript of the case or any official record: When Pilate decided a case against a non-citizen, the matter ended there; if guilty, the punishment was carried out the same day,[8] be it scourging, fine, slavery, exile or crucifixion.

"Who are the accusers?" Pilate asked, seeking the *delatores* (*accusators*),[9] persons to start and pursue a criminal case since the Roman law, like that of the Hebrews, did not provide the office of state prosecutor.

The *gospel* writers tease us with their scanty quotes; but we can fill in some of the gaps with safety.

High Priest Caiaphas spoke for "the Jews" who acted as *accusators*. "What accusation do you make against this man?"[10] Pilate repeated.

Caiaphas, the master Bureaucrat of them all, stepped forward, raised his head forty-five degrees so he could shout up at the governor.

"By his own admission, last evening in the palace of the High

Priest, in the High Priest's official audience chamber, during the hour immediately following midnight, before the High Priest himself and in the presence of several hundred other witnesses, this man said that he was the Christ!"[11]

"He called himself what?" Pilate asked in ignorance.

"The Christ," Caiaphas repeated. "He said that he was a king."

"A king?" Pilate mulled the thought aloud. "A king?"

He turned to the prisoner standing slightly behind and to Caiaphas' left and demanded in a more threatening voice: "Are you the King of the Jews?"[12]

Chapter 35

THE SEARCH FOR A CHARGE

"I asked, are you the King of the Jews?"[1] Pilate repeated, more curious than hostile.

Even the tired Bureaucrats stood quiet, straining to hear the response.

"You have said so,"[2] Jesus bar Joseph replied, his voice surprisingly strong in view of his physical condition, obvious to all that he suffered great pain.

In this *cognitio extra ordinem*[3] ("the trial and decision of a case"), authorized under Pilate's equestrian *imperium* ("the right to give orders"; "the official power of the Emperor") for the province of Judea, Pilate needed to select a charge against the accused: "The accuser alleges a misdeed, and the judge decides how to deal with it."[4]

The Roman system operated exactly opposite from the Jewish procedures which spelled out a specific transgression in advance, so the judges could decide whether the facts they heard in open court brought the defendant's conduct within the strict legal definition.

By contrast, Pilate began by seeking a description of the accused's acts, from his own mouth or from other witnesses; next, he alone would decide if he thought Jesus' conduct "bad" enough for a penalty; and if so, he would decide what name to call those acts, when he ordered scourging, slavery, exile or death.

Personal liberties could not develop: The Emperor ruled as law-giver, law-enforcer,[5] the Emperor also the final judge of appeals if and when anyone could reach him, the trial judges acting as his agents.[6]

In the early days of the Republic, the Senate appropriated to itself all three functions of government: Legislative, executive and judiciary.[7] Now, all lay in the hands of the Emperor:[8]

> Tiberius wanted the principate, or he would have found some way to evade it; the Senate feared and hated him, but shrank from re-establishing a republic based, like the old, upon theoretical sovereign assemblies.

> It wanted less democracy, not more; and it was pleased when Tiberius (A.D. 14) persuaded it to take over from the *comitia centuriata* (a military voting unit) the power of choosing public officials.

> The citizens complained for a time, mourning the loss of the sums they had received for their votes.

> The only political power now left to the common man was the right of electing the emperor by assassination. After Tiberius, democracy passed from the assemblies to the army, and voted with the sword.

Neither Tiberius nor his successors granted the citizen, whether aristocrat, equestrian or pleb, any personal rights, since this would reduce the Emperor's own power. The Emperor's right to rule rested on the power of the sword, and no one even dreamed of independent judges who could tell the Emperor, the army, or their agents, what they could or could not do.

The Roman system purposely avoided the concept of *precedent*,[9] Moses' format which bound judges to follow past decisions of other judges as they decided cases before them. *Precedent* also would reduce the Emperor's power; and no Emperor could ever permit this.

The rulings of various Roman judges, sitting at the same time but in different places and deciding cases with identical sets of facts, often produced conflicting results, as did their *rescripta* (legal proclamations).

The Romans opted for what they called the "ingenuity" of

each judge, even though this meant that each case turned on the fancy of the judge of the moment.[10]

Consistency never became a Roman legal goal. Greed, bribery, fraud, corruption, slander, extortion and murder supplied the values of their lives.

Chapter 36

PILATE'S CHOICES

Pilate sat confused, torn between several options, but with two prime goals: (1) preserve the Emperor's peace, and (2) guard the status quo with the Temple Bureaucrats who helped him rule. The guilt or innocence of the accused did not concern him in the least.

To sort out the case, he needed to know whether Caiaphas and his Temple clique brought him one of their religious squabbles, or valid evidence of a *crimen maiestatis*:[1] "A crime committed against the Roman people and its security ... high treason, sedition, criminal attack against a magistrate ... joining with the enemy, rousing the enemy against the Roman state, delivering a Roman citizen to the enemy, desertion from the battlefield."

This legal grab bag covered any thought, word or deed, of omission as well as commission, as defined by the magistrate trying the case, the convenient tool to dispose "legally" of an accused whom the magistrate found not acceptable.

The *accusators* no doubt explained to Pilate the Jewish *christos-massiah*,[2] emphasizing the "kingship" features of the "Kingdom of God" on earth, a rival to the kingdom of Rome. And Pilate, without doubt, wondered how this or any similar case would fit into Tiberius' new policy of Be-Good-To-Jews!

We need to weigh Pilate's wobblings against this background of political uncertainty, not of his fear of putting to death an innocent man, something that never entered his harsh military mind (*Luke* 23:1-5, 13-25):

> Then the whole company of them arose, and brought him before Pilate.

And they began to accuse him, saying, "We found this man perverting our nation, and forbidding us to give tribute to Caesar, and saying that he himself is Christ a King."

And Pilate asked him, "Are you the King of the Jews?" And he answered him, "You have said so."

And Pilate said to the chief priests and the multitudes, "I find no crime in this man." But they were urgent, saying, "He stirs up the people, teaching throughout all Judea from Galilee even to this place."

Pilate then called together the chief priests and the rulers and the people, and said to them, "You brought me this man as one who was perverting the people; and after examining him before you, behold, I did not find this man guilty of any of your charges against him; neither did Herod, for he sent him back to us. Behold, nothing deserving death has been done by him;

"I will therefore chastise him and release him." . . . .

Pilate addressed them once more, desiring to release Jesus; but they shouted out, "Crucify, crucify him!"

A third time he said to them, "Why, what evil has he done? I have found in him no crime deserving death; I will therefore chastise him and release him."

But they were urgent, demanding with loud cries that he should be crucified. And their voices prevailed.

So Pilate gave sentence that their demand should be granted. He released the man who had been thrown into prison for insurrection and murder, whom they asked for; but Jesus he delivered up to their will.

Pilate's offer to "chastise" Jesus' instead of ordering his death should not be construed as any great act of mercy. "Chastising" meant "flogging," which Roman law divided into three separate categories:[3] *fustes, flagella* and *verbena*. Also called *castigare* (*castigatio* "to chastise; castigate"), they applied this corporal punishment to both slaves (with a whip = *flagellum*) and to free persons (with a club = *fustis*) either as an additional penalty, or in place of a fine when the accused could not pay.

The lightest form (*fustigatio*) served also as a coercive measure for minor (sometimes trivial) offenses, really nothing more severe than a magistrate's "warning" when he decided that the matter did not require a full-blown trial (*cognitio*): The *fustes* served as a substitute for the *coercito* (summary punishment), without either escape or appeal, soldiers often receiving *castigatio* at the will of the commander of their Century.

Also called "scourging," the *flagella* often killed:[4]

The instrument used, the *horrible flagellum,* was made up of thongs of hardened leather studded with small pieces of bone and morsels of lead, and sometimes with sharp points called scorpions.

The sufferer, despoiled of his clothes, was bound by the hands to a low column, and was kept from moving out of the bending position, so that all the strokes might reach the mark, and that the executioner might wield them with greater force.

At the first blows, the skin became livid and bloody; soon it was torn to shreds, and the flesh came off in strips. There was no limit to the punishment except the fatigue or satiety of the torturers, and often their ferocity was proportioned to the greater patience of the victim.

We read in the passions of certain martyrs that veins, muscles, and intestines and the whole anatomy of the body were exposed to the horror-stricken gaze of the onlookers.

Not infrequently it happened that the condemned man succumbed during the torture.

Not exactly the compassionate ruling of a kindly, merciful Roman governor seeking to protect an innocent accused from a group of blood-thirsty accusers.

Chapter 37

PILATE'S IMPERIUM

John (18:31) raises the key issue of the Jews' right to assess the death penalty:

> Pilate said to them: "Take him yourselves and judge him by your own law."

> The Jews said to him: "It is not lawful for us to put any man to death."

As governor of Judea, Pilate held the *imperium*,[1] his commission of office, sealed by the Emperor himself. The *imperium* awarded the right to rule, and embraced the *ius gladii*: "The power to punish criminal individuals (D.2.13) with all kinds of punishment, the death penalty included. In Rome it was the emperor himself who exercised the right in capital trials. He could delegate it to the supreme officials in the provinces (governors, *legati*) and to the prefects in Rome, at first only in a specific case, later generally."

Rome did not think a provincial governor capable of ruling without the *ius gladii*. Equally important, he could not assign any part of this grant of imperial power: *Nemo potest gladii potestatem sibi datam uel cuius alterius coercitionis ad alium transferre* = "No one is able to commit to another the power to inflict capital punishment, or indeed to commit to another the power to inflict any other form of punishment."[2]

Still, the Romans did not disturb the local judicial institutions in any of the provinces they ruled.[3] They reconciled the legal conflict between permitting the local courts to function and the imperial governor's lack of power to delegate the *ius gladii* by a legal fiction: While the local courts could try an accused, convict him and order punishment of death, they needed the Roman governor to confirm the sentence before it could be carried out.

Virtually a rubber stamp arrangement, the fiction preserved the practical "independence" of the local courts, and still sustained the governor's *ius gladii* in legal theory.

In Jerusalem, for example, when a Court of the Twenty-Three found an accused guilty of adultery, murder, incest, assault or homosexual relations, any of the 36 sins which carried the death penalty, plus the entrance by a non-Jew into the Court of the Israelites in the Temple, they passed the death sentence of stoning, burning, decapitation or strangling. Pilate ratified the execution automatically, unless some unusual circumstance prevented it.

This solution also rested upon practical political realities: "It is largely based upon the necessity of preventing anti-Roman groups from eliminating the leaders of the pro-Roman factions in the cities [provinces] by judicial action."[4]

Rome needed to protect her friends and collaborators, like the Committee of Ten and other Sadducees in Judea; and she could not do this if any unsupervised *ius gladii* found its way into native hands.

Senatus-consultum ultimum: "That the consuls should see to it that no harm should come to the state."[5]

When *John* lets "the Jews" remind Pilate that, "It is not lawful for us to put any man to death," he means that it is not lawful for the Jews to carry out the death sentence without the governor's approval.

In addition, *John* reports a plea by the Committee of Ten to Pilate to find a *crimen maiestatis* in view of their double failure to obtain a death penalty verdict in the two earlier trials in the Jewish courts.

John (19:12-15) gives us the one, single, compelling argument that finally moved Pilate:

> Upon this Pilate sought to release him but the Jews cried out, "If you release this man, you are not

Caesar's friend; every one who makes himself a king sets himself against Caesar."

When Pilate heard these words, he brought Jesus out and sat down on the judgment seat at a place called The Pavement, and in Hebrew, Gabbatha.

Now it was the day of Preparation of the Passover; it was about the sixth hour. He said to the Jews, "Here is your King!" They cried out, "Away with him, away with him, crucify him!" Pilate said to them, "Shall I crucify your King?"

The chief priests answered, "We have no king but Caesar."

Loyalty to Caesar! Only the Temple Bureaucrats voiced this sentiment!

Pilate perhaps thought of the earlier letter someone smuggled to Tiberius on Capri complaining of Pilate's bringing the standards bearing the busts of the Emperor into Jerusalem shortly after his arrival in 26 A.D., and Tiberius' angry reprimand to Pilate. He churned again over the new Be-Kind-To-Jews policy. By Jove, he sat squeezed in the middle more than ever!

Chapter 38

THE HEROD AND BARABBAS PERICOPES

Luke's pericope (23:6-12) is the only account of Jesus' appearance before Herod Antipas. We do not know the source of his tradition, or why it escaped the other *gospel* writers:

> When Pilate heard this, he asked whether the man was a Galilean. And when he learned that he belonged to Herod's jurisdiction, he sent him over to Herod, who was himself in Jerusalem at that time.
>
> When Herod saw Jesus, he was very glad, for he had long desired to see him, because he had heard about him, and he was hoping to see some sign done by him.
>
> So he questioned him at some length; but he made no answer. The chief priests and the scribes stood by, vehemently accusing him.
>
> And Herod with his soldiers treated him with contempt and mocked him; then, arraying him in gorgeous apparel, he sent him back to Pilate.
>
> And Herod and Pilate became friends with each other that very day, for before this they had been at enmity with each other.

Herod Antipas,[1] sixth son of Herod the Great, his mother

262

Malthace the Samaritan, Herod's wife Number Four, ruled as tetrarch (subordinate prince) of Galilee and Perea from his father's death in 4 B.C. until 39 A.D. We know from the *gospels* and *Josephus* that this Herod caused John the Baptist's beheading, and later made worried inquiries about Jesus, fearing that Jesus might be John raised from the dead to haunt him (*Matthew* 14:1-2):

> At that time, Herod the tetrarch heard about the fame of Jesus; and he said to his servants, "This is John the Baptist, he has been raised from the dead; that is why these powers are at work in him . . . . "

> . . . Now when Jesus heard this, he withdrew from there in a boat to a lonely place apart . . .

The *pericope* stands totally irrelevant to the trial before Pilate, unless we read it as Pilate's last, politic effort to duck a possible backlash of the Jesus case from Rome, whichever way he ruled.

But what of the failure to *Matthew, Mark* and *John* to even mention the Herod pericope? If they knew of it, perhaps they, too, considered the episode irrelevant.

We must treat the Barabbas[2] *pericope*, which all four *gospel* writers report, with much more respect.

Luke (23:18-19) gives us the best identification of Barabbas:

> But they all cried out together, "Away with this man and release to us Barabbas . . . " a man who had been thrown into prison for an insurrection started in the city, and for murder.

John (18:40) tells us simply:

> Now Barabbas was a robber.

Matthew (27:16) is less specific:

> And they had then a notorious prisoner called Barabbas.

Mark (15:6-11) gives these additional details in his *pericope*:

Now at the feast he used to release for them one prisoner whom they asked.

And among the rebels in prison, who had committed murder in the insurrection, there was a man called Barabbas.

And the crowd came up and began to ask Pilate to do as he was wont to do for them. And he answered them, "Do you want me to release for you the King of the Jews?" For he perceived that it was out of envy that the chief priests had delivered him up.

But the chief priests stirred up the crowd to have him release for them Barabbas instead.

The Barabbas pericope continues to cause grave mischief, since it is the principal episode in which "the crowd," "the multitudes," "the people," "the Jews" and "they" screamed for Jesus' crucifixion, against Pilate's noble efforts to save Jesus from "the Jews":

Matthew (27:17,20-23) describes it:

So when they had gathered, Pilate said to them, "Whom do you want me to release for you, Barabbas or Jesus who is called the Christ? . . . . "

Now the chief priests and the elders persuaded the people to ask for Barabbas and destroy Jesus.

The governor again said to them, "Which of the two do you want me to release for you?" And they said "Barabbas." Pilate said to them, "Then what shall I do with Jesus who is called Christ?"

They all said, "Let him be crucified."

And he said, "Why, what evil has he done?"

But they shouted all the more, "Let him be crucified."

Mark (15:12-14) reports in similar vein:

And again Pilate said to them, "Then what shall I do with the man whom you call the King of the Jews?"

And they cried out again, "Crucify him."

And Pilate said to them, "Why, what evil has he done?"

But they all shouted all the more, "Crucify him."

Luke (23:20-23) is in line:

Pilate addressed them once more, desiring to release Jesus; but they shouted out, "Crucify, crucify him."

A third time he said to them, "Why, what evil has he done? I have found in him no crime deserving death. I will therefore chastise him and release him."

But they were urgent, demanding with loud cries that he should be crucified. And their voices prevailed.

John (19:14-15) adds a dramatic embellishment:

... and he said unto the Jews, "Behold your king!"

But they cried out, "Away with him! Away with him! Crucify him!"

Pilate said unto them, "Shall I crucify your King?"

The chief priests answered, "We have no King but Caesar."

The grave mischief stems from our failure over 1900 years to properly identify "the crowd," "the multitudes," "the people," "the Jews" and "they" as this hand-picked group of Temple Bureaucrats, screened into the Antonia by Pilate's guards, while the people as a whole went their ways outside the fortress on this Day of Preparation, totally ignorant of the Roman trial going on inside the Antonia's walls.

In another place, *John* (19:6) gives us a more specific and far more accurate identification of the actors who "stirred up the crowd," and who actually comprised "the crowd":

> ... the chief priests *and officers* ...
> King James translation

> ... chief priests *and their henchmen* ...
> New English Bible translation

> ... the high priests *and their attendants* ...
> Moffatt translation

> ... chief priests *and officials* ...
> Bible in Modern English translation

> ... the chief priests *and the guards* ...
> Jerusalem Bible translation

The Barabbas[3] *pericope* troubles many scholars for other reasons:

(1) Neither the *talmud, Josephus*, Roman historians nor any other source mentions any custom of a praefectus releasing a prisoner to the people "at the feast";

(2) It shows a weak Pilate, not in control of his post, led passively by the "chief priests and elders," not the forceful, aggressive, cruel, belligerent Pilate whom *Josephus* and *Philo* describe; and

(3) It makes no sense for Pilate to release a murderer and leader of rebellion, in contradiction of Pilate's prime purpose in Jerusalem to keep the peace.

I accept the Barabbas *pericope* because it's there, in all four *gospels*, as further proof of the Temple Bureaucrats' willingness to sacrifice "one man for the many," as Caiaphas told the Small Sanhedrin after Jesus' acquittal of Sabbath-breaking in his first Jewish trial in the Court of the Temple Mount.

To preserve their status quo, the greedy Bureaucrats, not "the Jews," shouted "Crucify him! Crucify him! Crucify him!" They convinced Pilate that Jesus' preachings of Judaism's thrust of God-Is-Good posed a far greater threat than Barabbas' use of the sword, which Rome could handle in its more comfortable arua of armed force against armed force.

Chapter 39

SENTENCE: GOLGOTHA!

Finding the *crimen maiestatis* of sedition, Pilate decreed the death sentence, and delivered Jesus to his soldiers who knew the exact routine to follow. For some reason, this particular group preferred their mocking pantomimes to the usual, more cruel physical abuse: (*Mark* 15:16-20):

> And the soldiers led him away inside the palace (that is, the praetorium); and they called together the whole battalion.

> And they clothed him in a purple cloak, and plaiting a crown of thorns, they put it on him.

> And they began to salute him, "Hail, King of the Jews!"

> And they struck his head with a reed, and spat upon him, and they knelt down in homage to him.

> And when they had mocked him, they stripped him of the purple cloak, and put his own clothes on him!

> And they led him out to crucify him!

None the less, by the time the procession formed up to move from the Antonia to Golgotha, almost a mile away, Jesus bar Joseph staggered, seriously disabled. Within a furlong, he fell under the weight of the 110-pound *patibulum*,[1] the beam that would form the horizontal bar of the cross after being attached to the *stipes crucis*, the upright stake which remained permanently implanted in the ground at the execution site. A soldier grabbed a chance passerby,[2] forcing him to carry the *patibulum* through the winding streets, out of the city to the "Place of a Skull,"[3] an elevated knob just beyond the city's wall.

The traumas of the two earlier beatings sapped Jesus' strength.

Ten hours before, guards in the High Priest's palace clubbed him with staves, producing intense pain but only minor damage to the deep tissues and organs;[4] but now, primary shock developed, brought on by the inflammatory reactions within the body as it tried to heal itself from the destruction of the *horrible flagellum*. (*Shock*[5] = a condition of acute circulatory failure due to derangement of circulatory control or loss of circulating fluid, and brought on by injury. It is marked by pallor and clamminess of the skin, decreased blood pressure, feeble rapid pulse, decreased respiration, restlessness, anxiety, and sometimes unconsciousness).

The procession crawled along: The Roman centurion, inching his horse sideways to sweep the crowds from their path; a soldier carrying the wooden *titulus*[6] with the inscription in Greek, Latin and Hebrew which Pilate personally composed, "Jesus of Nazareth, the King of the Jews";[7] Jesus bar Joseph, staggering, falling, rising, but somehow moving forward; Simon the Cyrene with the *patibulum* across his shoulders; the two thieves sharing Jesus' fate, each bearing his own *patibulum*; the mess-unit of auxiliaries;[8] a dozen Bureaucrats dispatched by Caiaphas to observe and heckle; the ever-present gawkers and curiosity seekers.

When they reached Golgotha, the soldiers, professionals in this grisly mode of torture and death, laid Jesus bar Joseph atop the *patibulum*, his arms outstretched, and drove a seven-inch spike between the ulnar and radial bones just above each wrist:[9] The Romans learned years earlier that the nails tore through the tissues of the hands if driven through the palms, and could not support the weight of the body for long. In the lower forearm above the wrist, the nails glided between tendons, nerves and major blood vessels, causing severe pain but minimum soft tissue damage, and not much bleeding.

Four soldiers lifted up the *patibulum* with its nailed-on burden, to anchor it atop the upright *stipes crucis* which stood seven feet in height. They dropped an iron spike with a square head vertically into place, to keep the cross beam from slipping off the upright member.

They positioned Jesus' buttocks-crotch astraddle the *sedile*,[10] a wedge-shaped piece of wood attached to the *stipes crucis* about half way down, so that it crushed into the perineum (the space between the anus and scrotum).

Finally, they pressed his legs together, twisted them to the right, bent the thighs at the hips, pulling the legs up into a knee-bend position. They drove a single seven-inch spike through both calcaneal (heel) bones, attaching the feet to the lower part of the *stipes crucis*.

"On the cross" in regulation manner, Jesus bar Joseph and the two thieves now awaited death that could come mercifully within a matter of hours, more often in two or three days, depending upon the stamina of the individual. Although the Romans perfected the art of crucifixion over the centuries, they could not explain why some men lost consciousness quickly, and others died only after long agonies when the vultures and wild dogs came to gnaw on their flesh while they still breathed.

Crucifixion brought about a combination of factors: Pain; shock; fright; exhaustion; anoxia (reduction of oxygen in body tissues, especially the brain); hypostasis (the settling of blood in the lower extremities due to a feeble blood current); hypotension (abnormally low blood pressure); and finally, heart failure.

In many cases, suffocation caused the death:[11]

> With the weight of the body being supported by the *sedulum* (the *sedile*: wooden wedge attached to the upright *stipes crucis*), the arms were pulled upward. This caused the intercostal [between the ribs] and pectoral [breast, chest] muscles to be stretched.
>
> Furthermore, movement of the muscles was opposed by the weight of the body. With the muscles

of respiration thus stretched, the respiratory bellows became relatively fixed.

As dyspnea [difficult, labored breathing] developed and pain in the wrists and arms increased, the victim was forced to raise the body off the *sedulum*, thereby transferring the weight of the body to the feet.

Respiration became easier, but with the weight of the body being exerted upon the feet, the pain in the feet and legs mounted. When the pain became unbearable, the victim again slumped down on the *sedulum*, with the weight of the body pulling on the wrists and again stretching the intercostal muscles.

Thus the victim alternated between lifting his body off the *sedulum* in order to breathe and slumping down on the *sedulum* to relieve the pain in his feet.

Eventually, he became exhausted or lapsed into unconsciousness so that he could no longer lift his body off the *sedulum*.

In this position, with the respiratory muscles essentially paralyzed, the victim suffocated and died.

A cruel medical and anatomical paradox, the nailing to the cross caused less generalized tissue damage than the scourgings that preceded the crucifixion; and if the victim could be taken down before death became final, he might survive. *Josephus* reports a case in point:[12]

Once more, when I was sent by Titus Caesar with Cearelius and a thousand horse to a village called Tekoa, to prospect whether it was a suitable place for an entrenched camp,

and on my return saw many prisoners who had been crucified, and recognizing three of my acquaintances among them, I was cut to the heart and came and told Titus with tears what I had seen.

He gave orders immediately that they should be taken down and receive the most careful treatment. Two of them died in the physicians' hands; the third survived.

Each of Golgotha's actors settled into his own view of the waiting.

One group of Bureaucrats, thinking back to the false prophecy trial in the Great Sanhedrin, taunted Jesus bar Joseph:[13]

Aha! You who would destroy the temple and build it in three days, save yourself and come down from the cross!

Other Bureaucrats continued the heckling:[14]

He saved others; he cannot save himself. Let the Christ, the King of Israel, come down from the cross that we may see and believe.

The auxiliaries, bored with their roles, joined in:[15]

The soldiers also mocked him, coming up and offering him vinegar, and saying "If you are the King of the Jews, save yourself!"

Others played a different game:[16]

When the soldiers had crucified Jesus they took his garments and made four parts, one for each soldier; also his tunic. But the tunic was without seam, woven from top to bottom;

so they said to one another, "Let us not tear it, but cast lots for it to see whose it shall be." This was to fulfill the scripture, "They parted my garments among them, and for my clothing they cast lots."

So the soldiers did this.

For Jesus bar Joseph, the body's soothing mechanism of shock brought a partial respite from his pain, while letting his mind still function clearly; and the Psalms and the Prophets he learned in the *bet-ha-midrash* school and at his mother's knee flowed in and out of memory:[17]

> Yea, dogs are round about me, a company of evildoers encircle me; they have pierced my hands and feet. I can count all my bones: they stare and gloat over me; they divide my garments among them, and for my raiment they cast lots.

He looked sadly at the soldiers rolling their dice; but then, his struggle for breath forced him to lift himself off the *sedile*, his mind filling with the words of Second Isaiah:[18]

> But now thus says the Lord, who created you, O Jacob, he who formed you, O Israel: "Fear not, for I have redeemed you; I have called you by name, you are mine.
>
> "When you pass through the waters I will be with you; and through the rivers, they shall not overwhelm you; when you walk through fire you shall not be burned, and the flame shall not consume you.
>
> "For I am the Lord your God, the Holy One of Israel, your Savior."

He sucked his lungs full of air before the pain in his feet forced him to drop his weight once more upon the *sedile*; and again his thoughts returned to Second Isaiah, speaking of the whole people of Israel:[19]

> He [Israel] was despised and rejected by men; a man of sorrows, and acquainted with grief; and as one from whom men hide their faces he was despised, and we esteemed him not.

Surely he has borne our griefs and carried our
sorrows; yet we esteem him stricken, smitten by
God, and afflicted.

But he was wounded for our transgressions, he was
bruised for our iniquities; upon him was the
chastisement that made us whole, and with his
stripes we are healed.

All we like sheep have gone astray; we have turned
every one to his own way; and the Lord has laid
on him the iniquity of us all.

Jesus' physical plight called up another passage from the
Psalmist:[20]

I am poured out like water, and all my bones are
out of joint; my heart is like wax, it is melted within
my breast; my strength is dried up like a potsherd,
and my tongue cleaves to my jaws; Thou dost lay
me in the dust of death.

Summoning his last measures of strength, he mumbled "I
thirst!",[21] and one of the soldiers passed up vinegar on hyssop,
holding it to his mouth.

By the time the vinegar reached him, his need for air compelled him to again pull himself off the *sedile*; but his memories
floated out again to the words of Isaiah, speaking once more to
the whole people of Israel, the chosen nation of God:[22]

Because you are precious in my eyes, and honored,
and I love you, I give men in return for you, peoples
in exchange for your life.

"You are my witnesses," says the Lord, "and my
servant whom I have chosen, that you may know
and believe me and understand that I am He. Before
me no God was formed, nor shall there be any after
me."

His deep achings became intolerable, his mind staying clear.

He gasped loudly for air before the hurt in his feet made him sit again on the *sedile*. As he mouthed the Psalmist's words, those standing near heard:[23]

> My God, my God, why hast Thou forsaken me? Why art Thou so far from helping me, from the words of my groaning?

He lacked the strength to change his position again, once more going back to the Psalmist:[24]

> Into Thy hand I commit my spirit, Thou hast redeemed me, O Lord, faithful God.

Luke (23:46) puts the act of death simply:

> And having said this he breathed his last.

Mark (15:37) adds a slight detail:

> And Jesus uttered a loud cry, and breathed his last.

Matthew (27:49) uses different words of art:

> And Jesus cried again with a loud voice and yielded up his spirit.

They measured the fact of death only by the gross observation of the cessation of breathing. They saw Jesus' head sagged against his chest, his mouth agape; and all four *gospel* writers tell how Joseph of Arimathaea claimed the body (*Mark* 15:43-46):

> Joseph of Arimathaea, an honorable counsellor, which also waited for the kingdom of God, came, and went in boldly to Pilate, and craved the body of Jesus.

> And Pilate marvelled if he were already dead; and calling unto him the centurion, he asked him whether he had been any while dead.

And when he knew it of the centurion, he gave the body to Joseph.

And he bought fine linen, and took him down, and wrapped him in the linen, and laid him in a sepulchre which was hewn out of a rock, and rolled a stone into the door of the sepulchre.

PART 8

JESUS' MISSED "DUE PROCESS" MESSAGE

And Jesus came and spake unto
them, saying, . . . "Go ye therefore and teach all nations . . .

"Do not think that I have come
to destroy the Law and the
prophets, but to fulfill.

" . . . till heaven and earth
shall pass away, not one jot or one
tittle shall be lost from the
Law till all things have been
accomplished . . . "
Matthew 28:18-19
Matthew 5:17-18

Chapter 40

"NOT ONE JOT OR ONE TITTLE SHALL BE LOST FROM THE LAW . . . "

Jesus honored the Law of his God and his fathers, in the *torah*, as taught by the prophets, debated by the scribes, practiced by the judges and evolved into the Oral Law of the Pharisees as now reported in the *talmud*. Like the Psalmist (1:1-2), he lived in God's Law: "Blessed is the man who walketh not in the counsel of the ungodly, nor standeth in the way of sinners, nor sitteth in the seat of the scornful. But his delight is in the Law of the Lord; and in His Law doth he meditate day and night."

He left no doubt about his deep feelings for the Law (*Matthew* 5:17-18):

> "Do not think that I have come to destroy the Law and the prophets, but to fulfill.
>
> For amen, I say to you, till heaven and earth shall pass away, not one jot or one tittle shall be lost from the Law till all things have been accomplished . . . "

Writers of Hebrew during Jesus' time used horn-like marks to indicate syllables, perhaps show pronunciation, and give other aids to reading. They called these "jots" and "tittles," which took on the extra meaning of something small ("iota") and tiny, a dash or touch, perhaps only a shade or nuance.

Why Jesus' great love of the Law?

From the *torah* and *talmud* we can pull out these basic "due process" requirements already in place and followed in Jesus' trials in the Court of the Temple Mount and before the Great Sanhedrin:

(1) Both trials took place in the regular meeting places of the two courts, as demanded by *Deuteronomy* and the *talmud*;

(2) Both courts met openly and in public, as required by Israel's most ancient Law Codes, and fleshed out in the *talmud*;

(3) Both trials took place in the daytime, since they involved the death penalty;

(4) No person could be found guilty until competent witnesses proved the case against him in open court;

(5) No person could be convicted upon his own admission or confession of guilt (no man could be compelled to witness against himself);

(6) No person could be convicted except upon the testimony of two or more competent witnesses, never on one alone.

(7) No accused could be convicted on *zomen* (false witness); and if *any* of the evidence could be shown to be *zomen*, the entire case fell, and the accused acquitted;

(8) The prosecuting witnesses must face the accused in open court, their testimony delivered in person, not through an interpreter or written document;

(9) No accused could be convicted by a vote of less than a majority of *two* judges;

(10) No person could be convicted on an unanimous verdict, although he could be acquitted unanimously;

(11) If the "set" of witnesses did not agree in their "witness," the accused must be acquitted;

(12) No person could be twice placed in jeopardy for the same offense;

(13) No judge could be a witness in any case on which he sat as judge;

(14) Judges could rely only upon testimony they heard in open court, none from any other source;

(15) Each witness must testify to the whole of the matter, not to just a fragmented part;

(16) Each witness must withstand vigorous cross-examination, and the harder the cross-examination, the more worthy the judge making it;

(17) No person could be condemned unless personally present in court during his trial;

(18) Evidence by inference (circumstantial evidence) could not be used;

(19) Except for the sins of false witness, false prophecy, burglary in the nighttime, blasphemy and idolatry, no person could be convicted unless two witnesses warned him in advance that his act would be a sin, and the exact type of punishment he would receive if he persisted in his wrongdoing; and

(20) A person's conduct must be judged in the light most favorable to him, which presumed him innocent until competent evidence proved him guilty.

Jesus honored God's Law, for God's Law honors Man, any Man: The Rich Young Ruler who came to Jesus by night asking the way of salvation; the Widow who left her mite of two copper coins as a tithe at the Temple Treasury; the Centurion's Slave whom Jesus healed; the Flute Players in the house of the Ruler whose daughter lay dead; the despised Publican (tax collector) Zaccheus whose guilt made him hide in a tree; the Dumb Demoniac whose demon Jesus cast out; the Reapers in the fields; the Shepherd who lost one of his hundred sheep; the Pharisees and Sadducees who sought to trap Jesus on the Law of divorce; the Phoenician woman who wished only to touch the fringes of his garment; the Priests and Levites who performed in the Temple sacrifices; the preachers and worshipers in the villages and towns of both Galilees; Mary Magdalene with her seven devils; his own blood brothers (James, Joseph, Simon and Judas) who belittled him during his life time; the Hypocrites and Doctors of the Law who strained at gnats but swallowed camels; the lowest Brother who sinned against another brother; the Rich Man with the full table and Lazarus, the beggar, who lay at the Rich Man's gate, his sores licked by the dogs; the High Priest, the Committee of Ten, and the other Temple Bureaucrats.

All stood equal before God's Law, raised up in human dignity by it, no matter that their personal conduct of the moment debased it.

We continue to miss a key part of the *gospel* which Jesus sent out his disciples to preach: His *fulfillment* of the Law requires a legal system throughout the world that honors each and every man and woman, giving them "due process" rights that protect them from each other and from their rulers, the Hitlers and Stalins, Maos and Ortegas, kings and generals, especially "Temple" Bureaucrats who pollute governments everywhere and in every era.

Jesus' missed message calls for independent judges all over the world who can say to the rulers, "Stop! Go no further, for if you do, you will breach the Law of God which protects all of mankind from slavery and baseness, every man and woman across the face of the earth."

Jesus' *fulfillment* of the Law demands that we teach all men — Christian, Jew, Moslem, Hindu, Buddhist, non-believer alike — that Man does not live by bread alone. He can live fully only *in* the Rule of Law: Law that becomes his refuge and fortress no matter what befalls him; Law that lifts him up when all around him seek to press him down; Law that shields him from the threats of tyrants; Law that protects the widow and her orphans; Law that keeps the rich and powerful from gobbling up the weak; a Law of nations that makes obsolete wars and rumors of wars; Law that lets Man's soul soar to the gates of Heaven, to catch his fondest dreams; Law that lets him live in love and charity with his neighbors; Law that begets ethics and morals; Law that lets him move in peace on earth; Law that gives him hope for salvation in the world to come.

God's Law, the Law of the Holy One, Blessed be He: "Go ye into all the world and teach and preach it!"

Appendix 1

GOSPEL REPORTS OF THE ARRESTS, TRIALS AND DEATH OF JESUS

The *gospels* of *Matthew, Mark, Luke* and *John* give us our only reports of Jesus' legal trials (*gospel* = Greek: *euangelion* (*evangel*) = "good news.")

Their present appearance in neat, printed, bound form is a far cry from their beginnings. The authors/editors wrote each separate episode they describe on a papyrus sheet called a *pericope* ("cutting"). We do not know how they filed or stacked the separate sheets, or who actually placed them in the mixed-up, non-chronological order we find today.

The "books" of the Old Testament come to us in similar fashion, papyrus sheets to vellum scrolls to printed page.

The interesting *The Bible In Order* presents the books of both testaments in the chronological order of their writing, a markedly different arrangement than the printed order of the bibles we grew up with.

Further, chapter and verse divisions of the entire bible came quite late, after the arrival of printing, chapters first introduced by Cardinal Hugo de Sancto Caro in 1250, the verses inserted by printer Robert Stevens in 1257 as he rode horseback from Lyons to Paris. Both divisions came from efforts to make the printed results more readable, not as the products of scholars and theologians.

Our effort to discover the separate events of what is mislabeled the "trial" (singular) of Jesus demands that we separate out the *pericopes* of his:

(1) Trial in the Small Sanhedrin of the Temple Mount for Sabbath-breaking;

(2) Trial before the Great Sanhedrin in the Hall of the Hewn Stone for false prophecy;

(3) His grilling in the houses of the High Priests, after his arrest in Gethsemane; and

(4) His final trial before Pontius Pilate.

GOSPEL REPORTS OF THE ARRESTS, TRIALS, AND DEATH OF JESUS CHRIST

MATTHEW	MARK	LUKE	JOHN
80-90 A.D.	After 71 A.D.	80-95 A.D.	100-120 A.D.
Alexandria/Antioch (?)	Rome	Greece/Syria (?)	Asia Minor (?) (Ephesus)
To: Jewish Christians	To: Roman Christians	To: Non-Jews	To: Jews & Greeks

First Arrest and Trial
Before the Small Sanhedrin (bet din)
of the Temple Mount

Chapter 12:

9 And when he was departed thence, he went into their synagogue:

10 And, behold there was a man which had his hand withered. And they asked him, saying, Is it lawful to heal on the sabbath days, so that they might accuse him.

11 And he said unto them, What man shall there be among you, that shall have one sheep, and if it fall into a pit on the sabbath day, will he not lay hold on it, and lift it out?

12 How much then is man better than a sheep? Wherefore it is lawful to do well on the sabbath day.

13 Then saith he to the man, Stretch forth thine hand. And he stretched it forth; and it was restored whole, like as the other.

14 Then the Pharisees went out, and held a council* against him how they might destroy him.

Chapter 3:

1 He entered the synagogue on another occasion; and there was a man who had his hand paralyzed.

2 They accordingly watched Him, to see if He would cure him on the Sabbath day, in order that they might inform against Him.

3 He then told the man who had the withered hand to "Stand up!" and of them

4 He inquired, "Is it allowable to do good on the Sabbath, or to do harm? to save life, or to take it?" But they kept silent.

5 Then looking round upon them with indignation, being grieved at the stupidity of their hearts, He said to the man, "Extend your hand!"

He accordingly extended it; and his hand was restored to its natural condition.

6 The Pharisees then went out, and at once held a consultation with the Herodians against Him, as to how they could destroy Him.

Chapter 6:

6 On another Sabbath, He entered the Synagogue and taught; and a man was there whose right hand was withered.

7 The professors and Pharisees accordingly watched Him, to see if He would cure On the Sabbath; in order that they might lay an information against Him.

8 Divining their reasonings, however, He said to the man who had the withered hand, "Get up, and stand out among us."

9 So he arose and stood. Jesus then said to them, "I ask you plainly, Is it allowable on the Sabbath to benefit or to injure? to save a life or to destroy it?"

10 Then looking round upon them all, He said to the man, "Extend your hand!"

11 He did so; and his hand was restored like the other. But they became mad with annoyance; and discussed among themselves what they could do to Jesus.

Chapter 11:

47 Therefore the Sanhedrin, or Great Council, was called together and the Chief Priests said, "What are we to do? For this man performs many signs.

48 If we let him go on thus, every one will believe in him, and the Romans will come and destroy both our holy place and our nation."

49 But one of them, Caiaphas, who was high priest that year, said to them, "You know nothing at all;

50 You do not understand that it is expedient for you that one man should die for the people, and that the whole nation should not perish."

· · · ·

53 So from that day on they took counsel how to put him to death.

54 Jesus therefore no longer went openly among the Jews, but went from there to the country near the wilderness.

*"Sanhedrin" in many translations.

GOSPEL REPORTS OF THE ARRESTS, TRIALS, AND DEATH OF JESUS CHRIST

MATTHEW	MARK	LUKE	JOHN
	Second Arrest and Trial Before the Great Sanhedrin (bet din ha-gadbol) Chamber of the Hewn Stone		
		(Not Mentioned)	*(Not Mentioned)*

MATTHEW

Chapter 26:

57 Then those who has seized Jesus led him to Caiaphas the high priest, where the scribes and the elders had gathered.

59 Now the chief priests and the whole council* sought false testimony against Jesus that they might put him to death,

60 but they found none, though many false witnesses came forward. At last two came forward

61 and said, "This fellow said, 'I am able to destroy the temple of God, and to build it in three days.'"

62 And the high priest stood up and said, "Have you no answer to make? What is it that these men testify against you?"

63 But Jesus was silent.

MARK

Chapter 14:

53 And they led Jesus to the high priest; and all the chief priests and the elders and the scribes were assembled . . .

55 Now the chief priests and the whole council* sought testimony against Jesus to put him to death; but they found none.

56 For many bore false witness against him, and their witness did not agree.

57 And some stood up and bore false witness against him, saying,

58 "We heard him say, 'I will destroy this temple that is made with hands, and in three days I will build another, not made with hands.'"

59 Yet not even so did their testimony agree.

60 And the high priest stood up in the midst and asked Jesus, "Have you no answer to make? What is it that these men testify against you?

61 But he was silent and made no answer.

*"Whole council" is used for "Sanhedrin" in many translations.

GOSPEL REPORTS OF THE ARRESTS, TRIALS, AND DEATH OF JESUS CHRIST

MATTHEW	MARK	LUKE	JOHN

The Third Arrest (Gethsemane)

MATTHEW

Chapter 26:
47 While he was still speaking, Judas came, one of the twelve, and with him a great crowd with swords and clubs, from the chief priests and the elders of the people.

48 Now the betrayer had given them a sign, saying, "The one I shall kiss is the man; seize him."

49 And he came up to Jesus at once and said, "Hail, Master!" And he kissed him.

50 Jesus said to him, "Friend, why are you here?" Then they came up and laid hands on Jesus and seized him.

MARK

Chapter 14:
43 And immediately, while he was still speaking, Judas came, one of the twelve, and with him a crowd with swords and clubs, from the chief priests and the scribes and the elders.

44 Now the betrayer had given them a sign, saying, "The one I shall kiss is the man; seize him and lead him away safely."

45 And when he came, he went up to him at once, and said, "Master!" And he kissed him.

46 And they laid hands on him and seized him.

LUKE

Chapter 22:
47 While he was still speaking, there came a crowd, and the man called Judas, one of the twelve, was leading them. He drew near to Jesus to kiss him;

48 but Jesus said to him, "Judas, would you betray the Son of man with a kiss?"

JOHN

Chapter 18:
When Jesus had spoken these words, he went forth with his disciples across the Kidron valley where there was a garden which he and his disciples entered.

2 Now Judas, who betrayed him, also knew the place; for Jesus often met there with his disciples.

3 So Judas, procuring a band of soldiers and some officers from the chief priests and the Pharisees, went there with lanterns and torches and weapons.

4 Then Jesus, knowing all that was to befall him, came forward and said to them, "Whom do you seek."

5 They answered him, "Jesus of Nazareth." Jesus said to them, "I am he." Judas who betrayed him was standing with them.

6 When he said to them, "I am he," they drew back and fell to the ground.

7 Again he asked them, "Whom do you seek?" And they said, "Jesus of Nazareth."

8 Jesus answered, "I told you that I am he; so, if you seek me, let these men go."

9 This was to fulfil the word which he had spoken, "Of those whom thou gaves me I lost not one."

GOSPEL REPORTS OF THE ARRESTS, TRIALS, AND DEATH OF JESUS CHRIST

MATTHEW	MARK	LUKE	JOHN

Jesus' Friends Resist His Third Arrest

MATTHEW	MARK	LUKE	JOHN
Chapter 26: 51 And behold, one of those who were with Jesus stretched out his hand and drew his sword, and struck the slave of the high priest, and cut off his ear. 52 Then Jesus said to him, "Put your sword back into its place; for all who take the sword will perish by the sword. 53 Do you think that I cannot appeal to my Father, and he will at once send me more than twelve legions of angels? 54 But how then should the scriptures be fulfilled, that it must be so?"	*Chapter 14:* 47 But one of those who stood by drew his sword, and struck the slave of the high priest and cut off his ear.	*Chapter 22:* 49 And when those who were about him saw what would follow, they said, "Lord, shall we strike with the sword?" 50 And one of them struck the slave of the high priest and cut off his right ear. 51 But Jesus said, "No more of this!" And he touched his ear and healed him.	*Chapter 18:* 10 Then Simon Peter, having a sword, drew it and struck the high priest's slave and cut off his right ear. The slave's name was Malchus. 11 Jesus said to Peter, "Put your sword into its sheath; shall I not drink the cup which the Father has given me?"

Jesus Protests the Secret, Night-time Arrest

MATTHEW	MARK	LUKE	JOHN
Chapter 26: 55 At that hour Jesus said to the crowds, "Have you come out as against a robber, with swords and clubs to capture me? Day after day I sat in the temple teaching, and you did not seize me. 56 But all this has taken place, that the scriptures of the prophets might be fulfilled."	*Chapter 14:* 48 And Jesus said to them, "Have you come out as against a robber, with swords and clubs to capture me? 49 Day after day I was with you in the temple teaching, and you did not seize me. But let the scriptures be fulfilled."	*Chapter 22:* 52 Then Jesus said to the chief priests and captains of the temple and elders, who had come out against him, "Have you come out as against a robber, with swords and clubs? 53 When I was with you day after day in the temple, you did not lay hands on me. But this is your hour, and the power of darkness."	*(Not Mentioned)*

289

GOSPEL REPORTS OF THE ARRESTS, TRIALS, AND DEATH OF JESUS CHRIST

MATTHEW	MARK	LUKE	JOHN

The Disciples Forsake and Flee

MATTHEW	MARK	LUKE	JOHN
Chapter 26: 56 (cont'd) Then all the disciples forsook him and fled.	*Chapter 14:* 50 And they all forsook him and fled. 51 And a young man followed him, with nothing but a linen cloth about his body; and they seized him, 56 but he left the linen cloth and ran away naked.	*(Not Mentioned)*	*(Not Mentioned)*

Executive Sessions In the Houses of the High Priests

MATTHEW	MARK	LUKE	JOHN
Chapter 26:	*Chapter 14:*	*Chapter 22:* 54 Then they seized him and led him away, bringing him into the high priest's house . . .	*Chapter 18:* 12 So the band of soldiers and their captain and the officers of the Jews seized Jesus and bound him. 13 First they led him to Annas; for he was the father-in-law of Caiaphas, who was high priest that year. 14 It was Caiaphas who had given counsel to the Jews that it was expedient that one man should die for the people.

GOSPEL REPORTS OF THE ARRESTS, TRIALS, AND DEATH OF JESUS CHRIST

Executive Sessions In the Houses of the High Priests (cont'd)

MATTHEW	MARK	LUKE	JOHN
Chapter 26:	*Chapter 14:*	66 ... and they said,	19 The high priest then questioned Jesus about his disciples and his teaching.
63 And the high priest said to him, "I adjure you by the living God, tell us if you are the Christ, the Son of God." Jesus said to him, "You have said so. But I tell you, hereafter you will see the Son of man seated at the right hand of Power, and coming on the clouds of heaven."	61 ... Again the high priest asked him, "Are you the Christ, the Son of the Blessed?" And Jesus said, "I am; and you will see the Son of man sitting at the right hand of Power, and coming with the clouds of heaven."	67 If you are the Christ, tell us." But he said to them, "If I tell you you will not believe;	20 Jesus answered him, "I have spoken openly to the world; I have always taught in the synagogues and in the temple, where all Jews come together; I have said nothing secretly.
65 Then the high priest tore his robes, and said, "he has uttered blasphemy. What is your judgment?" They answered "He deserves death."	63 And the high priest tore his mantle, and said, "Why do we still need witnesses? You have heard his blasphemy. What is your decision?" And they all condemned him as deserving death.	68 and if I ask you, you will not answer.	21 Why do you ask me? Ask those who have heard me, what I said." When he had said this, one of the officers standing by struck Jesus with his hand, saying, "Is this how you answer the high priest?"
		69 But from now on the Son of man shall be seated at the right hand of the Power of God."	23 Jesus answered him "If I have spoken wrongly, bear witness to the wrong; but if I have spoken rightly, why do you strike me?"
		70 And they all said, "Are you the Son of God, then?" And he said to them, "You say that I am."	24 Annas then sent him bound to Caiaphas the high priest.
		71 And they said, "What further testimony do we need? We have heard it ourselves from his own lips."	

Jesus Mocked by the Temple Guard

MATTHEW	MARK	LUKE	JOHN
67 Then they spat in his face, and struck him; and some slapped him,	65 And some began to spit on him, and to cover his face, and to strike him, saying to him, "Prophesy!" And the guards received him with blows.	*Chapter 22:*	*(Not Mentioned -- unless 18:22 applies):*
68 saying, "Prophesy to us, you Christ! Who is it that struck you?"		63 Now the men who were holding Jesus mocked him and beat him;	22 When he had said this, one of the officers standing by struck Jesus with his hand ....
		64 they also blindfolded him and asked him, "Prophesy! Who is it that struck you?"	
		65 And they spoke many other words against him, reviling him.	

GOSPEL REPORTS OF THE ARRESTS, TRIALS, AND DEATH OF JESUS CHRIST

MATTHEW	MARK	LUKE	JOHN

Trial Before Pilate: The Search for a Charge

MATTHEW

Chapter 27:

1 When morning came, all the chief priests and the elders of the people took counsel against Jesus to put him to death;

2 and they bound him and led him away and delivered him to Pilate, the governor.

11 Now Jesus stood before the governor; and the governor asked him, saying, "Are you the king of the Jews?" Jesus said to him, "You have said so."

12 But when he was accused by the chief priests and elders, he made no answer.

13 Then Pilate said to him, "Do you not hear how many things they testify against you?"

14 But he gave them no answer, not even to a single charge; so that the governor wondered greatly.

MARK

Chapter 15:

1 And as soon as it was morning the chief priests with elders and scribes, and the whole council held a consultation; and they bound Jesus and led him away and delivered him to Pilate.

2 And Pilate asked him, "Are you the King of the Jews?" And he answered him, "You have said so."

3 And the chief priests accused him of many things.

4 And Pilate again asked him, "Have you no answer to make? See how many charges they bring against you."

5 But Jesus made no further answer, so that Pilate wondered.

LUKE

Chapter 22:

66 When day came, the assembly of the elders of the people gathered together, both chief priests and scribes; and they led him away to their council.

Chapter 23:

1 Then the whole company of them arose, and brought him before Pilate.

2 And they began to accuse him, saying, "We found this man perverting our nation, and forbidding us to give tribute to Caesar, and saying that he himself is Christ a King."

3 And Pilate asked him, "Are you the King of the Jews?" And he answered him, "You have said so."

4 And Pilate said to the chief priests and the multitudes, "I find no crime in this man."

5 But they were urgent, saying, "He stirs up the people, teaching throughout all Judea from Galilee even to this place."

JOHN

Chapter 18:

28 Then they led Jesus from the house of Caiaphas to the praetorium. It was early. They themselves did not enter the praetorium, so that they might not be defiled, but might eat the Passover.

29 So Pilate went out to them and said, "What accusation do you bring against this man?"

30 They answered him, "If this man were not an evildoer, we would not have handed him over."

31 Pilate said to them, "Take him yourselves and judge him by your own law." The Jews said to him, "It is not lawful for us to put any man to death."

32 This was to fulfill the word which Jesus had spoken to show by what death he was to die.

33 Pilate entered the praetorium again and called Jesus, and said to him, "Are you the King of the Jews?"

34 Jesus answered, "Do you say this of your own accord, or did others say it to you about me?"

35 Pilate answered, "Am I a Jew? Your own nation and the chief priests have handed you over to me; what have you done?"

GOSPEL REPORTS OF THE ARRESTS, TRIALS, AND DEATH OF JESUS CHRIST

MATTHEW   MARK   LUKE   JOHN

Trial Before Pilate: The Search for a Charge (cont'd)

36 Jesus answered, "My kingship is not of this world; if my kingship were of this world, my servants would fight, that I might not be handed over to the Jews; but my kingship is not from the world."

37 Pilate said to him, "So you are a king?" Jesus answered, "You say that I am a king. For this I was born, and for this I have come into the world, to bear witness to the truth. Every one who is of the truth hears my voice."

38 Pilate said to him, "What is truth?"

GOSPEL REPORTS OF THE ARRESTS, TRIALS, AND DEATH OF JESUS CHRIST

MATTHEW	MARK	LUKE	JOHN
		The Appearance Before Herod Antipas	
(Not Mentioned)	(Not Mentioned)	Chapter 23:	(Not Mentioned)

LUKE, Chapter 23:

6 When Pilate heard this, he asked whether the man was a Galilean.

7 And when he learned that he belonged to Herod's jurisdiction, he sent him over to Herod, who was himself in Jerusalem at that time.

8 When Herod saw Jesus, he was very glad, for he had long desired to see him, because he had heard about him, and he was hoping to see some sign done by him.

9 So he questioned him at some length; but he made no answer.

10 The chief priests and the scribes stood by, vehemently accusing him.

11 And Herod with his soldiers treated him with contempt and mocked him; then, arraying him in gorgeous apparel, he sent him back to Pilate.

12 And Herod and Pilate became friends with each other that very day, for before this they had been at enmity with each other.

GOSPEL REPORTS OF THE ARRESTS, TRIALS, AND DEATH OF JESUS CHRIST

MATTHEW	MARK	LUKE	JOHN

Trial Before Pilate: The Temple Bureaucrats Choose Barabbas

MATTHEW	MARK	LUKE	JOHN
Chapter 27: 15 Now at the feast the governor was accustomed to release for the crowd any one prisoner whom they wanted. 16 And they had then a notorious prisoner called Barabbas. 17 So when they had gathered, Pilate said to them, "Whom do you want me to release for you, Barabbas or Jesus who is called Christ?" 18 For he knew that it was out of envy that they had delivered him up. 19 Besides, while he was sitting on the judgment seat, his wife sent word to him, "Have nothing to do with that righteous man, for I have suffered much over him today in a dream." 20 Now the chief priests and the elders persuaded the people to ask for Barabbas and destroy Jesus. 21 The governor again said to them, "Which of the two do you want me to release for you?" And they said, "Barabbas."	*Chapter 15:* 6 Now at the feast he used to release for them one prisoner whom they asked. 7 And among the rebels in prison, who had committed murder in the insurrection, there was a man called Barabbas. 8 And the crowd came up and began to ask Pilate to do as he was wont to do for them. 9 And he answered them, "Do you want me to release for you the King of the Jews?" 10 For he perceived that it was out of envy that the chief priests had delivered him up. 11 But the chief priests stirred up the crowd to have him release for them Barabbas instead.	*Chapter 23:* 18 But they all cried out together, "Away with this man, and release to us Barabbas" 19a man who had been thrown into prison for an insurrection started in the city, and for murder.	*Chapter 18:* After he had said this, he went out to the Jews again, and told them, "I find no crime in him. 39 But you have a custom that I should release one man for you at the Passover; will you have me release for you the King of the Jews?" 40 They cried out again, "Not this man, but Barabbas!" Now Barabbas was a robber.

GOSPEL REPORTS OF THE ARRESTS, TRIALS, AND DEATH OF JESUS CHRIST

MATTHEW	MARK	LUKE	JOHN

Trial Before Pilate: Decree of Death

MATTHEW

Chapter 27:

22 Pilate said to them, "Then what shall I do with Jesus who is called Christ?" They all said, "Let him be crucified."

23 And he said, "Why, what evil has he done?" But they shouted all the more, "Let him be crucified."

24 So when Pilate saw that he was gaining nothing, but rather that a riot was beginning, he took water and washed his hands before the crowd, saying, "I am innocent of this man's blood, see to it yourselves."

25 And all the people answered, "his blood be on us and on our children!"

26 Then he released for them Barabbas, and delivered him to be crucified.

MARK

Chapter 15:

12 And Pilate again said to them, "Then what shall I do with the man whom you call the King of the Jews?"

13 And they cried out again, "Crucify him."

14 And Pilate said to them, "Why, what evil has he done?" But they shouted all the more, "Crucify him."

15 So Pilate, wishing to satisfy the crowd, released for them Barabbas; . . he delivered him to be crucified.

LUKE

Chapter 23:

13 Pilate then called together the chief priests and the rulers and the people,

14 and said to them, "You brought me this man as one who was perverting the people; and after examining him before you, behold, I did not find this man guilty of any of your charges against him;

15 neither did Herod, for he sent him back to us. Behold, nothing deserving death has been done by him;

16 I will therefore chastise him and release him" . . . .

20 Pilate addressed them once more, desiring to release Jesus;

21 but they shouted out, "Crucify, crucify him!"

22 A third time he said to them, "Why, what evil has he done? I have found in him no crime deserving death; I will therefore chastise him and release him"

23 But they were urgent, demanding with loud cries that he should be crucified. And their voices prevailed.

24 So Pilate gave sentence that their demand should be granted.

25 He released the man who had been thrown into prison for insurrection and murder, whom they asked for; but Jesus he delivered up to their will.

JOHN

Chapter 19:

4 Pilate went out again, and said to them, "Behold, I am bringing him out to you, that you may know that I find no crime in him."

5 So Jesus came out wearing the crown of thorns and the purple robe. Pilate said to them, "Here is the man!"

6 When the chief priests and the officers saw him, they cried out, "Crucify him, crucify him!" Pilate said to them, "Take him yourselves and crucify him, for I find no crime in him."

7 The Jews answered him, "We have a law, and by that law he ought to die, because he has made himself the Son of God."

8 When Pilate heard these words, he was the more afraid;

9 he entered the praetorium again and said to Jesus, "Where are you from?" But Jesus gave no answer.

10 Pilate therefore said to him, "You will not speak to me? Do you not know that I have power to release you, and power to crucify you?"

11 Jesus answered him, "You would have no power over me unless it had been given you from above; therefore he who delivered me to you has the greater sin."

GOSPEL REPORTS OF THE ARRESTS, TRIALS, AND DEATH OF JESUS CHRIST

MATTHEW	MARK	LUKE	JOHN
	Trial Before Pilate: Decree of Death (cont'd.)		12 Upon this Pilate sought to release him, but the Jews cried out, "If you release this man, you are not Caesar's friend; every one who makes himself a king sets himself against Caesar."
			13 When Pilate heard these words, he brought Jesus out and sat down on the judgment seat at a place called The Pavement, and in Hebrew, Gabbatha.
			14 Now it was the day of Preparation of the Passover; it was about the sixth hour. He said to the Jews, "Here is your King!"
			15 They cried out, "Away with him, crucify him!" Pilate said to them, "Shall I crucify your King?" The chief priests answered, "We have no king but Caesar."
			16 Then he handed him over to them to be crucified.

Pilate Orders Jesus Scourged

MATTHEW	MARK	LUKE	JOHN
Chapter 27: 26 ... and having scourged Jesus,	Chapter 15: 15 ... and having scourged Jesus,	(Not Mentioned)	Chapter 19: 1 Then Pilate took Jesus and scourged him.

GOSPEL REPORTS OF THE ARRESTS, TRIALS, AND DEATH OF JESUS CHRIST

MATTHEW	MARK	LUKE	JOHN

Jesus Mocked by Pilate's Mercenaries

MATTHEW	MARK	LUKE	JOHN
Chapter 27: 27 Then the soldiers of the governor took Jesus into the praetorium, and they gathered the whole battalion before him. 28 And they stripped him and put a scarlet robe upon him, 29 and plaiting a crown of thorns they put it on his head, and put a reed in his right hand. And kneeling before him they mocked him, they stripped him of the robe, and put his own clothes on him, and led him away to crucify him.	*Chapter 15:* 16 And the soldiers led him away inside the palace (that is, the praetorium); and they called together the whole battalion. 17 And they clothed him in a purple cloak, and plaiting a crown of thorns they put it on him. 18 And they began to salute him, "Hail, King of the Jews!" 19 And they struck his head with a reed, and spat upon him, and they knelt down in homage to him. 20 And when they had mocked him, they stripped him of the purple cloak, and put his own clothes on him. And they led him out to crucify him.	*(Not Mentioned)*	*Chapter 19:* 2 And the soldiers plaited a crown of thorns, and put it on his head, and arrayed him in a purple robe; 3 they came up to him saying, "Hail, King of the Jews!" and struck him with their hands.

GOSPEL REPORTS OF THE ARRESTS, TRIALS, AND DEATH OF JESUS CHRIST

The Crucifixion: Golgotha's Regimen

MATTHEW

Chapter 27:

33 And when they came to a place called Golgotha, (which means the place of a skull),

34 they offered him wine to drink, mingled with gall; but when he tasted it, he would not drink it.

35 And when they had crucified him, they divided his garments among them by casting lots;

36 then they sat down and kept watch over him there.

37 And over his head they put the charge against him, which read, "This is Jesus the King of the Jews."

38 Then two robbers were crucified with him, one on the right and one on the left.

39 And those who passed by derided him, wagging their heads

40 and saying, "You who would destroy the temple and build it in three days, save yourself! If you are the Son of God, come down from the cross."

MARK

Chapter 15:

22 And they brought him to the place called Golgotha (which means the place of a skull).

23 And they offered him wine mingled with myrrh; but he did not take it.

24 And they crucified him, and divided his garments among them, casting lots for them, to decide what each should take.

25 And it was the third hour when they crucified him.

26 And the inscription of the charge against him read, "The King of the Jews."

27 And with him they crucified two robbers, one on his right and one on his left.

29 And those who passed by derided him, wagging their heads, and saying, "Aha! You who would destroy the temple and build it in three days,

30 save yourself, and come down from the cross!"

LUKE

Chapter 23:

33 And when they came to the place which is called The Skull, there they crucified him, and

34 And Jesus said, "Father, forgive them for they know not what they do." And they cast lots to divide his garments.

35 And the people stood by, watching; but the rulers scoffed at him saying, "He saved others; let him save himself, if he is the Christ of God, his Chosen One!"

JOHN

Chapter 19:

17 So they took Jesus, and he went out, bearing his own cross, to the place called the place of a skull, which is called in Hebrew Golgotha.

18 There they crucified him, and with him two others, one on either side, and Jesus between them.

19 Pilate also wrote a title and put it on the cross; it read, "Jesus of Nazareth, the King of the Jews."

20 Many of the Jews read this title, for the place where Jesus was crucified was near the city; and it was written in Hebrew, in Latin, and in Greek.

21 The chief priests of the Jews then said to Pilate, "Do not write, 'The King of the Jews,' but, 'This man said, I am King of the Jews.'"

22 Pilate answered, "What I have written I have written."

23 When the soldiers had crucified Jesus they took his garments and made four parts, one for each soldier; also his tunic. But the tunic was without seam, woven from top to bottom;

24 so they said to one another, "Let us not tear it, but cast lots for it to see whose it shall be." This was to fulfill the scripture, "They parted my garments among them, and for my clothing they cast lots."

GOSPEL REPORTS OF THE ARRESTS, TRIALS, AND DEATH OF JESUS CHRIST

MATTHEW	MARK	LUKE	JOHN

The Crucifixion: Golgotha's Regimen (cont'd)

JOHN

25 So the soldiers did this. But standing by the cross of Jesus were his mother, and his mother's sister, Mary the wife of Cleophas, and Mary Magdalene.

26 When Jesus saw his mother and the disciple whom he loved standing near, he said to his mother, "Woman, behold, your son!"

27 Then he said to the disciple, "Behold, your mother!" And from that hour the disciple took her to his own home.

28 After this Jesus, knowing that all was now finished, said (to fulfill the scripture), "I thirst."

29 A bowl full of vinegar stood there; so they put a sponge full of the vinegar on hyssop and held it to his mouth.

GOSPEL REPORTS OF THE ARRESTS, TRIALS, AND DEATH OF JESUS CHRIST

MATTHEW	MARK	LUKE	JOHN

The Crucifixion: Jesus Mocked by the Temple Bureaucrats and Soldiers

MATTHEW	MARK	LUKE	JOHN
Chapter 27: 41 So also the chief priests, with the scribes and elders, mocked him, 42 "He saved others; he cannot save himself. If he is the King of Israel, let him come down now from the cross, and we will believe in him. 43 He trusts in God; let God deliver him now, if he desires him; for he said, 'I am the Son of God.'" 44 And the robbers who were crucified with him also reviled him in the same way.	*Chapter 15:* 31 So also the chief priests mocked him to one another with the scribes, saying, "He saved others; he cannot save himself. 32 Let the Christ, the King of Israel, come down now from the cross that we may see and believe." Those who were crucified with him also reviled him.	*Chapter 23:* 36 The soldiers also mocked him, coming up and offering him vinegar, 37 and saying, "If you are the King of the Jews, save yourself!" 38 There was also an inscription over him, "This is the King of the Jews." 39 One of the criminals who were hanged railed at him, saying, "Are you not the Christ? Save yourself and us!" 40 But the other rebuked him, saying, "Do you not fear God, since you are under the same sentence of condemnation? 41 And we indeed justly; for we are receiving the due reward of our deeds; but this man has done nothing wrong." 42 And he said, "Jesus, remember me when you come in your kingly power." 43 And he said to him, "Truly, I say to you, today you will be with me in Paradise."	*(Not Mentioned)*

The Crucifixion: Darkness Over All the Land

MATTHEW	MARK	LUKE	JOHN
Chapter 27: 45 Now from the sixth hour there was darkness over all the land until the ninth hour.	*Chapter 15:* 33 And when the sixth hour had come, there was darkness over the whole land until the ninth hour.	*Chapter 23:* 44 It was now about the sixth hour, and there was darkness over the whole land until the ninth hour, 45 while the sun's light failed;	*(Not Mentioned)*

301

GOSPEL REPORTS OF THE ARRESTS, TRIALS, AND DEATH OF JESUS CHRIST

MATTHEW	MARK	LUKE	JOHN
		Death on the Cross	

MATTHEW

Chapter 27:

46 And about the ninth hour Jesus cried with a loud voice, "Eli, Eli, lama sabachthani?" that is, "My God, my God, why hast thou forsaken me?"

47 And some of the bystanders hearing it said, "This man is calling Elijah."

48 And one of them at once ran and took a sponge, filled it with vinegar, and put it on a reed, and gave it to him to drink.

49 But the others said, "Wait, let us see whether Elijah will come to save him."

50 And Jesus cried again with a loud voice and yielded up his spirit.

MARK

Chapter 15:

34 And at the ninth hour Jesus cried with a loud voice, "Eloi, Eloi, lama sabachthani?" which means, "My God, my God why hast thou forsaken me?"

35 And some of the bystanders hearing it said, "Behold, he is calling Elijah."

36 And one ran and, filling a sponge full of vinegar, put it on a reed and gave it to him to drink, saying, "Wait, let us see whether Elijah will come to take him down."

37 And Jesus uttered a loud cry, and breathed his last.

LUKE

Chapter 23:

46 Then Jesus, crying with a loud voice, said, "Father, into thy hands I commit my spirit." And having said this he breathed his last.

JOHN

Chapter 19:

30 When Jesus had received the vinegar, he said, "It is finished"; and he bowed his head and gave up his spirit.

31 Since it was the day of Preparation, in order to prevent the bodies from remaining on the cross on the sabbath (for that sabbath was a high day), the Jews asked Pilate that their legs might be broken, and that they might be taken away.

32 So the soldiers came and broke the legs of the first, and of the other who had been crucified with him;

33 but when they came to Jesus and saw that he was already dead, they did not break his legs.

34 But one of the soldiers pierced his side with a spear, and at once there came out blood and water.

35 He who saw it has borne witness—his testimony is true, and he knows that he tells the truth—that you also may believe.

36 For these things took place that the scripture might be fulfilled, "Not a bone of him shall be broken."

37 And again another scripture says, "They shall look on him whom they have pierced."

GOSPEL REPORTS OF THE ARRESTS, TRIALS, AND DEATH OF JESUS CHRIST

MATTHEW	MARK	LUKE	JOHN
		Tearing of the Temple Curtain	
Chapter 27: 51 And behold, the curtain of the temple was torn in two, from top to bottom;	Chapter 15: 38 And the curtain of the temple was torn in two, from top to bottom.	Chapter 23: 45 . . . and the curtain of the temple was torn in two.	(Not Mentioned)
		Earthquake and Resurrection of the Saints	
Chapter 27: 51 . . . and the earth shook, and the rocks were split; 52 the tombs also were opened, and many bodies of the saints who had fallen asleep were raised, 53 and coming out of the tombs after his resurrection they went into the holy city and appeared to many.	(Not Mentioned)	(Not Mentioned)	(Not Mentioned)
		Jesus' Divinity Proclaimed by a Non-Jew	
Chapter 27: 54 When the centurion and those who were with him, keeping watch over Jesus, saw the earthquake and what took place, they were filled with awe, and said, "Truly this was the Son of God!"	Chapter 15: 39 And when the centurion, who stood facing him, saw that he thus breathed his last, he said, "Truly this man was the Son of God!"	Chapter 23: 47 Now when the centurion saw what had taken place, he praised God, and said, "Certainly this man was innocent!" 48 And all the multitudes who assembled to see the sight, when they saw what had taken place, returned home beating their breasts.	(Not Mentioned)

APPENDIX 2

THE GOSPELS

We must understand the background and purpose of the *gospels* to properly interpret their scanty reports of Jesus' several trials.

We do not know the identity of the writers, or exactly when and where they wrote, but the most likely speculations suggest:

Mark:	After 71 A.D.	Rome	For audience of Roman Christians
Matthew:	80-90 A.D.	Alexandria/ Antioch (?)	For audience of Jewish Christians
Luke:	80-95 A.D.	Greece/Syria (?)	For audience of non-Jews
John:	100-120 A.D.	Asia Minor (Ephesus) (?)	For audience of Jews and Greeks

THROUGH THE EYES OF BIBLE SCHOLARS

My presentation is a distillation of the works of biblical scholars, and of necessity involves sorting, selection, and my own subjective conclusions.

ORAL TRADITIONS ABOUT JESUS BECAME DILUTED

Desperate need prompted the writing of the *gospels*, since the oral traditions about Jesus became corrupted in the half-cen-

304

tury following his death: *Harper's Bible Commentary* (*Am. Ed.*) explains:[1]

> But hardly had the new movement (Christianity) reached Rome than its two chief advocates, Peter and Paul, died martyrs' deaths in the first persecution of Christianity by the Romans under Nero in A.D. 64.
>
> Until then the gospel had been spread by the preaching of the missionaries. So long as there were those alive who had been with the Master in Galilee and Jerusalem, and who were able to instruct the younger missionaries in the facts of the gospel story and the words of the Lord, there was no need of written books.
>
> There is good reason to think that before the deaths of Peter and Paul, a beginning had been made to gather collections of the sayings of Jesus, as well as groups of stories and parables and a connected narrative of the Passion, in addition to the Old Testament passages which bore some references to the events of Jesus' life and death.
>
> But with the passing of the first generation of eye-witnesses of the ministry of Jesus, with the expansion of the mission and the increasing demand for authoritative guidance for converts and catechumens, as well as the growing realization that the Second Coming of Christ was not an immediate possibility, the need was felt to have in writing a connected record of the ministry of Jesus, which had previously existed only as illustrative or homiletic material in the sermons of the missionaries.

AVAILABLE SOURCE MATERIALS

Dean Clarence T. Craig, former professor of New Testament in the Yale Divinity School and dean of Drew Theological Seminary, describes the materials available to the gospel writers in *The Beginning of Christianity*:[2]

> Several different classifications of the units of the tradition have been proposed. Personally, I prefer the one given by Dibelius, and it has the added advantage that these units are conveniently printed in his book, *The Message of Jesus Christ*. In addition to the preaching summaries, he makes five classifications of tradition.
>
> (1) *The old stories or paradigms*. These are short incidents which culminate in a word of Jesus, which was useful in the preaching. Some are healing stories; some are controversial incidents. They are usually told with a minimum of detail, and were capable of general application. As a rule, neither the time nor the location figure. The story of plucking of ears of corn on the sabbath (Mark 2:23-28) offers a good example of this type.
>
> (2) *Parables*. These were the most distinctive of the teachings of Jesus and constitute a definite literary form. Most of them have been preserved independent of the original context. In the adaptation of these stories to the new problems of the Christian church, secondary expansions took place. These must be recognized if we are to recover the parables which Jesus spoke. But unquestionably in the parables we find some of the most original of the teaching of Jesus.
>
> (3) *Sayings*. These may be grouped under various topics and types. No long speeches of Jesus were remembered. The short, pithy sayings were collected under various devices for the assistance of the memory. Sometimes a common word joined different sayings, such as the word 'light.' Words about the Pharisees were collected together, or sayings about John the Baptist.

(4) *The great miracle tales.* Here the storyteller's art was developed in the direction of greater detail and delight in incident for its own sake. On the one hand, these were more secular in tone, and on the other hand, they emphasized the marvels which Jesus performed. As we read such a story as the stilling of the waves (Mark 4:35-41), we can see the early Christian teacher in competition with the wonder tales of other religious heroes.

(5) *Legends.* Here are brought together not only stories from the life of a holy man, but what I would rather describe as epiphany stories that is, stories which bring out the divine significance of Jesus.

It should be remembered that this classification is according to type, and does not of itself carry with it any judgment about historicity. It is a mistake to suppose that one can pass directly from a classification according to literary form to a judgment on historical value. Form is only one of the factors to be taken into consideration.

It should never be forgotten that classification is simply a convenient device for facilitating understanding. Individual differences are not removed by classification of the traditions. Yet it is all important for the student to realize that in studying the tradition about Jesus we do not deal primarily with four books.

We deal with literally scores of units of tradition, each of which must be studied by itself. The connecting framework from the later evangelists is much less important for the recovery of Jesus than the separate building stones out of which the gospels have been built. And these had a long history in oral use in the life of the church.

PERHAPS 80 DIFFERENT GOSPELS

Christianity's basic simplicity soon developed into little more than perplexing chaos. We do not know how many "gospels" appeared, possibly hundreds. As late as 350 A.D., one scholar places the number at 80. *Luke* tells us in his introduction (1:1-4) why he decided to write his own version:

> The author to Theophilus: Many writers have undertaken to draw up an account of the events that have happened among us, following the traditions handed down to us by the original eyewitnesses and servants of the Gospel.
>
> And so I in my turn, your Excellency, as one who has gone over the whole course of these events in detail, have decided to write a connected narrative for you, so as to give you authentic knowledge about the matters of which you have been informed.

Other "gospel" writers, no doubt, approached their tasks fully convinced that they, too, gave the "authentic knowledge about the matters of which" they purported to know.

Several Greek Versions

Professor F.F. Bruce, Rylands professor of Biblical criticism, University of Manchester, explains:[3]

> And when he (Papias) adds that every man translated these Logia (sayings of Jesus) as best he could, this suggests that several Greek versions of them were current, which partly explains some of the differences in the sayings of Jesus, common to the first and third Gospels; for in many places where the Greek of these gospels differs, it can be shown that one and the same Aramaic original underlies the variant Greek renderings.

Standardized Forms of Tradition

A few more excerpts from the writings of New Testament

scholars give us greater feel for the character of the *gospels*. We return to Dean Clarence Tucker Craig:[4]

> Behind the earliest of our gospels lies a whole generation of preaching in which the tradition about Jesus was passed on by word of mouth. In this oral tradition, a certain amount of fixity was attained, and some parts may have been committed to writing.

> We are not to think, however, of the production of books, but the serving of the growing needs of the Christian communities. We are not to think of one or two eyewitnesses though of course there were not a few who had memories of the life of Jesus. We are to think of a generation of Christian teachers using more or less standardized forms of tradition.

> This period of oral transmission was most important, though we cannot reconstruct every step without an element of conjecture. It was probably during this period that most of the tradition passed from the Aramaic language, in which Jesus and the first disciples had spoken, to the Greek language, which was the most important one for the developing church.

Teaching Tools

The *gospel* writers produced preaching tools and teaching documents; they never intended crisp, precise, orderly biographies; nor did any of the writers ever intend to create date-filled histories to spell out all the details of the events they reported, such as Jesus' trials and death. Rudolf Bultmann explains the critical teaching thrust in his *Theology of the New Testament*:[5]

> *The message of Jesus* is a presupposition for the theology of the New Testament rather than a part of that theology itself . . . . Christian faith did not exist until there was a Christian *kerygma* (Greek

= "preaching"); i.e., a *kerygma* proclaiming Jesus Christ—specifically Jesus Christ the Crucified and Risen One—to be God's eschatological act of salvation. He was first so proclaimed in the *kerygma* of the earliest Church, not in the message of the historical Jesus, even though that Church frequently introduced into its account of Jesus' message, motifs of its own proclamation.

DIFFERENT SLANTS OF INDIVIDUAL WRITERS

In trying to pull historical information from the *gospels* to help us analyze Jesus' trials, we run into the further problems of the points of view of the different writers, and the audiences they wrote for. Professor Bruce tells us:[6]

All four [*gospels*] relate sayings and doings of Christ, but can scarcely be called biographies in our modern sense of the word, as they deal almost exclusively with the last two or three years of His life, and devote what might seem a disproportionate space to the week immediately preceding His death.

They are not intended to be 'Lives of Christ,' but rather to present four distinctive points of view, and originally for different publics, the good news concerning Him.

Even *Halley's Bible Handbook* (23rd Ed.), which gives the more fundamentalist view in most of its approaches, admits to the editing, selecting and "personality" influences of the individual writers:[7]

For Whom Written. The Four Gospels, ultimately intended for All Mankind, originally written for, or addressed to, certain Churches or individuals. Matthew's original, it is thought, may have been made for the Church in Jerusalem. From it other Churches secured copies. Mark, it is thought, may have intended his book for the Church in Rome. Copies, no doubt, were sent to other Churches. Luke wrote his Gospel for an individual named Theophilus, a high official in the Roman Government. John's Gospel is thought to have been intended originally for the Church in Ephesus. While God inspired these men to write exactly what He wanted them to write, for the use of All Mankind of all generations, yet they themselves must have had in mind the background of their immediate readers; which may have influenced their choice of material.

The Writers' Individualities. While they had their Readers in mind, yet each, in his writing, must have reflected his own personality. They had the Same Story to tell, the Story of a MAN. How He Lived, and What He Did and Said. But each told the Story in his own way, mentioning that which especially appealed to himself; which accounts for the differences in the books.

I attempt my own capsule of the writer's points of view, since I do not find one in the literature completely satisfactory.

Mark's Point of View

Mark, the first of the "official" *gospels*, probably written in Rome for non-Jewish Christians after 71 A.D., faced the great problem of explaining how Jesus could be the "Christ" and the "Son of God," but rejected and killed by mortal man. *Mark* handles this puzzle in two short passages (8:27-30):

> And Jesus went on with his disciples, to the villages of Caesarea Philippi; and on the way he asked his disciples, "Who do men say that I am?"

> And they told him, "John the Baptist; and others say, Elijah; and others one of the prophets."

> And he asked them, "But who do you say that I am?"

> Peter answered him, "You are the Christ."

And he charged them to tell no man.

Scholars label this admonition Jesus' "Messianic Secret."
Mark also lets the centurion at Jesus' crucifixion, a non-Jew,
declare Jesus' special status (15:39):

> And when the centurion, who stood facing him, saw
> that he thus breathed his last, he said, "Truly this
> man was the [a] Son of God."

Matthew's Point of View

Matthew perhaps appeared around 80-85 A.D. for an
audience of Jewish Christians. He relied heavily upon *Mark's*
work, copying many of *Mark's* passages verbatim. His chief thrust:
Jesus fulfilled the "Kingdom of God" as foretold in the Old
Testament, especially by the prophets. Jesus is the "Son of God,"
the new Moses, bringing a "new covenant" to all peoples, Jew as
well as gentile; and if the Jews want to reject Jesus, it doesn't really
matter.

This "Kingdom of God" is the same Messianic concept as
developed in the Old Testament. *Matthew* loads his manuscript
with Jesus' sayings, many of them lumped together in a literary
device we now call the "Sermon on the Mount."

Matthew uses more "sayings" than the other writers.

Luke's Point of View

Luke probably appeared about the same time as *Matthew*,
writing for a community of Greek Christians.

Luke decided that Jesus' "Second Coming," as Jesus
promised, would *not* take place immediately; so the people
should live their lives in Jesus' spirit while they waited.

Luke emphasized Jesus' exemplary character: Kind, loving,
compassionate, concern for *all* humanity (Jew and gentile alike);
a special affinity for the poor, the lowly outcasts, and with the
criminal.

John's Point of View

John came much later, 100-120 A.D., *totally Greek in style,
content, format and thrust*. The book became the keystone for the

312

later development of Christian theology (14:6):

> Jesus said to him, "I am the way, the truth and the life; no one comes to the Father but by me. If you had known me, you would have known my Father also; henceforth, you know him and have seen him."

John may be the most beautifully written book of all time, no doubt the most persuasive. The devout Christian accepts *John's* Jesus on faith, and without reservation.

THE EARLY CHURCH'S NEED FOR ACTION

This great manufacturing of "gospels," and the "heresies" which arose, all but swamped the early church. Should they consider Jesus *all* divine, *all* human, *part*-divine and *part*-human? The Doctrine of the Trinity (God the Father, God the Son, and Holy Ghost) came centuries later.

Harper's Bible Commentary explains their need to act:[8]

> By the second century of the Christian era, there was beginning to appear the type of legendary story about Jesus which always tends to grow up around the life of any saint or holy man. The apocryphal gospels which stem from this period and later, with their wealth of fantastic tales of Jesus' boyhood and miraculous powers, show us how wisely guided the Church was to canonize our four gospels and refuse to recognize any others.

> But in Matthew's gospel—particularly in some of the miraculous events which he records in connection with the Crucifixion and Resurrection—we can see the beginning of the dangerous process when piety begins to invent details to enhance the reputation of the dead.

> The fact that the writer of *Matthew* is content to draw so much of his material from *Mark* makes it quite certain that whoever he was, he was not

Matthew, one of the twelve apostles. No one who had belonged to that select company of the disciples would be willing to accept the secondhand evidence of John Mark, at best a youth on the fringe of Jesus' followers at the time of our Lord's ministry.

An early tradition, however, asserts that Matthew the apostle made a collection of the "oracles" of Jesus, presumably his sayings, and it may be that the teaching of Jesus, which features so prominently in this gospel, was first written down by Matthew whose name thus became attached to the whole gospel.

THE NEW TESTAMENT CANON

The Church developed the New Testament *canon*[9] ("carpenter's ruler"); but it came late and evolved slowly.

Each bishop in his own jurisdiction of Antioch or Alexandria, Constantinople or Rome, *decreed* which "books" could be read in the worship services of his churches; he excluded ("banned") the others.[10] Great theological battles raged over those "sanctified" and those "heretical."[11]

Finally, Athanasius (293-373 A.D.), Bishop of Alexandria, issued his now famous *Easter Letter* in 367 A.D. which included an authorized list of 27 "books."[12] The Council of Laodicea (363 A.D.) earlier gave its blessing to the Athanasius list, with this confirmation repeated by the Councils of Hippo (393 A.D.) and Carthage (397 A.D.).

Acrimonious debate among the bishops doomed the "questionable books, gave holy status to the accepted ones." The Carthage Council ordered:[13]

... none except canonical writings are to be read in church under the title of divine Scripture.

Our *canon* today is the same as Bishop Athanasius' list.[14]

ANTI-JEWISH PREJUDICES OF GOSPEL WRITERS

We dare not ignore two other key points in studying the *gospel* sources for historical help on Jesus' trials: All scholars admit that they contain the biases and prejudices of the writers, and *all are anti-Jewish in reporting Jesus' trials and death.*[15]

The Jewish revolt of 66-70 A.D. embarrassed the Romans terribly, requiring four years and their finest legions to suppress it. How could this new religion sweeping the Mediterranean world be founded on the life of a man crucified by the Roman governor in Judea on the charge of sedition against Rome? The way around this vexing hurdle: Place the blame for Jesus' death on the "the Jews" themselves, and present Roman governor Pilate as the Reluctant Dragon, pushed against his will into doing the dirty work of "the Jews" who wanted to get rid of Jesus on religious grounds only.

INSPIRATION TO THE 20TH CENTURY READER

Finally, we should listen to Professor Fred G. Bratton on the matter of "inspiration" in his excellent *A History of the Bible*:[16]

> To speak of inspiration raises a problem for the twentieth-century reader.

> Are all the Books of the Bible equally inspired?

> A careful scrutiny of the contents will readily convince one that there is a difference in the degree of inspiration .... The men who wrote these books were human and therefore capable of error; yet they were, for the most part, closely akin to the spirit of God and had unusual spiritual genius in their grasp of reality.

> They were able to express truths that stand the test of time and inspire mankind in any age or place. If this can be called inspiration, then it can be said that the Bible is really inspired.

Whatever has the quality of insight that inspires one to a nobler conception of life is inspiring, whether it is regarded as "inspired" or not. Conversely, whatever degrades one's ideas of God, man and human life is palpably uninspiring.

PROBLEMS IN TRANSLATION

Serious problems in translation also impede our efforts to find out what went on at Jesus' trials.

Since John Wycliffe risked his life to produce the Wycliffe Bible in 1380-82, we encounter more than two dozen other translations of the New Testament in English alone.[17]

Tyndale (1525)
Coverdale (1535)
Rogers: Matthews Bible (1537)
Traverner Bible (1539)
Geneva (1557)
Rheims-Douai (1610)
Authorized Version (King James) (1611)
Revised Version (1881-85)
American Standard Version (1901)
Weymouth (1903)
Moffatt (1913-24)
Centenary (1924)
Twentieth Century New Testament (1901-04)
The Holy Scriptures (1917)
Ballantine (1923)
Basic English (1941)
Goodspeed (1923)
Phillips (1958)
Rieu (1953-57)
New Testament in Modern English (1958)
Jerusalem (1966)
Today's English Version (1966)
New English (1970)
New American (1970)
New American Standard (1971)
The Living Bible (1971)
New International Edition (1973)
New World (Revised) (1973)

The "Original" Manuscripts

The goal of each translation is to reach back to the "original" scriptures, to make them more meaningful to each generation of readers by adapting the latest developments of language and communication skills; but each translation must follow a tortuous path backwards to the "originals" or fragments of the "originals."[18] None of them now available goes back before the latter part of the fourth century, some 300 years after the life and death of Jesus.

This skimpy outline of the "official," "original" manuscripts shows the problems:[19]

Greek Manuscripts:
Codex Sinaiticus (4th, or perhaps 5th cent.): Old and New Testaments, plus Epistle of Barnabas and Shepard of Herman = Alexandrian text.
Codex Alexandrinus (5th cent.): Both testaments plus noncanon writings.
Codex Vaticanus (4th cent.): Considered best extant text of New Testament.
Codex Ephraemi (5th cent.): Mixed type of text.
Codex Bezae Cantabrigiensis (6th cent., perhaps 5th): Bilingual (Greek and Latin) in Western text.
Washington (Freer) Manuscript (5th cent.): Four types of text.
Koridethi Gospels (7th to 9th cent.): Text is Caesarean and Byzantine.
The "Lake Group" (minuscules, 118, 131, 209, etc.) (10th to 12th cent.): Place of origin unknown.
The "Ferrar Group" (minuscules 13, 69, 124, 346, etc.) (11th to 12th cent.): Parent manuscript unknown.
The "Koine" or "Byzantine" text (EFGH etc. and most minuscules) (late 3rd cent. Antioch): Popular Greek text for several centuries.

Papyri:
Philadelphia Papyrus (3rd cent.)
Vienna Papyrus (6th-7th cent.)

Paris Papyrus (3rd cent.)
Berlin Papyrus (3rd cent.)
Ann Arbor Papyrus (3rd-4th cent.)
Dublin Papyrus (3rd cent., Chester Beatty Collection)
Barcelona Papyrus (ca. 200 A.D.)
Geneva Papyrus (ca. 200 A.D., Bodmer Collection)

Versions of New Testament:
Itala (the Old Latin version before Jerome's Vulgate = these manuscripts were African, European and Italian)
Vulgate (Jerome = 383 A.D.)
The Old Syriac (edited by Cureton, 1858)
The Sinaitic Syriac (discovered in 1892)
The Peshitta Syriac version (ed. by G.H. Gwilliam, 1901)
The Sahidic version (ed. by G. Horner, 1911)
The Bohairic version (ed. by G. Horner, 1898)

Different scholars consult some 2,500 "original" vellum and papyrus manuscripts, no two identical.[20] These range from complete "Bibles" or "Testaments," down to fragments of a verse or two, a chapter, or a part of a single "book."

Locations of "Original" Manuscripts

The manuscripts rest in such diverse locations[21] as the Coptic Institute (Coptic Church) in Cairo; the British Museum, London; the Vatican Library, Vatican City; University of Michigan, Ann Arbor; Pacific School of Religion, Berkeley; Trinity College, Cambridge; Historical Museum, Moscow; Houghton National Biblical Library, Harvard University; Smithsonian Institution, Washington; National Biblical Library, Paris; and two dozen other likely and unlikely places around the world.

Nothing exists even vaguely resembling an "official" repository for "original" Bible manuscripts.[22]

Nor do we use any official "*canon*" for these or any other "original" manuscripts. Various Bible scholars accord varying weight to the different manuscripts, with subjective bias and prejudice entering in.

MUST USE OUTSIDE SOURCES

We must use all the outside sources at our command to discover what happened in Jesus' trials, not to re-write the *gospels*, but to interpret them correctly, so that we know what *Matthew, Mark, Luke* and *John* try to tell us.

APPENDIX 3

THE TALMUD

Our interest in the *talmud*[1] involves mainly its *mishnah* portion which is the same in both the Jerusalem and Babylonia *talmuds*, much less in the *gemarah* part which came much later, although the *gemarah* helps in many interpretations.

I work with the Soncino Press (London) English translation which contains the Babylonian *talmud's* 2-1/2 million words, divided into 63 separate volumes ("tractates"), and 524 chapters, in 18 bound volumes.

Simply stated, the *talmud* gives us the Common Law of the Jews: Legal case reports, history, parables, sermons, legends, customs, medicine and stories.

BASIC QUESTION: DID RULES OF "DUE PROCESS" OPERATE AT JESUS' TIME?

One basic question controls our study: Did the "due process of Law" requirements we find in the *talmud* we work with today apply at Jesus' time and to his trials?

I answer with a resounding, "Yes, indeed!"

Legal Fiction of Source of Oral Law

We saw in Chapter 12, "Cross-Examination: The *Warning*," how Jewish traditions traced the Oral law (outside the written *torah*) all the way back to Moses at Mt. Sinai (1250 B.C.), down through Ezra's Great Synagogue (450-400 B.C.), to the learned academies, and to the judges sitting on the Court of the Temple Mount and the Great Sanhedrin during Jesus trials.

Obviously, this attitude involves considerable legal fiction: Legal systems cannot remain static; they must change to meet their society's changing needs. No group of legal minds, sociologists or political scientists (regardless of their era) can anticipate all these changes, then design laws to meet them *centuries in advance.* It is not realistic, therefore, to say that God's Law decreed in 1250 B.C. covered each and every need of the people as they moved from their nomadic wanderings in the desert, to become herdsmen and farmers, then traders and merchants, and finally city dwellers.

Although based firmly on the *torah*, the Oral Law of the Pharisees at the time of Jesus' trials in the Court of the Temple Mount and the Great Sanhedrin in the Hall of the Hewn Stone required a millennium to gel, as judges, elders and those learned in the Law worked out rules and procedures to protect the whole nation from within and without, and to let its people live their individual lives as freely as possible.

GENESIS OF PRESENT TALMUD

In his classic, *On Jewish Law and Lore*, scholar Louis Ginzberg gives this helpful insight:[2]

> No student of post-biblical literature (after the "canon" was closed) can fail to be struck by the fact that it is interpretative and commemorative.

> The literature of a people, however, is but a mirror of the ideas which rule that people, and in post-biblical times, the idea of "the Book" was all-powerful among the Jews. Nehemiah records a covenant entered into under the guidance of Ezra: "To walk in God's Law which was given by Moses, the servant of God and His ordinances and His statutes."

> By this solemn act, a "book"—the Pentateuch—became the written constitution of the new commonwealth [around 400 B.C.], its code of laws, and its way of life.

But a dead letter needs to be made living by interpretation. Hence the interpretative character of the post-biblical writings.

Old Talmudic sources call the spiritual leaders of Israel in the centuries between Ezra (about 450) and the age of the Maccabeans (175) *Soferim*, which means "men of the Book," interpreters of sacred Scripture, and not, as it is usually translated, "scribes." . . .

The enormous mass of "interpretation" thus accumulated during the centuries of the *Soferim* was further augmented in the century of the Jewish free state under the Hasmoneans . . .

The strong national feeling engendered by the victorious wars in defense of Jewish religion and morals led to ordinances and regulations aimed at the complete isolation of Israel from the surrounding world. At the same time, the development of commerce and trade under the Hasmonean rulers peremptorily called for the building up of a code of civil law. The few rules found in the Scripture bearing on this branch of the law were not sufficient and could not be made so, not even by the most subtle reasoning or the cleverest interpretation.

The time was certainly ripe for legislation . . . But how dare one tamper with sacred Scripture, in which the Divine Will is revealed?

The sages and scholars of that time about the middle of the Hasmonean era [120-90 B.C.] had the necessary temerity. They took a very important step towards formulating what might be called *de facto* though not *de jure*, a new code – they created the *Mishnah*.

These earlier scholars knew only one subject of study – scripture; their comments and interpretations were interwoven with the text, interpreted and commented upon.

The creators of the *Mishnah* detached the enormous bulk of unwieldy material from the biblical passages and studied it independently.

The new method was not only highly practical, since the numerous laws based on interpretation of Scriptural passages could now be studied in a concise and systematic way, but it also gave "the oral law" an independent existence.

Hitherto the law, practices, and customs that had no Scriptural basis could only be studied by being connected in one way or another with some text in Scripture. *Yet many of these orally transmitted laws and customs were as old as the oldest found in Scripture, and were no less revered by the people.* [Emphasis added.]

In the mishnaic method of study, a difference between the written *Torah* and the oral *Torah* hardly exists. The origins of the *Mishnah* and the rise at the same time of a militant Sadduceeism which reacted against over-emphasis of the oral law certainly stand in some causal nexus, though it is hard to tell which is the cause and which the effect.

The final compilation of the *Mishnah* toward the end of the second century C.E. (Common Era) [A.D.] by the Patriarch R. Judah completed a work at which scholars had labored for *three hundred years.* [Emphasis added.]

Early Attempts to Codify Oral Law

Another Jewish legal scholar, Hyman Goldin, adds his authority in *Hebrew Criminal Law and Procedure:*[3]

The code of Jewish traditional law, known as the "Mishnah" *par excellence*, was codified by Rabbi Judah ha-Nasi (born 135 C.E.)[A.D.]. It cannot be doubted, however, that an attempt to codify the *halakah* (Law), the traditional Law, was made by Jewish jurists at a much earlier date.

At what date the earlier or first Mishnah, the *Mishnah Rishonah* alluded to in the present Mishnah, first began to take definite form, cannot be stated with exactitude.

Isaac Halevy (*Berliner Magazin*, 1886) would have it that the beginnings of the first codification go back to the time of the Men of the Great Assembly, Ecclesia Magna, a supreme authority established under Ezra and Nehemiah (*circa* 450 B.C.E.)[B.C.]. M. Lerner (*Berliner Magazin*, 1886, pp. 1-20) believes that Hillel the Elder, and his contemporary Shammai, before the destruction of the second Temple (*circa* 32 B.C.E.), edited a Mishnah; while M. Hoffman (*Die Erste Mishnah und die Controversen der Tannaim*, Berlin, 1882) is of the opinion that an attempt to embody the *halakah* into a code was first made by the *Zikne Bet Shammai*, and the *Zikne Bet Hillel*, the elders of the school of Shammai and the elders of the School of Hillel [contemporaries of Jesus].

Thereafter the synod of Jabneh (Jamnia = 90-95 C.E.), under the presidency of Rabban Gamaliel II, and Rabbi Eleazar ben Azarish, immediately after the destruction of the second Temple by Titus, undertook to collect their wording and their differences; thus, there arose the collection of laws known as *Eduyot* (*Berakot*, 28a).

About a half century later, Rabbi Akiba undertook to make a methodical arrangement of the mass of laws incorporated in the *Eduyot* collection. He sifted the vast traditional material, and edited a systematic collection, known as *Mishnah Rabbi Akiba*, by arranging different subjects in different treatises (Sanhedrin 86b; Abbot d' Rabbi Nathan, XVIII,1).

The Look Backward for Legal Precedent

By way of summary, we can trace the due process and substantive law provisions of "*the mishnah*" of Judah ha-Nasi (180-200 A.D.) which we work with today all the way back to centuries before Jesus' trials, back through the *mishnah Rabbi Akiba* (50-130 A.D.) which arranged the *eduyot* collection of the synod of Jabneh (Jamnia = 90-95 A.D.), back through the academies of Shammai and Hillel (older contempories of Jesus) who gave us the present divisions of "*the mishnah*," back to the first *mishnah*, the *mishnah rishonah*, at the time of the Men of the Great Assembly under Ezra and Nehemiah (450 B.C.), which took its life and words from the *torah* of Moses and his worthy successors.

We can rely on this continuity because "*the mishnah*" specifically refers to the earlier ones, the editors bound by the concept of *precedent* as the natural offspring of the Covenant Constitution, *precedent* to guide and bind the judges as they decided actual cases that came before them. Ever the look backward in search of the prior rule, that rule a part of God's divine Law.

Rabbi Judah The Prince and his associate editors approached their compilation of "*the mishnah*" the same way modern revisers tackle local, state and Federal law codes, in efforts to simplify and "modernize" them; but the fascinating results of all these revisions is not the novel, creative, innovative changes they produce, rather how much everything remains the same.

The Reluctance to Change

Ancient peoples accepted change far less than we do today, living by the *mos maiorum*[4]: "The way of the ancients." No one would dare tamper with God's basic rules of "due process" which sprang from the *torah* over the centuries before Jesus' trials.

Our own criminal codes today remain basically the same as at the adoption of the U.S. Constitution in 1789, and differ only slightly from the laws of Elizabethan England. We can trace some provisions all the way back to the great Codes of Ancient Israel, evolved long before Jesus' time.

No one ever created a new legal system in advance; law systems evolve and mature over a period of centuries; and the look is always backward.

Ancient Definition of Murder Holds Today

Take the definition of murder, for example. We find almost identical language in the criminal codes of all fifty United States, the court decisions interpreting the code provisions flowing from the same mold. *California Penal Code* section 189 is typical:

> All murder which is perpetrated by . . . *lying in wait* . . . is murder in the first degree.

The phrase "lying in wait" comes right out of *Deuteronomy* 19:11:

> If a man hates his neighbor, and *lies in wait* for him, and attacks him, and wounds him mortally . . . then the elders of his city shall send and fetch him from there, and hand him over to the avenger of blood, so that he may die. [Emphasis added.]

Fourth Amendment comes from Deuteronomy

Americans pride themselves on the Fourth Amendment to the U.S. Constitution which makes them "secure in their persons, houses, papers and effects against unreasonable searches and seizures." Many think its source the English Bill of Right of 1689, or the Magna Carta of 1215. Actually, its rationale also comes from *Deuteronomy* (24:10):

> When you make your neighbor a loan of any sort, *you shall not go into his house* to fetch his pledge. *You shall stand outside*, and the man to whom you make the loan shall bring his pledge out to you. [Emphasis added.]

Murder Victim Must Die Within Year

Another Common Law rule holds that if the victim of an assault does not die within one year, the assailant cannot be prosecuted for murder, even if the death takes place the day after the year passes. Proof of the medical cause of death is unreliable in most cases where the victim lingers past 365 days after the assault, the danger of a miscarriage of justice too great to take a chance on convicting an innocent man. We find the rationale for the rule in *Exodus* 21:18-20:

> When men quarrel and one strikes the other with a stone or with his fist and the man does not die but keeps his bed, then if the man rises again and walks abroad with his staff, he that struck him shall be clear; only he shall pay for the loss of his time, and shall have him thoroughly healed.

> When a man strikes his slave, male or female, with the rod and the slave dies under his hand, he shall be punished. But if the slave survives a day or two, he is not to be punished;

BASIC "DUE PROCESS" COMES FROM TORAH

The basic "due process" requirements come from the *torah* whose canon closed centuries before Jesus' time. I repeat here only a few specific citations:

"Due process" generally: *Numbers* 35:12

No double jeopardy: *Exodus* 23:7

Open, public trials: *Deuteronomy* 16:18

Proscriptions against false witness: *Deuteronomy* 19:16-19

No condemnation on the testimony of only a single witness: *Deuteronomy* 19:15

The Common Law cases reported in the *talmud (mishnah)* merely interpret and flesh-out the ancient Law Codes in the *torah*.

ACUTE NEED TO WRITE ORAL LAW CAME IN 70 A.D.

The acute need to reduce the centuries of Oral Law to writing came in 70 A.D., the Romans finally crushing the Jewish War of Independence (66-70). This ended the Temple Clique and all the Sadducees: We hear not a word from any of them again!

The Pharisees saw that for Judaism to survive, they must drastically change its Oral Law format. Tradition holds that conspirators smuggled Rabbi Jachanon ben Zakkai through the Roman lines in a coffin, landing him in Jabneh (Jamnia) west of Jerusalem, where he and his group of scholars began work on the *mishnah* which finally reached Judah The Prince's "the *mishnah*" which we find today.

Again, they looked backward less than a year, to record the Laws and rulings during the days of the Temple, of the Jewish courts including the Courts of Twenty-Three and the Great Sanhedrin which sat in the Hall of the Hewn Stone. The goal: Record and preserve, so that the defeated and dispersed nation could live as nearly like the olden days as possible, save one great difference: The Temple would probably never be restored!

This explains why they went to such great pains to write down the details of the various courts during the Temple era: Court of the Three; Court of the Twenty-Three; the Great Sanhedrin; where they sat; in what bench arrangement; their jurisdiction; who could serve as judges; court etiquette; rules of procedure; their format of debating the Law; and above all, the substantive "due process" requirements evolved over 1200 years before.

To say, as some critics do, that the producers of all the various *mishnahs* (Judah the Prince worked with as many as thirteen earlier ones to compose his lasting masterpiece) sat around and dreamed up some "Utopian" legal system that never knew practical life in a real nation, shows the critics' lack of knowledge of legal history generally, and the exacting goals of the writers of the *mishnahs* specifically.

APPENDIX 4

JEWISH COURT ORGANIZATION AT THE TIME OF JESUS' TRIALS

The *talmud's* Fourth Division, *nezikin* ("damages") furnishes the bulk of our knowledge of the organization of the Jewish courts during the Second Temple era, although other chapters contain scattered cases and rulings.

Of the Fourth Division's ten tractates (chapters), *sanhedrin* and *makkoth* ("stripes") serve as our detailed sources on what we now call criminal matters.

The organization of our Anglo-American courts in both civil and criminal matter is patterned almost exactly on the ancient Jewish model, and based on the concept of *jurisdiction*,[1] the power and authority of a court to act.[2]

The Court of Three[3] exercised the same type of "limited jurisdiction" as our present-day municipal courts, justice courts, magistrate's courts, police courts or courts of special sessions. Situated throughout the countryside in rigidly drawn judicial districts (as well as sitting in Jerusalem), the Courts of Three tried civil cases: Charges of seduction, slander, suits on indemnity, bailments, the valuation of slaves, the redemption of pledges, fourfold and fivefold restitution; and lesser transgressions punishable by flagellation.

The Court of Three also held preliminary hearings in more serious criminal cases, to see whether they should be expanded into a trial by a larger court.

The Court of Twenty-Three (*bet din*), also called the Small

Sanhedrin, served as the court of "general jurisdiction,"[4] comparable to the U.S. district courts, superior courts, circuit courts, recorder's courts and England's High Courts.

The Great Sanhedrin[5] (*bet din ha-gadol*), also called the Court of the Seventy-One, functioned as the highest court of the land, comparable in almost every respect to the United States Supreme Court (except the number of judges). Sitting in the Hall of the Hewn Stone, it heard appeals from the inferior courts throughout the nation.

Additionally, it could try (original trial jurisdiction) cases involving:[6]

(1)   An idolatrous tribe;

(2)   The false prophet;

(3)   The rebellious elder; and

(4)   Offenses committed by the High Priest himself.[7]

Since Courts of the Twenty-Three of the several tribes (by this time, administrative districts) could be organized only by a decision of the Great Sanhedrin, it held supervisory powers over the entire judicial system.[8]

AUTHORITIES CITED

— A —

ABRAHAMS, I.: *Studies in Pharisaism and the Gospels*, KTAV Pub. House, N.Y. (1967).

Aid to Bible Understanding, Watch Tower Bible and Tract Society, Brooklyn (1971).

All Scripture Is Inspired of God and Beneficial, Watch Tower Bible and Tract Society of New York, Brooklyn (1963).

ARETAEUS: *On the Causes and Indications of Acute and Chronic Diseases (4 Vol.); On the Treatment of Acute and Chronic Diseases (4 Vol.)*. (Early Greek Physician).

ARGYLE, A. W.: *The Gospel According to Matthew*, Cambridge University Press, England (1963).

ARMSTRONG, April Ousler: *The Tales Christ Told*, Doubleday, Garden City (1958).

AVI-YONAH, Michael: *2nd Temple Reconstruction (Holyland Hotel)*, Jerusalem (1966).

— *The Holy Land*, Thames and Hudson, London (1972).

— B —

BAECK, Leo: *The Pharisees and Other Essays*, Schocken Books, New York (1966).

BAMMEL, Ernest: *The Trial of Jesus*, SCM Press Ltd., London (1970).

BARBET, Pierre: *A Doctor at Calvary (translated by the Earl of Wicklow)*, P. J. Kenedy & Sons, New York (1953).

BARCLAY, William: *The Bible and History*, Abingdon Press, Nashville (1968).

BERGER, Adolf: *Encyclopedic Dictionary of Roman Law*, The Philosophical Society, Philadelphia (1953).

BIRCHALL, Ann Corbett, P.E.: *Greek Gods and Heroes*, British Museum Publications, London (1974).

BISHOP, Jim: *The Day Christ Died*, Harper, New York (1957).

Black's Law Dictionary, West Pub. Co., St. Paul (1968).

BLINZLER, J.: *The Trial of Jesus*, E. T., Cork (1959).

BRANDON, S. G. F.: *Jesus and the Zealots*, Scribner's Sons, New York (1967).

— *The Trial of Jesus of Nazareth*, Dorset Press, New York (1968).

BRATTON, Fred G.: *A History of the Bible*, Beacon Press, Boston (1967).

BRIGHT, John: *A History of Israel*, Westminster Press, Philadelphia (1959).

BRUCE, F.: *New Testament Documents. Are They Reliable?* Wm. Eerdmans Pub. Co., Grand Rapids (1960.

BRUNNER, Theodore: *The Sedecula on the Cross: Literary Evidence in Support of the Giv'at ha miyar Find*, L.A. *Times*, Aug. 1, 1971, Sec. C, pg. 1.

BUCHLER, Adolf: *Types of Jewish-Palestinian Piety from 70 B. C. E. to 70 C. E. The Ancient Pious Man*, Jews College, London (1922).

BUCKLAND, W. W.: *A Text-Book of Roman Law from Augustus to Justinian*, University Press, Cambridge (1962).

BULTMANN, Rudolf: *Theology of the New Testament*, Scribner's Sons, New York (1955).

BURNS, Edward McNall: *Western Civilization (7th Ed.)*, W. W. Norton, New York (1968).

BURROWS, Millar: *The Dead Sea Scrolls*, Viking Press, New York (1955).

– C –

CARMICHAEL, M. A.: *The Death of Jesus*, Macmillan Company, New York (1962).

CECIL, Russell L. and LOEB, Robert F.: *A Textbook of Medicine*, W. B. Saunders, Philadelphia (1959).

CHANDLER, Walter M.: *The Trial of Jesus—From a Lawyer's Standpoint*, Harrison Company, Publishers, Atlanta (1956).

COHEN, A.: *Everyman's Talmud*, E. P. Dutton & Co., New York (1949).

COHN, Haim: *The Trial and Death of Jesus*, Harper & Row, New York (1971).

CRAIG, Clarence T.: *The Beginning of Christianity*, Abingdon Press, Nashville (1953).

CULLMANN, Oscar: *Salvation in History*, SCM Press, Ltd., London (1967).

CUMONT, Franz: *The Mysteries of Mithra*, Dover Publications, Inc., New York (1956).

– D –

DANBY, Herbert: *The Mishnah*, Oxford University Press, England (1933).

DANIEL-ROPS, Henri: *Daily Life in the Time of Jesus*, The New American Library, New York (1964).

DAUBE, David: *Collaboration with Tyranny in Rabbinic Law*, Oxford University Press, London (1963).

—*Roman Law—Linguistic, Social and Philosophical Aspects*, University Press, Edinburgh (1969).

—*Studies in Biblical Law*, KTAV Publishing House, New York (1960).

DEPASQUALE, Nicholas P., BURCH, George E.: *Death by Crucifixion*, American Heart Journal 66:3 (1963).

DERRETT, J. Duncan M.: *Law in the New Testament*, Atheneum Press, N. Y. (1976).

DE VAUX, Roland: *Ancient Israel, Its Life and Institutions*, Darton, Longman & Todd, London (1973).

DIXON, Roger: *The Christ Trial*, Pinnacle Books, New York (1973).

DODD, C. H.: *Historical Traditions In the Fourth Gospel*, Cambridge University Press, England (1965).

DOMINICK, Mabel A.: *The Bible and the Historical Design*, Plimpton Press, Norwood, Massachusetts (1936).

DURANT, Will: *The Story of Civilization: Part III: Caesar and Christ*, Simon and Schuster, New York (1944).

— E —

EDERSHEIM, Alfred: *The Life and Times of Jesus the Messiah*, Wm. Eerdmans, Pub., Grand Rapids (1971).

— *The Temple (Its Ministry and Services)*, Wm. Eerdmans Pub. Co., Grand Rapids (1958).

EHRLICH, J. W.: *The Holy Bible and the Law*, Oceana Publications, New York (1962).

Encyclopedia Britannica, Encyclopedia Britannica, Inc., Chicago (1974).

Encyclopaedia Judaica, Keter Pub. House, Jerusalem (1971).

EPSTEIN, Rabbi I. (Ed.): *The Babylonian Talmud*, Soncino Press, London (1935).

EUSEBIUS: *Ecclesiastical History*, English translation by Lake, Harvard University Press, Cambridge (1926).

— F —

FINEGAN, Jack: *Encountering New Testament Manuscripts (A Working Introduction to Textual Criticism)*, Wm. Eerdmans Pub. Co., Grand Rapids (1974).

FINKEL, Asher: *The Pharisees and the Teacher of Righteousness*, E. J. Brill, Leiden/Koln, Leiden (1874).

FINKELSTEIN, Louis: *Akiba — Scholar, Saint and Martyr*, Atheneum Press, New York (1970).

— *Pharisaism in the Making*, KTAV Pub. House, New York (1972).

— *The Jews — Their History (4th Ed.)*, Schocken, New York (1972).

FLUSSER, David: *Jesus*, Herder and Herder, N. Y. (1960).

FREEDMAN, H. and SIMON, Maurice: *Midrash Rabba*, The Soncino Press, London (1939).

FULLER, Reginald H.: *The Formation of the Resurrection Narratives*, SPCK, London (1972).

— G —

GERSH, Harry: *The Sacred Books of the Jews*, Stein and Day, New York (1968).

334

GERSHFIELD, Edward M.: *Studies in Jewish Jurisprudence*, Hermon Press, New York (1971).

GINZBERG, Louis: *On Jewish Law and Lore*, Jewish Publication Society, Philadelphia (1955).

— *The Legends of the Jews*, Jewish Publication Society, Philadelphia (1925).

GOGUEL, Maurice: *Jesus and the Origins of Christianity*, Harper and Brothers, New York (1933).

GOLDIN, Hyman E.: *Hebrew Criminal Law and Procedure*, Twayne Pub., New York (1952).

GOLDIN, Judah: *The Living Talmud*, New American Library, New York (1955).

GOODENOUGH, Erwin R.: *Jewish Symbols in the Greco-Roman Period (13 Vols.)*, Princeton University Press, New Jersey (1968).

GORMAN, Ralph: *The Last Hours of Jesus*, Sheed & Ward, New York (1960).

GRAETZ, Heinrich: *History of the Jews (6 Vols.)*, The Jewish Publication Society of America, Philadelphia (1893).

GRANT, Michael: *Jesus — A Historian's View of the Gospels*, Scribner's Sons, New York (1977).

— *The Army of the Caesars*, Scribner's Sons, New York (1974).

— *The Jews and the Roman World*, Scribner's Sons, New York (1973)

GRANT, Robert: *A Historical Introduction to the New Testament*, Collins, London (1963).

GRAYZEL, Solomon: *A History of the Jews*, The New American Library, New York (1967).

GREENSLADE, S. L.: *The Cambridge History of the Bible*, England (1963).

GUIGNEBERT, Charles: *Ancient, Medieval and Modern Christianity*, University Books, New Hyde Park, New York (1961).

— *Jesus*, University Books, New Hyde Park, New York (1956).

— *The Jewish World in the Time of Jesus*, University Books, New Hyde Park, New York (1959).

— H —

Halley's Bible Handbook, Zondervan Pub. House, Grand Rapids (1927-1965).

HERFORD, R. Travers: *The Ethics of the Talmud: Sayings of the Fathers*, Schocken Books, New York (1962).

HERSCHEL, Abraham J.: *The Prophets*, The Jewish Publication Society of America, Philadelphia (1962).

HOEHNER, Harold W.: *Herod Antipas*, Cambridge University Press, England (1972).

HOSKYNS, Sir Edwyn and DAVEY, Noel: *The Riddle of the New Testament Documents, Are They Reliable?* Wm. Eerdmans Pub. Co., Grand Rapids (1943).

HOUTS, Marshall: *From Evidence to Proof*, Charles C Thomas, Springfield (1956).

— *Lawyer's Guide to Medical Proof (4 Vols.)*, Matthew Bender & Co., New York (1966-1989).

HUNTER, Archibald M.: *The Parables Then and Now*, Westminster Press, Philadelphia (1971).
— *The Gospel According to John*, Cambridge University Press, London (1965).
HUNTER, William A.: *Introduction to Roman Law*, Sweet & Maxwell, London (1934).

— J —

JAUBERT, Annie: *The Date of the Last Supper*, Alba House, Staten Island, New York (1965).
JEREMIAS, Joachim: *Jerusalem in the Time of Jesus*, SCM Press, London (1960).
— *The Parables of Jesus*, SCM Press, London (1972).
— *The Prayers of Jesus*, SCM Press, Ltd., London (1974).
— *Rediscovering the Parables*, Scribner's Sons, New York (1966).
JOHNSON, Paul: *A History of Christianity*, Atheneum Press, New York (1976).
JOLOWICZ, H. H. and NICHOLAS, Barry: *Historical Introduction to the Study of Roman Law*, University Press, Cambridge (1972).
Josephus (translations this bibliography by Whiston and Thackery.)

— K —

KADUSHIN, Rabbi J.: *Jewish Code of Jurisprudence: Talmudic Law Decisions*, The Jewish Jurisprudence Co., New Rochelle (1923).
KAUFMANN, Yehezkel: *The Religion of Israel*, Schocken Books, New York (1972).
KENT, Charles Foster: *Israel's Laws and Legal Precedents*, Scribner's Sons, New York (1907).
KENYON, Kathleen: *Royal Cities of the Old Testament*, Barrie & Jenkins, London (1971).
KILPATRICK, G. D.: *The Trial of Jesus*, Friends of Dr. Williams' Library, London (1953).
KINNEY, John M., DECOSSE, Jerome J., et al.: *Medicine Updates Trauma: Now A Disease Entity, Trauma, Vol. 15., No. 2*, Matthew Bender & Co., New York (1973).
KITOV, Eliyahu: *The Book of Our Heritage*, Feldheim Publishers, Jerusalem (1973).
KLAUSNER, Joseph: *The Messianic Idea in Israel from its Beginning to the Completion of the Mishnah*, George Allen and Unwin, London (1943).
— *Jesus of Nazareth*, The Macmillan Campany, New York (1926).
KUNKEL, Wolfgang: *An Introduction to Roman Legal and Constitutional History*, Clarendon Press, Oxford (1973).

–L–

LADD, George Eldon: *Jesus and the Kingdom*, World Books, Waco (1964).

LARUE, Gerald A.: *Old Testament Life and Literature*, Allyn and Bacon, Inc., Boston (1968).

LIGHTFOOD, Neil R.: *Lessons from the Parables*, Baker Book House, Grand Rapids (1965).

LINNEMANN, Eta: *Jesus of the Parables*, Harper & Row, New York (1966).

–M–

MACROBIUS: *Saturnalia* II, 4, 11.

MAERTENS, Thierry: *Bible Themes (A Source Book)*, Darton, Longman & Todd, London (1964).

MAIER, Paul L.: *First Easter– The True and Unfamiliar Story*, Harper & Row, New York (1973).

MANTEL, Hugo: *Studies in the History of the Sanhedrin*, Harvard University Press, Cambridge (1965).

MARMOR, Leonard, M. D.: *"Shock," Trauma, Vol. 13, No. 1*, Matthew Bender & Co., New York (1971).

MATTHEWS, I. G.: *The Religious Pilgrimage of Israel*, Harper & Brothers, New York (1947).

MC RUER, J. C.: *The Trial of Jesus*, Blandford Press, London (1964).

MENDELSOHN, S.: *The Criminal Jurisprudence of the Ancient Hebrews*, Hermon Press, New York (1968).

Mishna, The (see DANBY, Herbert. and EPSTEIN, Rabbi I., this bibliography)

MOORE, George Foote: *Judaism In the First Centuries of the Christian Era, (3 Vols.)*, Harvard University Press, Cambridge (1927).

MOULE, C. F. D.: *The Gospel According to Mark*, Cambridge University Press, London (1965).

MOWINCKEL, Sigmund: *The Psalms in Israel's Worship*, Oxford University Press, England (1962).

MOWRY, Lucetta: *The Dead Sea Scrolls and the Early Church*, University of Notre Dame Press, London (1962).

–N–

NAMARA, Martin: *Targum and Testament. (Aramaic Phrases of the Hebrew Bible: A Light on the New Testament)*, Wm. Eerdmans Pub., Grand Rapids (1968).

NEGENMAN, Jan H.: *New Atlas of the Bible, (Ed. by H. H. Rowley)*, Doubleday & Company, Inc., Garden City, New York (1969).

NEIL, William: *Harper's Bible Commentary*, Harper & Row, New York (1962).

NEUSNER, Jacob: *Invitation to the Talmud*, Harper & Row, New York (1973).

– *The Rabbinic Traditions About the Pharisees Before 70 (3 Vols.)*, E. J. Brill, Leiden (1971).

— P —

PAUL, Shalom M. and DEVER, William G.: *Biblical Archaeology*, Keter Pub. House, Jerusalem (1973).

Pentateuch and Haftorahs — (Hebrew Text/English Translation/and Commentary), Soncino Press, London (1973).

PEROWNE, S.: *The Life and Times of Herod the Great*, Hodder and Stroughton, London (1956).

PETRACOS, Basil Chr.: *Delphi*, Hesperus Ed., Athens (1971).

PHILLIPS, Anthony: *Ancient Israel's Criminal Law*, Schocken Books, New York (1970).

PHILO: *The Embassy to Gaius*, Loeb Classical Library, Harvard University Press, Cambridge (1971).

PRAT, Ferdinand: *Jesus Christ, His Life, His Teaching and His Work (2 Vols.)*, Bruce Pub. Co., Milwaukee (1950).

PRITCHARD, James B.: *Ancient Near Eastern Texts Relating to the Old Testament*, Princeton University Press, New York (1969).

— R —

REICKE, Bo: *The New Testament Era. The World of the Bible from 500 B.C. to A.D. 100*, Adam & Charles Black, London (1964).

RHYMER, Joseph: *The Bible in Order*, Doubleday, Garden City (1975).

ROBINSON, H. Wheeler: *The Religious Ideas of the Old Testament*, Scribner's Sons, New York (1919).

ROWLEY, H. H.: *The Faith of Israel*, SCM Press, London (1956).

RUBENS, Alfred: *A History of Jewish Costume*, Funk & Wagnalls, New York (1967).

RUCKSTUHL, Eugen: *Chronology of the Last Days of Jesus*, Desclee Co., New York (1965).

RUNES, Dagobart D.: *The Talmud of Jerusalem*, Philosophical Library, New York (1956).

RUSSELL, D. S.: *The Jews from Alexander to Herod*, (New Clarendon Bible), Oxford University Press, England (1967).

— S —

Sabbath and Festival Prayer Book, The Rabbinical Assembly of American and the United Synagogues of American, New York (1974).

SALM, C. Luke: *Studies in Salvation History*, Prentice-Hall, Englewood Cliffs, New Jersey (1964).

SAPIR, Baruch and NEEMAN, Dov: *Capernaum (Kfar-Nachum)*, Historical Sites Library, Tel-Aviv (1967).

SARNA, Nahum: *Understanding Genesis*, Schocken Books, New York (1970).

SCHAUSS, Hayyim: *The Jewish Festivals*, Union of American Hebrew Congregations, New York (1930).

SCHMIDT, J. E.: *Attorneys' Dictionary of Medicine and Word Finder*, Matthew Bender & Co., New York (1971-1989).

SCHULZ, Fritz: *Classical Roman Law*, Adam and Charles Black, London (1954).

SCHURER, Emil: *A History of the Jewish People (2nd Ed.)*, Edinburgh (1891).

Self-Pronouncing Edition of the Holy Bible, The World Syndicate Pub. Co., Cleveland.

SENDREY, Alfred: *Music in Ancient Israel*, Philosophical Library, New York (1969).

SHERWIN-WHITE, A. N.: *Roman Society and Roman Law in the New Testament*, Clarendon Press, Oxford (1961).

SMITH, Wilbur M.: *The Biblical Doctrine of Heaven*, Moody Press, Chicago (1968).

SOLTAU, Henry W.: *The Tabernacle, the Priesthood, and the Offerings*, Christian Publications, Harrisburg (1965).

STRACK, Hermann L.: *Introduction to the Talmud and Midrash*, Atheneum Press, New York (1974).

— T —

Talmud, The Babylonian, Soncino Press, London (1935).

TCHERIKOVER, Victor: *Hellenistic Civilization and the Jews*, Atheneum Press, New York (1970).

THACKERY, H. St. J.: *Josephus (9 Vols.)* Loeb Classical Library, Harvard University Press, Cambridge (1926).

The Book of the Bible, Golden Press, New York (1972).

The Holy Scriptures of the Old Testament (Hebrew and English), The British & Foreign Bible Society, London (1972).

The Interpreter's Dictionary of the Bible, Abingdon Press, Nashville (1962).

The Torah. The Five Books of Moses. A New Translation of the Holy Scriptures According to the Masoretic Text, Jewish Publication Society, Philadelphia (1967).

THROCKMORTON, Burton H. Jr.: *Gospel Parallels (A Synopsis of the First Three Gospels)*, Thomas Nelson, Inc., New York (1967).

— V —

VAN DEN BUSSCHE, Henri: *Understanding the Lord's Prayer*, Sheed & Ward Ltd., London (1963).

VAN DER LOOS, H.: *The Miracles of Jesus*, E. J. Brill, Leiden (1968).

VAN PAASSEN, Pierre: *Why Jesus Died*, Dial Press, New York (1949).

VAUGHAN, Curtis: *The New Testament from 26 Translations*, Zondervan Pub. House, Grand Rapids (1967).

— W —

WASSERMAN, Abraham: *Flavius Josephus (Selections from his Works)*, Viking Press, New York (1974).

WHISTON, William: *Josephus (Complete Works)*, Gregel Pub., Grand Rapids (1960).

WILSON, William: *The Execution of Jesus*, Scribner's Sons, New York (1970).

WINGO, Earle L.: *The Illegal Trial of Jesus*, Bobbs-Merrill Co., Indianapolis (1954).

WINTER, Paul: *On the Trial of Jesus*, Walter de Gruyter, New York (1961).

CITATIONS

PROLOGUE: FORMAT AND APPROACH

[1]Grant, Robert: *A Historical Introduction to the New Testament*, pg. 140.

[2]Eusebius: *Ecclesiastical History*: III: 39, 12-16.

[3]Jaubert, Annie: *The Date of the Last Supper*; Ruckstuhl, Eugen: *Chronology of the Last Days of Jesus*.

[4]*The Interpreter's Dictionary of the Bible*, pg. 646.

[5]See also *Aid to Bible Understanding*, pg. 1600; Freedman, H. and Simon, Maurice: *Midrash Rabba*, pgs. 126, Vol. X (Index) & Vol. I:70; Ginzberg, Louis: *The Legends of the Jews*, pg. I:135.

[6]Since its publication in 1961, Paul Winter's book, *On the Trial of Jesus*, has received almost reverential treatment. Winter recognizes the "timetable problem," but then deals with it illogically. He concludes that we must *eliminate* some of the separate and distinct "scenes," rather than the more reasonable solution of lengthening the time span into which the episodes fit (pgs. 7-8):

> When individual evangelists collected what had been related and assumed the task of arranging their material to provide a framework of their own theological notions, they found not one, but several relevant traditions. Side by side with what we may call "primary tradition," there now were a number of secondary traditions which had developed from the former.

> Rather than omit anything they considered of importance, the evangelists assembled all they could collect, combining secondary and primary traditions, and reanimating the narrative for purposes of illustration, exposition, exhortation and apologetics.

> Successive stages in the development of the tradition, in which later forms had grown up from the earlier, now became co-ordinated. Thus the Gospels contain no less than seven different descriptions of a scene of a judicial or quasi-judicial character, together with five descriptions of a scene of the maltreatment and mockery of Jesus.

> The original themes had been multiplied in the secondary traditional assigning to them new and different contexts. Each evangelist retained what he himself had found, and enlarged it by his specific contribution.

> In this way a discrepancy came about between the various evangelical accounts. The point in time occupied in one Gospel by a certain event is in another assigned to quite a different one. The narrow shape of the primary tradition is distorted; here and there bulges have occurred; the same incidents are reported over and over again, with modifications, in different places.

> The sequence of events now recorded in the four Gospels could not

possibly have taken place within the space of six or seven hours, the actual time-lag between Jesus' arrest and crucifixion. Hence modern writers have attempted to stretch this span of time by postulating a period of several days, thereby hoping to accommodate all the details about the trial contained in the Gospels.

Yet it is impossible to weave together all these disconnected facts into one harmonized account of the trial of Jesus, whether we assume that it lasted a few hours or several days. The writers who have tried to make room for every scene and detail in the various descriptions act in disregard of the evangelists' intentions.

Each evangelist aimed at giving a complete and unbroken account of the proceedings. It is illegitimate to interpose an interval of two days between the "events" reported in successive lines of a certain Gospel, and fill this interval with descriptions taken from another Gospel.

Both Winter and Justice Haim Cohn (*The Trial and Death of Jesus*) recognize the basic "timetable problem," but then take different tacks to reach their ultimate conclusions: *Winter* = The Jewish trials really are fictional and did not take place at all; *Cohn* = The Jews were trying to save Jesus.

They employ the thrust that the Gospel reports cannot be accurate; instead, they are historical monstrosities.

My position is just the opposite! The *gospels*, our only direct sources, are safe historical documents, *provided* we recognize them for what they are: Brief, incomplete outlines of a series of separate judicial and executive episodes that were spaced over a period of weeks, months or years.

The *gospel* accounts of Jesus' trials have been incredibly misinterpreted for centuries. Even writers who appreciate the sophistication of the Jewish legal system during Jesus' time fall into the "timetable trap": Since the system would not permit a Jewish trial (singular) to take place within the time frame set by the *gospels*, ergo, the Jewish trial was "illegal" on a dozen grounds. For slants on this theme, see Wingo, Earle L.: *The Illegal Trial of Jesus*; Brandon, S.G.F.: *The Trial of Jesus of Nazareth*; Chandler, Walter M.: *The Trial of Jesus From A Lawyer's Standpoint*; Carmichael, M.A.: *The Death of Jesus*; Maier, Paul L.: *First Easter— The True and Unfamiliar Story*; Wilson, William: *The Execution of Jesus*; Dixon, Roger: *The Christ Trial*; Bammel, Ernest: *The Trial of Jesus*; Gorman, Ralph: *The Last Hours of Jesus*; McRuer, J.C.: *The Trial of Jesus*; Bishop, Jim: *The Day Christ Died*; Van Paassen, Pierre: *Why Jesus Died*; Blinzler, J.: *The Trial of Jesus*; Kilpatrick, G.D.: *The Trial of Jesus*.

There are other books and many articles in the periodical literature, all playing variations on the same basic theme. I recently heard a lecturer spend an hour on, "The 19 Illegalities In Jesus' Jewish Trial"!

[7]*The Torah. The Five Books of Moses. A New Translation of the Holy Scriptures According to the Masoretic Text; Pentateuch and Haftorahs* (Hebrew Text/English Translation/and Commentary); *Encyclopaedia Judaica*, pgs. 15:1235-1258; *The Holy Scriptures of the Old Testament* (Hebrew and English).

[8]*Encyclopaedia Judaica*, pgs. 13:232-267, at pg. 232:

The so-called "law of Moses" (cf. I Kings 2:3; II Kings 14:6; Ezra 3:2, 7:6, etc.) has long been divided into five books, hence the Hebrew *hummash* or *hamishah humshei Torah* and the Latin *Pentateuch* derived from the Greek. Though it is not known when the division was made, it seems that it was in existence long before the destruction of the Second Temple.

[9]For discussions of when the *canon* ("carpenter's ruler") of the *Torah* closed ("set"), see Bratton, Fred G.: *A History of the Bible*, pgs. 103-124; Russell, D.S.: *The Jews from Alexander to Herod*, pgs. 112, 116, 131, 176, 191; *Encyclopaedia Judaica*, pg. 13:232; *The Interpreter's Dictionary of the Bible*, pgs. 1:498-520.

[10]Neil, William: *Harper's Bible Commentary*, pgs. 131-133.

[11]Strack, Hermann, L.: *Introduction to the Talmud and Midrash*; Goldin, Judah: *The Living Talmud*; Runes, Dagobart D.: *The Talmud of Jerusalem*; Herford, R. Travers: *The Ethics of the Talmud: Sayings of the Fathers*; Neusner, Jacob: *Invitation of the Talmud*; Cohen, A.: *Everyman's Talmud*; Gersh, Harry: *The Sacred Books of the Jews*; Finkelstein, Louis: *Akiba - Scholar, Saint and Martyr*; *Encyclopaedia Judaica* (general index for multiple related entries); Ginzberg, Louis: *On Jewish Law and Lore*, pgs. 3-5; Goldin, Hyman E.: *Hebrew Criminal Law and Procedure*, pgs. 99-100; Durant, Will: *The Story of Civilization: Part III: Caesar and Christ*, pg. 31; Klausner, Joseph: *The Messianic Idea in Israel*, pgs. 391-392.

[12]*Encyclopaedia Judaica*, pgs. 5:189-195; Finkelstein, Louis: *The Jews, Their History* (4th Ed.), pg. 172; Ginzberg, Louis: *The Legends of the Jews*; Gersh, Harry: *The Sacred Books of the Jews*, pg. 185; Freedman, B.A. and Simon, Maurice: *Midrash Rabbah*, (10 vols).

[13]Thackery, H. St. J.: *Josephus* (9 vols); Whiston, William: *Josephus* (Complete Works); Wasserman, Abraham: *Flavius Josephus* (*Selections from His Works*).

PART 1

THE JEWISH-TEMPLE STATE

Chapter 1

YOM KIPPUR: DAY OF ATONEMENT

[1]Tractate ("Volume") *Yoma* of the *Babylonian Talmud* (English translation by Dr. I. Epstein, editor) gives us a 480-page, detailed description of the Day of Atonement rituals in the Second Temple during Jesus' lifetime.

A number of books and other sources summarize these exacting provisions: *Encyclopaedia Judaica*, pgs. 5:1376-1388; Kitov, Eliyahu: *The Book of Our Heritage*, pgs. 307-310, 318, 319, 330; Schauss, Hayyim: *The Jewish Festivals*, pgs. 119-142; Jeremias, Joachim: *Jerusalem in the Time of Jesus*, pgs. 37, 56, 67, 97, 149, 159, 161, 162, 177, 194, 226, 264.

Many books on Jewish history and the literature of the Old Testament detail the Day of Atonement because of its significance to Judaism; for example, Grayzel, Solomon: *A History of the Jews*, pgs. 119, 156, 243, 417; and Larue, Gerald A.: *Old Testament Life and Literature*, pgs. 187, 193, 197, 199, 329, 335, 336, 369, 386, 403.

For an excellent discussion of the parallel themes of "atonement" in the Old and New Testaments, see Maertens, Thierry: *Bible Themes (A Source Book)*, pgs. II:205-208.

[2]*Talmud*: Tamid 30b.

[3]*Encyclopaedia Judaica*, pgs. 5:1377-1378; Edersheim, Alfred: *The Temple (Its Ministry and Services)*, pgs. 304-329; Schauss, Hayyim: *The Jewish Festivals*, pg. 125.

[4]Of the four *gospels*, *John* most explicitly spells out Jesus' appearances at the Temple ceremonies: 2:13; 2:23; 5:1; 7:14; 7:37; 10:22; 11:55; 13:1.

[5]Josephus: *Wars of the Jews*, 6:422 and 2:280, gives these figures for the festival of Passover, and for a date that approximates 65 A.D. Still, it is reasonable to assume that they apply generally to Day of Atonement celebrations during Jesus' time some thirty to forty years earlier.

For an example of the scholar's approach to "numbers" in *Josephus* and other sources, see Jeremias, Joachim: *Jerusalem in the Time of Jesus*, pgs. 77-84.

[6]Sendrey, Alfred: *Music in Ancient Israel*, pgs. 227, 325, 394-405, 408.

[7]*Talmud*: Yoma 16a; *Encyclopaedia Judaica*, pg. 15-966; Edersheim, Alfred: *The Temple (Its Ministry and Services)*, pg. 46.

[8]*Encyclopaedia Judaica*, pgs. 15:63-64; Edersheim, Alfred: *The Temple (Its Ministry and Services)*, pg. 28.

[9]The exact number, location and direction of Jerusalem's walls is still not settled. By the time of the Second Temple's destruction in 70 A.D., at least three walls were known, although only two may have been built before Jesus' lifetime. The historical and archeological problems of identifying these separate walls has produced a substantial body of literature. For a summary, see *Encyclopaedia Judaica*, pgs. 9:1378-1405; also, Avi-Yonah, Michael: *The Holy Land*, pgs. 15, 64, 69, 200, 275; Kenyon, Kathleen: *Royal Cities of the Old Testament*; Paul, Shalom M. and Dever, William G.: *Biblical Archeology*; Avi-Yonah, Michael: *2nd Temple Reconstruction (Holyland Motel)*; Edersheim, Alfred:*The Temple (Its Ministry and Services)*, pg. 31.

[10]*Talmud*: Tamid: V, 6, 33a.

[11]High Priest 18-37 A.D. Caiaphas was the son-in-law of Annas, High Priest 6-15 A.D. who headed one of the four great families of Sadducees who exercised totalitarian authority over the bureaucracy of the Temple-State, which ruled Judea.

[12]Jonathan, son of Annas, brother-in-law of Joseph Caiaphas, bore the title of *sagan* (deputy), also called, "Captain of the Temple." Jonathan went on to serve an incredibly short term as High Priest in 37 A.D. when Caiaphas was deposed: His term lasted only 40 days, from Passover to Pentecost.

[13]*Talmud*: Yoma 16b; *Encyclopaedia Judaica*, pgs. 15:960-969; Edersheim, Alfred: *The Temple (Its Ministry and Services)*, pg. 47; Soltau, Henry W.: *The Tabernacle, the Priesthood, and the Offerings*.

[14]*Talmud*: Yoma 35b; 39b.

[15]Almost every book on Judaism or the history of the Jews discusses their approach to the name of God; so the literature on this still speculative subject is vast.

By way of example, the index under the heading, "Names of God" in *Encyclopaedia Judaica* contains five dozen entries. *The Interpreter's Dictionary of the Bible*, pgs. 2:407-417, "GOD, Names of," gives a terse summary of the subject.

[16]*Talmud*: Yoma 71b.

[17]Edersheim, Alfred: *The Temple (Its Ministry and Services)*, pg. 304; *Acts* 27:9. Also, *Encyclopaedia Judaica*, pg. 5:1382.

[18]*Talmud*: Yoma 70a; 71b; 72a.

[19]*Talmud*: Yoma 87b.

[20]*Talmud*: Pesahim 54a. See also Moore, George Foote: *Judaism In the First Centuries of the Christian Era*, 1:526.

[21]*Talmud*: Yoma 21a.

[22]*The Interpreter's Dictionary of the Bible*, pgs. 3:879-880:

> The third order (after the High Priest and Priests) of the [Temple] hierarchy is that of the Levites. They are subordinate cultic officials, the *clerici minores*, who have charge of the lower duties of the sanctuary (Num. 1:40, 3:28, 32; 8:15; 31:30, 47; I Chr. 23:25-32).

> Levites are installed by a ceremony consisting of lustration, shaving the body, sacrifice, the laying on of hands, and solemn presentation to God (Num. 8:5-13).

> Their function is to assist the priests and serve the congregation (Num. 1:50; 3:6, 8; 16:9; 18:2; I Chr. 23:28, 32; Ezra 3:8-9). They are responsible for the care of the courts and chambers of the sanctuary, the cleansing of the sacred vessels, the preparation of the cereal offerings, and the service of praise (I Chr. 23:28-32).

> Some are mentioned particularly as being porters or gatekeepers (I Chr. 9:19; 26:1, 19; II Chr. 8:14), some as treasurers (I Chr. 26:20), and some as choristers and musicians (Ezra 3:10; Neh. 12:27; cf. I Chr. 6:31-32; 16:4-5, 7; 25:1-8; II Chr. 8:14), although on other occasions singers and porters are listed separately as distinct from the Levites (Ezra 2:40-42; 10:23; Neh. 7:43-45, 73; 12:27).

> The Levites have also a teaching function as interpreters of the law (Neh. 8:7, 9; cf. II Chr. 17:7-9; 35:3), but this eventually passed into the hands of the scribes (*see* Scribe).

> Levites assist the priests in the administration of justice (I Chr. 23:4; 26:29; II Chr. 19:8-11) and in the charge of the treasury (Ezra 8:33-34; cf. I Chr. 26:20 ff).

[23]*Talmud*: Yoma 11a; 37a.

[24]Sendrey, Alfred: *Music in Ancient Israel*, Section VI, pgs. 262-420.

[25]Josephus: *Antiquities of the Jews*: XX, 216; Mowinckel, Sigmund: *The Psalms in Israel's Worship*, pg. II:82. Although the references probably describe events of an earlier period, it is reasonable to assume that the fierce Bureaucratic rivalries within the Temple Bureaucracy continued unabated throughout the entire period of the Second Temple. This is the congenital nature of bureaucracy, no matter what or where its time or place. See also Nt. 89, *infra*.

[26]*Talmud*: Yoma 30a. In addition to the immersions, there were ten separate "sanctifications."

[27]Edersheim, Alfred: *The Temple (Its Ministry and Services)*, pg. 309.

[28]*Talmud*: Yoma 32a.

[29]*Talmud*: Yoma 30a; 34b.

[30]See Chapter 8, "The Nazareth Threat," for a description of the Pharisees

and the Sadduccees, the two major religious/political parties who vied for power in the Temple-State. The other two groups, *essenes* and *zealots*, exercised practically no general influence in the administration of the Temple Bureaucracy, the *essenes* withdrawing to Qumran (Dead Sea Scrolls country), and the revolutionary *zealots* operating primarily in the Galilee.

[31]*Talmud*: Yoma 60a.

[32]*Ibid.*, 35b.

[33]*Ibid.*, 36a.

[34]*Ibid.*, 58a.

[35]*Ibid.*, 58a.

[36]*Ibid.*, 32b; 75b.

[37]*Ibid.*, 48a.

[38]The references in *Talmud*: Yoma to the dress of the High Priest during the rituals of the Day of Atonement are voluminous, Sections 31b, 32a and 32b representative of the obsession with bureaucratic minutiae. To keep from bogging down in the details, see the adequate summary in Edersheim, Alfred: *The Temple (Its Ministry and Services)*, pgs. 305-306.

[39]*Talmud*: Yoma 45a.

[40]Note 38, *supra*.

[41]The five immersions and "ten sanctifications" are mentioned frequently in *Talmud*: Yoma, as in 71a, the "sanctifications" as ritual washings of the High Priest's hands and feet, the "washings" interspersed with changes of garments, as described in *Talmud*: Yoma 70a.

[42]*Talmud*: Yoma 2a; 4b-5a.

[43]*Talmud*: Yoma 2a; 4a; 8b; 10a; 18b-19a.

[44]*Talmud*: Yoma 4a.

[45]*Talmud*: Yoma 13a-14b.

[46]*Talmud*: Yoma 13a; 47a. By definition, this would include many, perhaps most, Galileans. See Ch. 7, "Jesus' Fellow-Galileans: 'The People of the Land.'"

[47]*Talmud*: Yoma 18a.

[48]*Talmud*: Yoma 18a-18b.

[49]*Talmud*: Yoma 18b.

[50]*Talmud*: Yoma 2a; 5a; 12a.

[51]*Talmud*: Yoma 18b; 19b.

[52]*Talmud*: Yoma 16a-16b; Edersheim, Alfred: *The Temple (Its Ministry*

and Services), pgs. 51-59.

[53]*Ibid.*

[54]*Ibid.*

[55]*Talmud*: Yoma 58a; 59a; Edersheim, Alfred: *The Temple (Its Ministry and Services)*, pgs. 54-56.

[56]Edersheim, Alfred: *The Temple (Its Ministry and Services)*, pg. 316, summarizes the one-by-one order of the sprinklings.

[57]Daniel-Rops, Henri: *Daily Life in the Time of Jesus*, pg. 214.

[58]1 Samuel 10:23-24. Throughout history, roles of leadership often rested upon men taller than average. This fact tempts speculation that Jesus was, indeed, taller than most; but it is speculation only. There are also short men who capture control of their times, as Napoleon.

[59]The tedious steps in the elaborate, all-day rituals, spelled out carefully in *Talmud*: Yoma, are condensed in *Encyclopaedia Judaica*, pgs. 3:976-980, and Edersheim, Alfred: *The Temple (Its Ministry and Services)*, Chapter XVI, pgs. 303-328, "The Day of Atonement."

[60]*Ibid.*; *Leviticus* 16:12-14.

[61]*Talmud*: Kelim, I:6.

[62]Josephus: *Wars of the Jews*, V:5:5, 219.

[63]*2 Samuel* 6:16-19.

[64]*Talmud*: Yoma 52b-53a.

[65]*Ibid.*

[66]Again, Edersheim, Alfred: *The Temple (Its Ministry and Services)*, pg. 307, for the order of the sacrifices.

[67]*Talmud*: Yoma 41b; 62a-62b.

[68]*Talmud*: Yoma 66a.

[69]*Talmud*: Yoma 41b.

[70]*Ibid.*

[71]*Talmud*: Yoma 21a; 66b.

[72]*Talmud*: Yoma 67a; 68b.

[73]*Talmud*: Yoma 66a; 67a; 67b.

[74]*Psalm* 51:13-14.

[75]*Talmud*: Yoma 68b.

[76]*Ibid.*

[77]*Talmud*: Yoma 53b.

[78]*Talmud*: Yoma 53b; 57a; 58a; 58b.

[79]*Talmud*: Yoma 52b; 53a.

[80]*Talmud*: Yoma 25a-25b; 26a-26b; 27a-27b; 45a; 45b; 46a; 46b; Edersheim, Alfred: *The Temple (Its Ministry and Services)*, pg. 307.

[81]Edersheim, Alfred: *The Temple (Its Ministry and Services)*, pg. 307.

[82]*Leviticus* 16:29; *Talmud*: Yoma 74a-74b.

[83]*Talmud*: Yoma 73b.

[84]*Talmud*: Yoma 4b.

[85]*Talmud*: Yoma 31b; 32a; 32b; 70a; 70b.

[86]*Talmud*: Yoma 70a.

[87]*Talmud*: Pesahim 57a.

[88]*Ibid.*

[89]For an excellent description of the shameless graft and corruption within the Temple Bureaucracy, see Jeremias, Joachim: *Jerusalem in the Time of Jesus*, pgs. 92-99.

Although he wrote about a period some three decades after Jesus' time, *Josephus'* description of the insensitivities of the Bureaucrats applied to the time of Jesus' trials: Josephus: *Histories of the Jews*, XX: 8:8, 180:

> There now was enkindled mutual enmity and class warfare between the high priests, on the one hand, and the priests and the leaders of the populace of Jerusalem, on the other.
>
> Each of the factions formed and collected for itself a band of the most reckless revolutionaries and acted as their leader. And when they clashed, they used abusive language and pelted each other with stones.
>
> And there was not even one person to rebuke them. No, it was as if there were no one in charge of the city, so that they acted as they did with full license.
>
> Such was the shamelessness and effrontery which possessed the high priests that they actually were so brazen as to send slaves to the threshing floors to receive the tithes that were due to the priests, with the result that the poorer priests starved to death.
>
> Thus did the violence of the contending factions suppress all justice.

So it is ever with Bureaucracy!

[90]See Chapter 4, "The Committee of Ten."

[91]*Talmud*: Pesahim 57a.

[92]*Talmud*: Yoma 68b.

[93]*Psalm* 19:14.

[94]*Talmud*: Yoma 35b; 39b.

[95]*Ibid.*

[96]*Talmud*: Yoma 70a.

[97]Avi-Yonah, Michael: *2nd Temple Reconstruction.*

[98]Josephus: *Histories of the* Jews, XV:9, 3; Perowne, S.: *The Life and Times of Herod the Great*, pg. 118.

[99]Avi-Yonah, Michael: *Model of Ancient Jerusalem.*

Chapter 2

THE TEMPLE: BUREAUCRACY'S POWER SEAT

[1]Josephus: *Histories of the Jews*, X:8, 1-7.

[2]*Ibid.*

[3]*Psalm* 137:1-4.

[4]Josephus: *Histories of the Jews*, IX:14, 1-3.

[5]*Ibid.*; *Encyclopaedia Judaica*, pgs. 15:1003-1006.

[6]Psalm 137:5-6.

[7]Kaufmann, Yehezkel: *The Religion of Israel*; Rowley, H.H.: *The Faith of Israel*, pgs. 48-73, "The Nature of God."; Robinson, H. Wheeler: *The Religious Ideas of the Old Testament*, pgs. 51-76, "The Idea of God."; Sarna, Nahum: *Understanding Genesis.*

[8]The national depression that engulfed the Exiles in their Babylonian Captivity is poignantly expressed in the books of *Lamentations* in the Old Testament and *Baruch* in the Apocrypha.

[9]*Encyclopaedia Judaica*, pgs. 15:579-583; Grayzel, Solomon: *A History of the Jews*, pgs. 136 et seq.; Bright, John: *A History of Israel*, pgs. 439-441; Kaufmann, Yehezkel: *The Religion of Israel*, pgs. 162, 302, 451; Rowley, H.H.: *Worship in Ancient Israel (Its Forms and Meaning)*, pgs. 213-245, "The Synagogue."

[10]*Ibid.*; Sapir, Baruch and Neeman, Dov: *Capernaum (Kfar-Nachum).*

[11]Note 9, *supra*; *Encyclopaedia Judaica*, pgs. 3:976-980.

[12]*Sifre Deuteronomy*, 41.

[13]Note 9, *supra*.

[14]Note 9, *supra*.

[15]Note 8, *supra*.

[16]Josephus: *Histories of the Jews*, XI:1, 1-3.

[17]*Ibid*.

[18]*Ibid*.

[19]*The Interpreter's Dictionary of the Bible*, pgs. 3:876-889, "Priests and Levites."

[20]Jeremias, Joachim: *Jerusalem in the Time of Jesus*, pgs. 194-195.

[21]*Ibid*., at pgs. 377-378.

[22]Jeremias, Joachim: *Jerusalem in the Time of Jesus*, pgs. 98-99.

[23]Josephus: *Histories of the Jews*, XX:10:1:230.

[24]Russell, D.S.: *The Jews from Alexander to Herod*, pg. 36:

> Jason sought appointment to the High-Priestly office in return for a large sum of money to be paid to Antiochus and the pledge of his wholehearted support in the Hellenization of the Jews (cf. 1 Macc. I:13-15; 2 Macc 4:15). Antiochus [Greek king ruling Judea at that time] at once agreed.

> To him such an appointment was an astute political move, for, quite apart from the financial advantage gained, Jason was the avowed leader in Jerusalem of the pro-Syrian party. Jason accordingly assumed office (174 B.C.) and set in motion his agreed policy of Hellenization.

> The King gave him permission to build a gymnasium in Jerusalem and to enroll Jewish youths in it. Games were organized in which the athletes, according to Greek custom, ran naked on the track; even young priests left the altar to take part in the sports. They removed their mark of circumcision; they wore the distinctive cap of Hermes, the patron of Greek sports; they changed their Hebrew names to the Greek style, and conformed in almost every way to Greek custom and fashion.

[25]Russell, D.S.: *The Jews from Alexander to Herod*, pg. 37:

> It is not in the least surprising that the orthodox Jews in Jerusalem were greatly incensed at these things. Quite apart from Jason's obnoxious policy of Hellenization, it was to them intolerable that a High Priest should be appointed to this divine office by a Gentile King.

> Their feelings were tempered only by the fact that he at least belonged to the High-Priestly family, and it is probably for this reason that they took no active measures against him.

> But Jason's position was far from secure. The Tobiads, although they had supported his appointment to the High Priesthood, now found that

his policy of Hellenization was not radical enough, and determined to obtain the office for Menelaus (Hebrew, *Menahem*), one of their own number.

The sources disagree about this man's identity; but if, as the writer of 2 Maccabees records (cf. 3:4, 4:23), he was a Benjamite, then he was not even a member of a priestly family.

The opportunity came when Jason sent Menelaus to Antiochus with certain moneys which he owed the King. Menelaus grasped his opportunity, pledging to the King a more thorough policy of Hellenization than Jason's and offering three hundred talents more than his rival had been able to give. Antiochus accepted, and Menelaus returned to Jerusalem as the new High Priest.

[26] Josephus: *Antiquities of the Jews*, XIII:9, 1.

[27] *Encyclopaedia Judaica*, pgs. 8:473-475.

[28] Note 24, *supra*.

[29] Note 20, *supra*.

[30] Information on the names of the High Priests, their successions to office, and their terms of office is scattered throughout the *talmud* and *Josephus*. This list is a combination of two authoritative lists in Jeremias, Joachim: *Jerusalem in the Time of Jesus*, pgs. 377-378; and Edersheim, Alfred: *The Life and Times of Jesus the Messiah*, pg. 2:702.

[31] *Talmud*: Yoma 38a.

[32] *Ibid*.

[33] *Talmud*: Yoma 58b.

[34] *Talmud*: Pesahim 65b.

[35] Typical of the detailed *talmudic* references concerning matters of the economy is *talmud*: Menahoth 86b, 87a which relates to wine. Similar references can be located for almost every other commodity.

[36] *Talmud*: Menahoth 85b.

[37] Jeremias, Joachim: *Jerusalem in the Time of Jesus*, with special references to "I Industries," "II Commerce," and "VII Decisive Factors in Determining the Economic Circumstances of the People of Jerusalem."

[38] *Talmud*: Baba Mezi's 88a.

[39] *Ibid*.

[40] *Talmud*: Pesahim 57a.

[41] Jeremias, Joachim: *Jerusalem in the Time of Jesus*, pg. 204.

[42] *Ibid*., 26, 27, 84, 205, 252.

[43]*Ibid.*

[44]*Ibid.*

[45]*Ibid.*, 22, 26.

[46]*Ibid.*, 22, 29.

[47]*Ibid.*, 28, 47.

[48]*Ibid.*, 28; *Deuteronomy* 16:16-17.

[49]*Encyclopaedia Judaica*, pg. 15:582.

Chapter 3

THE TEMPLE AND THE TEMPLE MOUNT

[1]Josephus: *Histories of the Jews*, XI:1-4.

[2]*Talmud*: Sukkah 51b.

[3]1 *Kings* 5-7.

[4]2 *Chronicles* 1-5.

[5]The Babylonians assaulted Judea three different times:597, 593 and 586 B.C., the Jews defending their nation and Temple so tenaciously the first two times that the Babylonians decided that they could only win a decisive victory by burning the Temple.

[6]*Judges* 2:17:

> And yet they would not harken unto their judges, but they went awhoring after other gods, and bowed down themselves unto them; they turned quickly out of the way which their fathers walked in . . . .

[7]Josephus: *Histories of the Jews*: XI:1-4.

[8]*Ibid.*, at XV:1.

[9]*Ibid.*, at XV: ii, 2.

[10]*Ibid.*, at XV:9,3.

[11]*Ibid.*

[12]Descriptions of the physical dimensions of the Temple Mount and the Temple structures proper (both internal and external) are scattered throughout such diverse sources as the biblical books of *Kings*, *Chronicles* and *Ezekiel*, and in *Josephus* and the *talmud*. Tractate *middoth*, for example, gives a plan of the Second Temple with exact measurements of its main features, probably drawn up (possibly in Greek) while the Temple still stood. The editors of the *talmud*

included it as a guide for rebuilding the destroyed Second Temple which, they all assumed, God would bring about.

Many scholars, combing the many sources, have assembled a guide to the Temple measurements. As with other subjects, we find considerable conflict in their interpretations of the ancient writings.

The size of the "cubit," the standard unit of linear measurement, causes the most difficulty, as explained in *The Interpreter's Dictionary of the Bible*, pg. 4:836:

> Undoubtedly the cubit was the length of the forearm to the tip of the middle finger; but, as human arms are of different lengths, the Israelites' cubit was not absolute. There are more than a hundred occurrences of the word for "cubit" . . .

For convenience, modern writers project the ancient cubit as eighteen inches; but this is misleading since we encounter several "cubits," including a "royal cubit" of approximately twenty-one inches: *Talmud*: Kelim 17:9-10:

> The (measure of the) cubit of which they have spoken applies to the cubit of middle size. There were two cubits by the Palace of Shushan (Gate), one at the north-eastern corner and another at the south-eastern corner. That at the north-east was longer than the cubit of Moses by half a fingerbreadth; that at the south-east was longer than the other by half a fingerbreadth; thus it was one fingerbreadth longer than the cubit of Moses.
>
> And why was there ordained a larger cubit and a smaller cubit? So that the craftsmen might undertake their tasks according to the measure of the smaller cubit, and thereby escape the guilt of Sacrilege.
>
> R. Meir says: All [the measurements in the Temple] were according to the cubit of the middle size excepting those of the Golden Altar and the horns and the Circuit and the Base [of the Altar]. R. Judah says: The [standard of the] cubit used for the (Temple) building was six handbreadths and that for the utensils five handbreadths.

For most of the Temple measurements, for economy of time and space, I cite Edersheim, Alfred: *The Temple (Its Ministry and Services)*. For this particular measure of the Temple Mount, see *Encyclopaedia Judaica*, pgs. 15:988-989.

[13]Edersheim, Alfred: *The Temple (Its Ministry and Services)*, pg. 44.

[14]*Ibid.*, pg. 37.

[15]*Encyclopaedia Judaica*, pg. 15:963.

[16]Edersheim, Alfred: *The Temple (Its Ministry and Services)*, pg. 35.

[17]*Ibid.*, pg. 37.

[18]*Ibid.*, pg. 37.

[19]*Ibid.*, pg. 47.

[20]*Ibid.*, pg. 44.

[21]*Ibid.*, pg. 43.

[22]*Ibid.*, pg. 44.

[23]*Ibid.*, pg. 44.

[24]*Ibid.*, pg. 44.

[25]*Talmud*: Baba Mezi'a 88a.

[26]Jeremias, Joachim: *Jerusalem in the Time of Jesus*, pgs. 33, 34, 41, 19.

[27]Edersheim, Alfred: *The Temple (Its Ministry and Services)*, pg. 45.

[28]Jeremias, Joachim: *Jerusalem in the Time of Jesus*, pg. 28; *Deuteronomy* 16:16-17.

I am, perhaps, overly conservative in my approach to numbers. See also Note 27, pg. 69:

> That strict discipline both in regard to priests and worshippers would, however, be necessary, may be inferred even from the immense number of worshippers which thronged Jerusalem and the Temple.
>
> According to a late computation, the Temple could have held 'within its colossal girdle' 'two amphitheaters of the size of the Colosseum.' As the latter is reckoned to have been capable, inclusive of its arena and passages, of accomodating 109,000 persons, the calculation that the Temple might contain at one time about 210,000 persons seems by no means exaggerated.
>
> It will readily be believed what immense wealth this multitude must have brought to the great national sanctuary.

[29]*Matthew* 21:10-17; *Mark* 11:11; *Luke* 19:45-46; *Mark* 11:15-19; *Luke* 19:47-48.

[30]Note 39, *infra*.

[31]Edersheim, Alfred: *The Temple (Its Ministry and Services)*, pgs. 38, 46-47.

[32]*Ibid.*, 38, 46.

[33]*Encyclopaedia Judaica*, pgs. 15:965-966.

[34]Graetz, Heinrich: *History of the Jews*, pg. II:10.

[35]Edersheim, Alfred: *The Temple (Its Ministry and Services)*, pg. 47.

[36]*Ibid.*

[37]*Encyclopaedia Judaica*, pgs. 15:966-968.

[38]*Ibid.*

[39]*Ibid.*

[40]*Ibid.*

[41]*Ibid.*

[42]Josephus: *Wars of the Jews*: V:5:3, 201.

[43]Josephus: *Wars of the Jews*: V:5:3, 201:

> ... Of the gates, nine were completely overlaid with gold and silver, as were also their door-posts and lintels; but one, that outside the sanctuary, was of Corinthian bronze, and far exceeded in value those plated with silver and set in gold.

> Each gateway had two doors, and each door was thirty cubits in height and fifteen in breadth.

Talmud: Middoth 11, 3:

> MISHNAH ... ALL THE ORIGINAL GATES WERE CHANGED FOR GATES OF GOLD EXCEPT THE GATES OF NICANOR, BECAUSE A MIRACLE WAS WROUGHT TO THEM: SOME SAY, HOWEVER, IT WAS BECAUSE THE COPPER OF THEM GLEAMED [like gold].

[44]*Talmud*: Sukkah, 51b.

[45]Josephus: *Wars of the Jews*: V:5,4,6,222.

[46]Edersheim, Alfred: *The Temple (Its Ministry and Services)*, pg. 51.

[47]*Ibid.*

[48]Josephus: *Wars of the Jews*: V:5:6, 226.

[49]*Talmud*: Middoth 111:4.

[50]*Talmud*: Middoth 111:5.

[51]*Encyclopaedia Judaica*, pgs. 15:968; 16:920; 2:200.

Chapter 4

THE COMMITTEE OF TEN

[1]*John* 7:1.

[2]*Matthew* 26:47.

[3]*Mark* 14:53.

[4]*Luke* 23:1,13,18.

[5]Throughout history, "the committee" approach has stifled our creativity and reach for new horizons. Fortunately, strong leaders appear from time to

time to inch us above the monotonous, unproductive mediocrity of "the committee," one of the special burdens of Bureaucracy whose main goal is to preserve the status quo. "The committee" operates without individual responsibility for actions which are condemned later, its members absolving themselves of personal fault by pointing the finger of blame at their fellows. "The committee" format of the Temple-State developed into Judaism's greatest weakness during Jesus' lifetime, permitting grave economic injustices and thwarting social reform. It finally fell during the great Jewish Rebellion of 66-70 A.D., which was probably as much a revolt against the Committee of Ten's Temple Bureaucracy than against the Romans.

[6]Flusser, David: *Jesus*, pg. 119. Confirmed in personal conversations at Hebrew University, Jerusalem, November-December, 1974.

[7]*Talmud*: Kethuboth, 12a-12b; 105a; 107b; Rosh Hashanah, 22a; Oholoth XVII:5.

[8]Schurer, Emil: *A History of the Jewish People*, (2nd Ed.).

[9]Reicke, Bo: *The New Testament Era. The World of the Bible from 500 B.C. to A.D. 100.* pgs. 146-148.

[10]Chapter 31, "Herod," details these events.

[11]*Encyclopaedia Judaica*, pg. 12:67.

[12]Goodenough, Erwin R.: *Jewish Symbols in the Greco-Roman Period*, pgs. 9:96-97.

[13]Goodenough, ibid. contains at least a dozen other references attesting the properties of "ten." See also, *Exodus* 34:28; *Deuteronomy* 4:13; 10:4; *Leviticus* 26:26; *Joshua* 17:5.

[14]Jeremias, Joachim: *Jerusalem in the Time of Jesus*, pgs. 88-99, 158-159, 169-198.

[15]We find numerous references in the *talmud* and in *Josephus* to the practice of purchasing the High Priesthood.
Typical is *talmud: Yoma* 8b:

> Originally, indeed, it was called the "cell of the *buleute*" but because money was being paid for the purpose of obtaining the position of high priest and the (high priests) were changed every twelve months ("they were removed by the king when a higher price was offered him for the priesthood"), like those counsellors, who are changed every twelve months, therefore it came to be called the "cell of the counsellors."

[16]See Chapter 2, "The Temple: Bureaucracy's Power Seat."

[17]Rubens, Alfred: *A History of Jewish Costume*, pgs. 5-18.

[18]Goodenough, Erwin R.: *Jewish Symbols in the Greco-Roman Period*, pgs. 2:214-295 (Fig. 1031). Other pages further detail the type of amulets worn by

Hellenized, non-orthodox Jews during this period.

[19]*Talmud*, Yoma 16a-16b; 17a; 19a; 47a.

PART 2

THE SYNAGOGUE PREACHERS

Chapter 5

THE SYNAGOGUE AT CAPERNAUM

[1]*Encyclopaedia Judaica*, pgs. 5:136-139:

> CAPERNAUM, ancient village on the N.W. shore of the sea of Galilee. Its name is derived from the Hebrew *Kefar* ('village of') *Nahum* (an unknown personage). It is first mentioned by Josephus as a village on his line of advance toward the issue of the Jordan into the Sea of Galilee and is described by him as 'a highly fertile spring called by the inhabitants Capharnaum' (Wars, 3:519-20). In the New Testament it appears as the place of residence chosen by Jesus on the shore of the lake and it is sometimes even termed 'his own city' (Matt. 4:13; 9:1), and it is also stated that he preached in the synagogue of Capernaum one Sabbath (Mark 1:21; John 6:59). It was the seat of a customs house (Matt. 9:9) and at least five of the apostles, including the very first ones, were fishermen from Capernaum. Although Jesus in the end reproved the people of Capernaum for their lack of belief (Matt. 11:23; Luke 10:15), a Judeo-Christian community continued there into talmudic times (Eccles. R. 1:8).

[2]*Encyclopaedia Judaica*, pgs. 15:582-583.

[3]Sapir, Baruch and Neeman, Dov: *Capernaum (Khar-Nachum)*, pgs. 55-58. I rely on the assumptions of the archeologists and biblical scholars that the architecture and appointments of the Third Century (A.D.) synagogue, described by the authors and partially restored, does not differ radically from the synagogue which stood on the same site during Jesus' time, the one in which he preached and worshiped.

[4]*Ibid.*, at pg. 61.

[5]An elaboration upon *Numbers* 24:5, in *Sabbath and Festival Prayer Book*, pg. 2.

Although this is a modern work, it shows perfectly how, through all their history, the Jews developed liturgy from the Scriptures, the Scriptures the source of all Temple and Synagogue worship, as well as the Law.

[6]Note 3, *supra*, at pgs. 59, 65.

[7]Note 3, *supra*, at pgs. 58, 62-63.

[8]Note 3, *supra*, at pg. 66.

[9]"Loving-kindness" served as a favorite, recurrent theme, appearing dozens of times in the Old Testament, especially in the Psalms. The liturgical format of the synagogue service drew heavily from the Psalms. We know that Jesus followed this established pattern, since many of his words in the gospels, especially his last words on the cross, come directly from the Psalms.

[10]The Hebrew word is *chazan*. See *Encyclopaedia Judaica*, pgs. 15:582-583.

[11]*Psalm* 24:3-5.

[12]Note 3, *supra*.

[13]These descriptions of the thrust of the worship service are those of Rabbi Robert Bergman, Israel Academy, Irvine, California, in lectures and private conversations. I prefer his dramatic imagery to the more formal explanations in the mass of literature that has developed on the liturgy of the synagogue.

[14]*Matthew* 4:23; 9:35; *Mark* 1:39; *Luke* 13:10; 4:15; 4:44; 12:11-12; 21:12.

[15]*Encyclopaedia Judaica*, pgs. 14:1370-1372; 4:585; 10:388; 13:422; 5:763; 13:1352; 15:786.

[16]Note 13, *supra*.

[17]Note 13, *supra*.

[18]Note 13, *supra*.

[19]Rowley, H.H.: *Worship in Ancient Israel. (Its Forms and Meaning)*, pgs. 232-233; *Encyclopaedia Judaica*, pgs. 3:335-336.

[20]The Herbrew word is *meturgeman*.

McNamara, Martin: *Targum and Testament. (Aramaic Phrases of the Hebrew Bible: A Light on the New Testament)*, pg. 48.

[21]*Encyclopaedia Judaica*, pg. 15:811:

> TARGUM. In its verbal form the Hebrew root *tirgem* means both 'to explain' and 'to translate.' The nominal form means 'translation.'
>
> Although technically it can apply to translation into, and from, any language, the word is employed in rabbinical literature almost exclusively for both the translation of the Bible into Aramaic (cf. Meg. 3a) and the Aramaic portions of the Bible, including individual words (*e.g.*, Gen. 31:47; cf. Shab. 115a; Yad. 4:5).
>
> The Targum, i.e., the Aramaic translation par excellence, is the Targum Onkelos, which was regarded as so authoritative that the weekly portion is enjoined to be read privately 'twice in the original and once in the Targum' (Ber. 8a), a custom which is still maintained in orthodox circles.

McNamara, Martin: *Targum and Testament (Aramaic Phrases of the Hebrew Bible: A Light on the New Testament)*, pg. 167:

> The targumic tradition was a sacred tradition, originating in the liturgy.

> The Palestinian Targum, being recited every Sabbath in the synagogues, would have been well known to Christ and his Apostles, as well as to the Jewish converts to Christianity. That Christ should have made use of the religious traditions of his people when addressing his message to them is altogether natural. He came not to destroy the Law but to fulfil it, to bring it to perfection.

> The task which he completed was being prepared right through the Old Testament period. This preparation included the progress in the understanding of revelation found in the targumic paraphrases.

> Jesus was a Jew of the Jews. His language and mental make-up were theirs. It is, then, not surprising that the manner in which he, and later the Apostles, presented the gospel to the Jews was that already known to them.

A considerable body of literature exists on the question of what language(s) Jesus spoke: Hebrew? Aramaic? Or both? To me, the question is persuasively answered by deduction from two known facts:

(1) He preached to the people in their synagogue (Note 14, *supra*) in the language they understood (Aramaic = the Semitic Language *spoken* by the Jews in First Century Palestine, having about the same relationship to Hebrew as modern Spanish to Italian): *Encyclopaedia Judaica*, pgs. 3:259-287; and

(2) He read from the *haftorah* ("Prophets") in the language in which it was written (*Hebrew*): *Luke* 4:16-22:

> And he came to Nazareth, where he had been brought up; and he went to the synagogue, as his custom was, on the sabbath day. And he stood up to read;

> and there was given to him the book of the prophet Isaiah. He opened the book and found the place where it was written,

> "The Spirit of the Lord is upon me, because he has anointed me to preach good news to the poor.

> "He has sent me to proclaim release to the captives and recovering of sight to the blind, to set at liberty those who are oppressed, to proclaim the acceptable year of the Lord."

> And he closed the book, and gave it back to the attendant, and sat down; and the eyes of all in the synagogue were fixed on him.

> And he began to say to them, "Today this scripture has been fulfilled in your hearing."

> And all spoke well of him, and wondered at the gracious words which proceeded out of his mouth;

These passages tell us that Jesus spoke at least biblical Hebrew *and* Aramaic. Since almost all educated Jews of the period and locality also knew *koine*, the Greek of the common people, the probabilities are that he was trilingual. He could well have also known classical Greek.

[22]McNamara, Martin: *Targum and Testament (Aramaic Phrases of the Hebrew Bible: A Light on the New Testament)*, pg. 49.

[23]*Ibid.*, at pg. 48.

[24]Note 14, *supra*.

Chapter 6

THE PREACHER FROM NAZARETH

[1]*Luke* 15:11-12.

My presentation follows closely Eta Linnemann's *Jesus of the Parables*, Chapter 4, "The Parable of the Prodigal Son." She gets more drama and understanding into this coverage than any treatment of the parables I know. I use some of her exact words.

[2]Much literature exists on the parables, Jesus' primary teaching format. For example: Armstrong, April Ousler: *The Tales Christ Told*; Hunter, Archibald M.: *The Parables Then and Now*; Lightfoot, Neil R.: *Lessons From the Parables*; Jeremias, Joachim: *Rediscovering the Parables*; Linnemann, Eta: *Jesus of the Parables*.

We do not know exactly (or even vaguely) where Jesus used the parable of the "Prodigal Son" (or when); so it could just as well have been in the synagogue at Capernaum as in another of his many synagogue sermons.

Klausner, Joseph: *Jesus of Nazareth*, pg. 259:

> The writers of the first Gospels were Jews in spirit.
>
> As Jews they aimed not at writing a history of Christianity or a biography of Jesus, but at showing how the will of God showed itself in certain events. Hence we must not expect a chronological account of the ministry of Jesus in Mark or Matthew, or even in Luke (whose aim was to connect the life of Jesus with historical personages and events), and we cannot, therefore, compose a scientific biography of Jesus according to modern methods.
>
> We have defined for us only the *opening* point of his ministry (his baptism by John in the Jordan), and the *closing* point (his crucifixion by Pontius Pilate at Jerusalem).
>
> There is a difficulty in fixing the intervening points.
>
> Mark's purpose being religious and not historical or biographical, he strings events together according to the parables and sayings of Jesus,

and places together in conjunction events (and even sayings and parables), however distant in time, if only they possess an inner, logical connexion.

[3]The Jews' basic laws of property (rights of ownership; acquisition; hereditary succession; and drafting of documents) appear in Tractate *Baba Bathra*, the Babylonian *talmud*, although we find decisions and commentaries on the subject scattered throughout the other sixty-two volumes.

[4]*Luke* 15:13.

[5]*Encyclopaedia Judaica*, pgs. 13:72-77.

The popularity of the parables is attested by the general index to the Epstein translations of the *Babylonian talmud* which contains forty entries under "Parables." Since the index is, in effect, fragmentary and incomplete, these forty entries barely scratch the surface of the use of the parable format in the *talmud*.

Talmud: Sanhedrin 38b:

> When R. Meir used to deliver his public discourses . . . . a third consisted of parables. R. Johanan also said: R. Meir had three hundred parables of foxes, and we have only three left [Probably of those collected by R. Meir, since many other fox fables are found throughout the *talmud* and Midrash].

Talmud: Sanhedrin 46b:

> A parable is stated; To what is this matter comparable? To twin brothers (who lived) in one city; one was appointed king, and the other took to highway robbery. At the king's command, they hanged him . . . . "

[6]*Luke* 15:14.

[7]*Encyclopaedia Judaica*, pgs. 6:8-19; Grayzel, Solomon: *A History of the Jews*, see appropriate entries in general index; Russell, D.S.: *The Jews From Alexander to Herod*, see appropriate entries in subject index under "Dispersion."

[8]*Luke* 15:15.

[9]*Talmud*, Baba Kamma 82b.

[10]*Luke* 15:16-17.

[11]Jeremias, Joachim: *The Parables of Jesus*, pg. 130.

[12]*Luke* 15:17-19.

[13]Edersheim, Alfred: *The Life and Times of Jesus the Messiah*, pg. 2:261.

[14]*Luke* 15:20.

[15]*Luke* 15:21.

[16]*Luke* 15:22-24.

[17]These introductory, transitional phrases in the *talmud* are too numerous to count.

[18]Theologians and commentary writers enjoy a field day with the role of the elder brother, each giving it his/her own twist. For example, Hunter, Archibald M.: *The Parables Then and Now*, pg. 17:

> Julicher's achievement was to prove, by and large, that the parables are not allegories to be spelt out point by point like the clues of a crossword puzzle. On the contrary, they exist mostly to make one point, though, as in the Prodigal Son, there may be a subsidiary one, (viz. the rebuke of the self-righteous Pharisee), and the details are part of the dramatic machinery of the story.

[19]Jeremias, Joachim: *The Parables of Jesus*, pgs. 130-133; Edersheim, Alfred: *The Life and Times of Jesus the Messiah*, pgs. 2:262-263.

[20]*Ibid.*

[21]*Ibid.*

[22]*Ibid.*

[23]*Ibid.*

[24]*Ibid.*

[25]*Ibid.*

[26]Birchall, Ann Corbett, P.E.: *Greek Gods and Heroes*; Petracos, Basil Chr.: *Delphi*; Burns, Edward McNall: *Western Civilization* (7th Ed.), pgs. 1:137-254.

[27]*Luke* 15:25-27.

[28]*Luke* 15:28-29.

[29]*Luke* 15:30.

[30]*Luke* 15:31-32.

[31]*Matthew* 15:32-39; 14:13-21; *Mark* 6:30-44; 8:1-10; *Luke* 9:10-17.

[32]The central thrust of an extremely important part of Jesus' message becomes clearer when we substitute the word "Bureaucrat" for the objects of his criticism: "Hypocrites" (*Matthew* 15:7); "Chief priests" (*Matthew* 21:23-32); "Publican" (*Luke* 19:2); "Sinners" (*Matthew* 9:13; *Mark* 2:17; *Luke* 5:32); "Publicans" and "Sinners" (*Luke* 15:1).

[33]Jesus performed no great feat to establish a national "name recognition" reputation in a country almost the exact geographical size as the state of New Jersey, 120 miles in north-south length and 20-30 in width, with a permanent population of 500,000-600,000. *Torah*, Temple, festivals, Holy Days, all kinds of religious celebrations, End of Days, Kingdom of God, repentance, the Messiah,

baptism, prayer, sacrifice, eternal life, resurrection of the body, all monopolized conversation as much as talk of obtaining the necessities of this physical life. Anyone who taught something new, or presented the old in a dramatic suit of clothes, became an immediate celebrity.

[34]*Mark* 1:22.

Chapter 7

JESUS' FELLOW-GALILEANS: THE "PEOPLE OF THE LAND"

[1]Josephus: *Life*: 235.

[2]Josephus: *Wars of the Jews*: III:1-2; *Talmud* Shebi'ith: 9:2.

[3]Daniel-Rops, Henri: *Daily Life in the Time of Jesus*, pgs. 18, 233.

[4]*Ibid.*, at pg. 18.

[5]Guignebert, Charles: *The Jewish World in the Time of Jesus*, pg. 8-9.

[6]*Ibid.*, at pg. 9.

[7]*Ibid.*

[8]Finkelstein, Louis: *Akiba: Scholar, Saint and Martyr*, pg. 62.

[9]*Talmud*: Baba Bathra 38a.

[10]*Ibid.*, 38a-38b.

[11]Note 5, *supra*, pgs. 6-7.

[12]*Ibid.*

[13]*Matthew* 4:15.

[14]Daniel-Rops, Henri: *Daily Life in the Time of Jesus*, pg. 47.

[15]*The Interpreter's Dictionary of the Bible*, pgs. 1:810-812.

[16]*Encyclopaedia Judaica*, pgs. 2:221-229.

[17]Josephus: *Life*: 232; *Talmud*: Baba Bathra 75b; *Talmud*: Sanhedrin 19a.

[18]Daniel-Rops, Henri: *Daily Life in the Time of Jesus*, pg. 49.

[19]Guignebert, Charles: *The Jewish World in the Time of Jesus*, pg. 8.

[20]This table is an elaboration of a similar one found in Dominick, Mabel A.: *The Bible and the Historical Design*, pgs. 113-114.

[21]Josephus: *Wars of the Jews*: II:117.

[22]Josephus: *Histories of the Jews*: XVIII:1-11.

[23]Josephus: *Histories of the Jews*: XVIII:23-24.

[24]Guignebert, Charles: *The Jewish World in the Time of Jesus*, pg. 11.

[25]*Matthew* 10:4; *Luke* 6:16.

[26]Daniel-Rops, Henri: *Daily Life in the Time of Jesus*, pgs. 150-152.

[27]*Ibid.*, at pg. 151.

[28]*Encyclopaedia Judaica*, pg. 2:833.

[29]*Talmud*: Aboth 2:5.

[30]*Talmud*: Pesahim 49b.

[31]*Talmud*: Yoma 13a; Hagigah 23a.

[32]*Talmud*: Demai 11:1.

[33]*Talmud*: Sabbath 13a.

[34]*Ibid.*, glossary.

[35]*Talmud*: Hagigah 18b.

[36]*Talmud*: Berakoth 52b.

[37]*Talmud*: Nedarim 18b.

[38]*Talmud*: Kethuboth.

[39]*Talmud*: Kethuboth 95b et seq.

[40]*Talmud*: Kethuboth 96a.

[41]*Talmud*: Kethuboth 9b.

[42]*Talmud*: Kethuboth 59a, 64b; Baba Bathra 122a; Hullin 135a.

[43]*John* 2:46.

Chapter 8

THE NAZARETH THREAT

[1]See Chapter 7, "Jesus' Fellow-Galileans: The People of the Land,'" and Chapter 31, "Herod."
The Interpreter's Dictionary of the Bible, pg. 2:347:

> The religious worship in this northerly Gentile region [the Galilee] was related to the many popular cults which had spread around the Mediterranean . . . . Shrines to numerous deities must have existed in

the larger cities of Gentile Galilee, especially in a Roman town like Tiberias, and would have been found even in the more Jewish towns. They represented the normal and traditional worshp of the Gentile majority in Galilee.

Van der Loos, H.: *The Miracles of Jesus*, pg. 6, et seq. speaks of the world at Jesus' time as "miracle minded" and an age which demanded miracles.

[2]Josephus: *Antiquities of the Jews*: XVIII: 116-119 (2).

[3]*Luke* 9:14; *John* 6:10.

[4]*Matthew* 14:17; *Mark* 6:38; *Luke* 9:13; *John* 6:9; 5:11,12.

[5]*Matthew* 9:6; 11:5; 15:31; 21:14; *Mark* 2:9,11; *John* 5:11,12.

[6]*John* 9:1-7.

[7]*Matthew* 9:32-33; 12:22; *Luke* 1:20.

[8]*Matthew* 8:23-26.

[9]*Matthew* 8:5-13; *Luke* 7:1-10.

[10]*Matthew* 9:33; *Mark* 16:9; *Luke* 8:2.

[11]*Mark* 11:20.

[12]*Matthew* 3:7.

[13]*Matthew* 16:4; 12:38.

[14]*Matthew* 23:13,15,27.

[15]*Matthew* 23:24.

[16]*Matthew* 23:23.

[17]*Matthew* 23:27.

[18]*Matthew* 23:29.

[19]*Matthew* 23:30.

[20]*Matthew* 23:37-39; *Luke* 13:34-35.

[21]*Mark* 2:2-12; *Luke* 16:18.

[22]*Luke* 19:2-10.

[23]*Matthew* 11:19.

[24]*Matthew* 6:12-15; 18:21-35; *Mark* 11:25; *Luke* 11:4.

[25]*Matthew* 23:25-26.

[26]*Mark* 2:27.

[27]*John* 6:15.

[28]*Luke* 20:20.

[29]*Interpreter's Dictionary of the Bible*, pgs. 4:160-163; *Encyclopaedia Judaica*, pgs. 14:620-621.

Any history of the Jews carries some description of the Sadducees: Moore, George Foot: *Judaism In the First Centuries of the Christian Era (3 Vols.)*, pgs. 1:68 et seq., is a good source; but since the Sadducees disappeared with the destruction of the Temple in 70 A.D., they really did not leave much of permanent value. They served important roles for the Jewish people during the Second Temple, particularly the Roman era; but left only a negligible, indirect, long-range impact on Judaism.

[30]*Interpreter's Dictionary of the Bible*, pgs. 3:774-781; *Encyclopaedia Judaica*, Note 1, *supra*, pgs. 13:363-366.

The Pharisees played a dominant role in Judaism through the ages; so we can analyze substantial literature on them. See Neusner, Jacob: *The Rabbinic Traditions About the Pharisees Before 70*, (3 vols.); Baeck, Leo: *The Pharisees and Other Essays*; Finkelstein, Louis: *Pharisaism in the Making*; Finkel, Asher: *The Pharisees and the Teacher of Righteousness*; Abrahams, I.: *Studies in Pharisaism and the Gospels*.

Judaism owes its survival to the Pharisees who immediately began to put into writing Jewish history, traditions, lore and Law after the destruction of the Temple in 70 A.D.

[31]*Ibid.*

PART 3

THE SOPHISTICATED JEWISH LEGAL SYSTEM: THE TRIAL FOR SABBATH-BREAKING

Chapter 9

THE FIRST JEWISH TRIAL

[1]*Matthew* 12:14.

[2]*Talmud*: Sanhedrin gives the basic rules of procedure for trials in the Jewish courts. These rules applied during Jesus' lifetime.

Goldin, Hyman E.: *Hebrew Criminal Law and Procedure*, gives an excellent summary of the *talmud's* lengthy coverage.

[3]Bratton, Fred Gladstone: *A History of the Bible*, pgs. 155-179; Goguel, Maurice: *Jesus and the Origins of Christianity*, I:134-161; Hoskyns, Sir Edwyn and Davey, Noel: *The Riddle of the New Testament Documents. Are They*

368

Reliable? pgs. 10-20; Argyle, A.W.: *The Gospel According to Matthew*; Moule, C.F.D.: *The Gospel According to Mark*; Tinsley, E.J.: *The Gospel According to Luke*; Hunter, A.M.: *The Gospel According to John*; *The Interpreter's Dictionary of the Bible* (4 Vols.), pgs. III:302; III:267; III:180; and II:932; Negenman, Jan H.: *New Atlas of the Bible* (Ed. by H.H. Rowley), pgs. 185-187; *The Book of the Bible*, pgs. 163-166.

See also, Rhymer, Joseph: *The Bible in Order*, which arranges the books of both Old and New Testaments in the chronological order of their writing, an order markedly different from the traditional bibles with which we grew up. Paul's epistles, for example come before the *gospels* and *Acts*.

For the fundamentalist view of how the bible came about, see *All Scripture Is Inspired of God and Beneficial*, and *Halley's Bible Handbook*, pgs. 413 and 527.

[4]*Encyclopaedia Britannica*, pgs. 2:949; Dodd, C.H.: *Historical Traditions in the Fourth Gospel*, pg. 21; Bratton, Fred G.: *A History of the Bible*, pg. 333; Reicke, Bo: *The New Testament Era. The World of the Bible from 500 B.C. to A.D. 100*, pg. 122.

[5]Greenslade, S.L.: *The Cambridge History of the Bible*, pgs. 3:408-445.

[6]*Self-Prouncing Edition of the Holy Bible*, pg. 15: "Information Concerning the Bible."

[7]*Ibid.*

[8]Craig, Clarence T.: *The Beginning of Christianity*, pgs. 59-61.

Chapter 10

THE SMALL SANHEDRIN OF THE TEMPLE MOUNT

[1]Many scholars have combed the *torah*, *talmud* and other sources and produced summaries on court organization, jurisdiction, substantive rules of Law and procedures during the period of the Second Temple. These concepts, of course, grew over 1200 years before Jesus' time, dating back to at least the Covenant Constitution Moses worked out with God at Sinai in 1250 B.C. Representative texts include:

Daube, David: *Studies in Biblical Law*; Kent, Charles Foster: *Israel's Laws and Legal Precedents*; Goldin, Hyman: *Hebrew Criminal Law and Procedure*; Mantel, Hugo: *Studies in the History of the Sanhedrin*; Mendelsohn, S.: *The Criminal Jurisprudence of the Ancient Hebrews*; Gershfield, Edward M.: *Studies in Jewish Jurisprudence*; Kadushin, Rabbi J.: *Jewish Code of Jurisprudence: Talmudic Law Decisions*; Ehrlich, J.W.: *The Holy Bible and the Law*.

[2]I have not found any sources which describe a special meeting room (chamber) for the Court of the Temple Mount. We do know that city walls were

thick enough to contain rooms and "cells." Prof. Avi-Yonah's meticulous *2nd Temple Reconstruction*, Holyland Hotel, dramatically shows the use of marble columns, Greek arches and openness to blend the cloistered areas under the outside city walls into the adjacent courts, in this case, the Court of the Gentiles.The sitting chamber of the Court of the Temple Mount would need a roof or shelter of some kind from the rain, since there is nothing to indicate that the rainy season caused the regular Monday and Thursday meetings of the Court to be suspended (Gershfield, Edward M.: *Studies in Jewish Jurisprudence*, pg. 195; Mendelsohn, S.: *Criminal Jurisprudence of the Ancient Hebrews*, pg. 97; *Talmud*: Baba Kama 82a). The walkway above the cloister area would provide this protection from the elements.

Further, this location of the Court of the Temple Mount is in keeping with the 1000-year tradition of "the Gate" as the site where the elders dispensed justice and made their administrative decisions for the people (De Vaux, Roland: *Ancient Israel, Its Life and Institutions*, pgs. 152-157.)

[3]*Deuteronomy*, 16:18.

[4]The Law recognized thirty-six death penalty offenses: Eighteen moral abuses, arising from illegal sexual relations; twelve acts which violated the religious Laws (Sabbath- breaking fell into this category); three offenses against parents; one offense of assault or murder; one offense of forcible abduction, kidnapping or selling into slavery; and one offense of treason (including that of *rebellious elder* who committed treason against God by not following the legal precedents of decided cases) (Goldin, Hyman E.: *Hebrew Criminal Law and Procedure*, pgs. 26-28).

[5]The Law used four methods of execution: (1) Stoning, (2) Burning, (3) Decapitation, and (4) Strangulation; stoning considered the most severe form of punishment, with strangulation the least severe. Note 4, *ibid*, pgs. 28-37.

[6]This transcript of the Sabbath-breaking trial in the Court of the Temple Mount is, of course, my own invention. I supply all names, except Jesus', but I bend over backwards to make the dialogue and procedural steps entirely realistic.This is possible from years of study of the debates reported in the *talmud* of the judges as they decided actual cases. I use not only the exact words and phrases of the judges, but also try to capture the tone and flavor of a trial in a Court of Twenty-Three, Israel's court of general trial jurisdiction during the Second Temple period. The underlying theme of any of their trials concerned itself with (1) fairness, (2) an objective search for the facts, (3) "due process" protection of the rights of the accused, and (4) the correct application of God's Law.

[7]Goldin, Hyman E.: *Hebrew Criminal Law and Procedure*, pg. 121.

[8]*Talmud*: Aboth 1:2. "Master" and "Holy Master" appear frequently throughout the *talmud* as terms of respect for learned scholars, elders and judges. *Numbers* XI:28 reports Joshua addressing Moses as "My Lord Moses." These titles of respect were part of the culture of the time in which Jesus lived.

[9]*The Interpreter's Dictionary of the Bible*, pgs. 3:774-781, "Pharisees."

[10]For clarity and readability, but without the slightest disservice to substance, I combine the Danby and Epstein translations of the *mishnah* and *talmud* (Danby, Herbert: *The mishnah*, pgs. 387-388, Ch. 4:5; and *Sanhedrin* 37a-37b.) The dramatic "Inspire with Awe" was used routinely during Jesus' time. My arrangement of the original words is simply an effort to give them more readability in the light of modern language developments. I have also shortened the requirement considerably.

[11]*Encyclopaedia Judaica*, pg. 16:589; *Talmud*: Sanhedrin 40a.

[12]Note 10, *Ibid.*

[13]*Daniel* 13 (in the apocrypha).

[14]*Talmud*: Sanhedrin 32b; 37a.

[15]*Talmud*: Shabbath 127a.

[16]*Ibid.*

[17]*Talmud*: Sanhedrin 6b.

[18]*Talmud*: Sanhedrin 86b.

[19]*Deuteronomy* 1:17.

[20]*Encyclopaedia Judaica*, pg. 16:589; Goldin, Hyman E.: *Hebrew Criminal Law and Procedure*, pgs. 118-121; *Talmud*: Sanhedrin 40a (where the term *hakiroth* is used).

[21]Josephus: *Against Apion*: II, 164-165.

[22]*Encyclopaedia Judaica*, pgs. 14:1587-1593.

[23]*Talmud*: Sanhedrin 15b; 18b; 2b; 32a; 86a; *Deuteronomy* 18:20.

Chapter 11

DIRECT EXAMINATION: THE HEALING ACT

[1]Mendelsohn, S.: *Criminal Jurisprudence of the Ancient Hebrews*; pg. 127.

[2]*Talmud*: Sanhedrin 40a.

[3]*Luke* 6:6-11.

[4]The number "17" is my own invention. I find no source giving the political break-down of the members of any of the courts at the time. There is sufficient material, however, to support the conclusion that the Pharisees were the dominant political party, and that the Temple Bureaucracy (Sadducees) did not

feel safe to try to rule without the collaboration of the Pharisees.

For a succinct background discussion of the rise and continuing influence of the Pharisees through the Second Temple period, see Russell, D.S.: *The Jews from Alexander to Herod*, pgs. 71-76, 155-164. See also Jeremias, Joachim: *Jerusalem in the Time of Jesus*, pgs. 246-267, "Appendix: The Pharisees" and "The Lay Nobility," pgs. 222-232; Josephus: *Histories of the Jews*, XVIII:17.

[5]We find a large body of literature on the scribes, explaining their history and functions, particularly at the time of the Second Temple. It is well summarized in *The Interpreter's Dictionary of the Bible*, pgs. 4:246-248.

Chapter 12

CROSS-EXAMINATION: THE WARNING

[1]*Talmud*: Sanhedrin 40a. The last of the *searching inquiries*, "Did you warn him?" is a technical phrase, unique to Ancient Israel's sophisticated legal system. Before any accused could be convicted, at least two complaining witnesses must testify that they (or someone in their presence) *warned* the accused that his threatened conduct would be a transgression of God's law (*Talmud*: Sanhedrin 8b), and further told him what the specific punishment would be if he persisted in his wrongdoing.

The *warning* concept (also called preadmonition) expressed the Jews' emphasis on Law "involvement," as distinguished from Law "enforcement" practiced by their neighbors.

Moses' basic organization from the days of Sinai and the desert still held: "Moses chose able men out of Israel, and made them heads over the people at all times . . . rulers of thousands, of hundreds, of fifties, and of tens" (*Exodus* 18:25-26). If the people kept sin out of their own "ten," there would be no Law-breaking in a "fifty," a "hundred" or a "thousand."

The Jews who *warned* their fellows against transgressing God's Law did not bear the stigma of busybodies, nosy vigilantes, rats or finks: All knew their responsibilities to keep God's public peace, to prevent God's law from defilement; and none dared shirk this duty (Mendelsohn, S.: *The Criminal Justice of the Ancient Hebrews*, pg. 97).

Only in this aura of Law "involvement" could enforceable human rights develop, the *warning* serving as the prime tool to make the "involvement" concept workable.

Outside the Temple Mount in Jerusalem, no policemen patrolled the rest of the country. Concerned citizens pressured all in the community to respect God's Law. When evildoers failed to heed the proper *warning*, complaining citizens accused them before the courts, either a Court of the Three or a Court of the Twenty-Three, and a trial took place, controlled by strict rules of legal procedure.

372

[2]*Encyclopaedia Judaica*, pg. 16:589.

[3]For a quick summary of the personalities of Hillel and Shammai, and their schools, see Cohen, Dr. A.: *Everyman's Talmud*, pgs. xx-xxiii.

[4]*Talmud*: Sanhedrin 88b; *Tosefta* Sanhedrin 1:7, 1; *Tosefta* Nagiga 2.

[5]*Talmud*: Sanhedrin 40a; Maimonides, H.: *Sanhedrin*, 8; Mendelsohn, S.: *The Criminal Jurisprudence of the Ancient Hebrews*; pg. 142:

> The probationer advances to the judicial bench, whence he delivers his argument. If his argument proves untenable, he remains among the judges for the rest of that day only; but if he is clever, and serves to save the life of the prisoner, he remains there for ever after as an active member of the court (Tosefta Sanhedrin IX, 43; *Talmud* Sanhedrin 42a).

[6]Although the six divisions of the *talmud* ("Orders") date from Hillel, an older contemporary of Jesus, the present chapter division and numbering scheme came later. I use it for convenience to identify reference passages as though it actually did exist during Jesus' Sabbath-breaking trial.

[7]*Talmud*: Sanhedrin 41a; *Encyclopaedia Judaica*, pg. 13:227.

[8]*Talmud*: Kethuboth 32a; Sanhedrin 72b; 88b; 81b.

[9]*Exodus* XII:19; *Deuteronomy* XVI:3; *Leviticus* III:17, XX:17-21, XXIII:29, 30.

[10]*Talmud*: Makkoth 1:8.

[11]Goldin, Hyman E.: *Hebrew Criminal Law and Procedure*, pg. 122:

> It must be noted that under the Mosaic Law, the testimony of any set of witnesses, whether it be composed of two or of one hundred witnesses, is considered as one inseparable entity. If, therefore, one of the witnesses should for any reason be disqualified, the testimony of the whole set is rendered invalid and inadmissible, and the accused is consequently acquitted.

See also *Talmud*: Makkoth 6b; Sanhedrin 24b. et seq.; 27b et seq.

[12]*Talmud*: Makkoth 6b; Sanhedrin 24b et seq.; 27b et seq.

[13]The judges' obsession to obtain impartial testimony runs throughout the *talmud*. A number of references imply that the "victim" may not be impartial since he may receive some indirect benefit from the prosecution of the accused.

[14]Note 11, *supra*.

[15]*Deuteronomy* 19:18-21.

[16]Gershfield, Edward M.: *Studies in Jewish Jurisprudence*, pg. 193.

[17]*Talmud*: Sanhedrin 36b.

[18]*Gershfield*, Note 16, at pg. 194.

[19]*Talmud*: Sanhedrin 17a.

[20]*Talmud*: Sanhedrin 7a.

Chapter 13

CROSS-EXAMINATION: SABBATH-BREAKING

[1]*Talmud*: Sanhedrin 27a; 27b; 28a; 33b; 34a.

[2]*Deuteronomy* 19:16-21.

[3]Goldin, Hyman E.: *Hebrew Criminal Law and Procedure*, pgs. 122, 123:

> After the direct examination, the witnesses were subjected to cross-examination.
>
> This cross-examination consisted of inquiries that had no direct bearing upon the issue involved, but simply tested the veracity of the witnesses. In cases involving civil matters, such inquiries might have concerned the color of the clothes worn by the plaintiff or the defendant during the alleged negotiations, or whether the parties to the action had been sitting or standing at the time, or whether the object involved in the proceedings had been wrapped in a silk or a woolen cloth.
>
> In cases of homicide, the witnesses would have been asked if the accused or the victim had worn light or dark clothes, or if the color of the surrounding area had been white or black, and other similar questions
> . . . .

See also *Talmud*: Sanhedrin 40a.

[4]*Matthew* 12:9-14; *Mark* 3:16; *Luke* 6:6-11. *Mark* and *Luke* report Jesus calling "the man" to come to him. *Matthew* omits this part of the episode.

[5]*Talmud*: Shabbath 53b.

[6]*Ibid.*, 66b.

[7]*Ibid.*, 67a.

[8]*Ibid.*, 75a.

[9]*Ibid.*, 81a.

[10]*Ibid.*, 109a.

[11]*Ibid.*, 84b.

[12]*Ibid.*, 147b.

[13]*Ibid.*, 66b.

[14]*Mark* 2:27.

[15]The idiom, "a favorable verdict," appears in lieu of "acquittal" or "not guilty," dramatically implying the basic thrust of the Second Temple Jewish legal system: The protection of personal rights, within the framework of maintaining public order which, of course, is the first obligation of any goverment, any time, any place.

[16]*Talmud*: Sanhedrin 32a; 33b; Yoma: 18a.

[17]*John* 11:49-50.

[18]Daube, David: *Collaboration with Tyranny in Rabbinic Law.*

PART 4

THE TRIAL FOR FALSE PROPHECY: WHAT DID JESUS REALLY PREACH?

Chapter 14

THE GREAT SANHEDRIN IN THE HALL OF THE HEWN STONE

[1]Goldin, Hyman E.: *Hebrew Criminal Law and Procedure*, pgs. 76, 214.

[2]The literal translation of *bet din ha-gadol* is "the greatest house of justice" or "the largest house of justice." See *Encyclopaedia Judaica*, pgs. 15:968; 2:200; 16:920.

[3]*Talmud*: Yoma 25a.

[4]*Ibid.*

[5]Russell, D.S.: *The Jews from Alexander to Herod*, pg. 74.

[6]*Talmud*: Sanhedrin 36b-37a.

[7]*Talmud*: Sanhedrin 37a.

[8]*Talmud*: Sanhedrin 36b; 17b; 29b; 34b; 35a; 40a.

Chapter 15

THE CHARGE: FALSE PROPHECY

[1]*Mark* 13:1-4; 14:58.

[2]*Matthew* 27:40.

[3]*Matthew* 23:37-39; *Luke* 13:34-35.

[4]*Encyclopaedia Judaica*, 13:1151 et seq. See also Herschel, Abraham J.: *The Prophets*, pgs. 5, 472-473.

[5]My paraphrase of *Matthew* 24:1-3; *Mark* 13:1-4; *Deuteronomy* 13:3; 13:5.

[6]*Encyclopaedia Judaica*, pgs. 13:1168-1171.

[7]*Deuteronomy* 13:8-11; *Talmud*: Sanhedrin 89a.

[8]*Deuteronomy* 18:22.

[9]*Talmud*: Sanhedrin 2a.

Chapter 16

"THE KINGDOM OF GOD"

[1]*John* 7:1.

[2]*Luke* 20:20.

[3]*Deuteronomy* 13:5.

[4]*Luke* 3:10.

[5]*The Interpreter's Dictionary of the Bible*, pg. 3:880.

[6]*Matthew* 3:4.

[7]Josephus: *Histories of the Jews*: XVIII:(2), 116-117.

[8]*Matthew* 3:7-10.

[9]*Matthew* 3:5-6.

[10]*Matthew* 3:2.

[11]Josephus: *Histories of the Jews*: XVIII:(2), 117-118.

[12]*Hosea* 1:10.

[13]All three Synoptic gospels describe John's baptism of Jesus: *Matthew* 3:13-17; *Mark* 1:9-11; *Luke* 3:21-22.

[14]Moore, George Foote: *Judaism In the First Centuries of the Christian Era*, pgs. 421-422.

[15]*Talmud*: Makkoth, glossary, pg. 179.

[16]Midrash Rabba: *Deuteronomy* XI:10.

[17]*Talmud*: Sotah, 13b.

[18]*Talmud*: Makkoth 23b.

[19]*Talmud*: Yoma 9b.

[20]*Talmud*: Sotah 48b.

[21]Josephus: *Histories of the Jews*: XVII:(2), 118-119.

[22]*Matthew* 19:14; *Mark* 2:8; *Luke* 5:33.

[23]*Matthew* 4:17.

[24]*Matthew* 11:11; *Luke* 7:28. For a discussion of Jesus' terminology, see Ladd, George Eldon: *Jesus and the Kingdom*, pg. 106.

[25]*Amos* 5:18.

[26]*Genesis* 1.

[27]*Amos* 5:24.

[28]*Zechariah* 14:9.

[29]See Ladd, Note 24, *supra*, at pgs. 66-71.

[30]*Ibid.*, at pg. 51.

[31]Ladd, in Note 24, *supra*, at pgs. 66-71.

[32]*Ibid.*, at pgs. 42-48.

[33]*Isaiah* 2:4.

[34]*Isaiah* 11:16.

[35]*Luke* 16:23.

[36]Ladd, in Note 24, *supra*, at pgs. 48, 58-59, 60, 72-97.

[37]Ladd, in Note 24, *supra*, at pg. 118:

> New Testament scholars generally agree that the burden of Jesus' message was the Kingdom of God (*Mark* 1:15; *Matthew* 4:17.) The same message was entrusted to the twelve disciples (*Matthew* 10:7) and to a band of seventy on a later mission (*Luke* 10:9, 11).

And at pages 160-161:

> Jesus' message about the kingdom was not merely instruction or prophecy or promise; it was the proclamation of good news: It was gospel.

In the synagogue at Nazareth, Jesus claimed that this gospel was no longer hope but event (*Luke* 4:18). The time of fulfillment had come. Jesus had been anointed to preach the good news . . . to the poor, to proclaim . . . release to the captives, to proclaim . . . the acceptable year of the Lord.

In the proclamation of the gospel, promise had become fulfillment.

Chapter 17

"HEAR, O ISRAEL, THE LORD OUR GOD . . ."

[1]*Encyclopaedia Judaica*, pg. 14:1372.

[2]*Ibid.*

[3]*Talmud*: Berakoth 10b.

[4]*Talmud*: Berakoth 16a.

[5]*Talmud*: Berakoth 20a.

[6]*Matthew* 22:36-38; *Mark* 12:28-30; *Luke* 10:25-28.

Chapter 18

"THE SON OF GOD"

[1]*Matthew* 14:33.

[2]*Matthew* 8:29; *Mark* 5:1-8; *Luke* 8:26-28.

[3]*Matthew* 4:3; *Luke* 4:3.

[4]Moore, George Foote: *Judaism in the First Centuries of the Christian Era*, pgs. 2:202 et seq.

[5]*Genesis* 1:26; 9:6.

[6]*Genesis* 2:7.

[7]*Psalms* 8:5-6.

[8]*Ecclesiasticus, or the Wisdom of Jesus Son of Sirach* 17:6-8.

[9]*Ibid.*, at 17:11.

[10]*Wisdom of Solomon*, 2:23-24; 3:2-6.

[11]I combine portions of *The Thanksgiving Psalms of the Dead Sea Scrolls*, Nos. XVI (x. 3-14) and XVI (xi. 3-12), as translated and published in Burrows, Millar: *The Dead Sea Scrolls*.

[12]From the viewpoint of hard courtroom proof, *Matthew, Mark* and *Luke* offer the most persuasive evidence of what Jesus actually said about himself. *John's* Greek format, totally and completely different from the other three gospel writers, is perhaps the most important and beautiful book ever written; but *John's* literary poetry makes it difficult to separate out Jesus' true words from *John's* magnificent embellishments.

What others say and write about Jesus as the "son of God," the *kerygman* (*Greek* "preaching") of the last 1900 years, differs greatly from *Matthew, Mark* and *Luke's* bare-bones reports of Jesus' teaching and preaching about himself.

Chapter 19

"MY FATHER WHO IS IN HEAVEN"

[1]Buchler, Adolf: *Types of Jewish-Palestinian Piety from 70 B.C.E. to 70 C.E. The Ancient Pious Men*; Matthews, I.G.: *The Religious Pilgrimage of Israel.*

[2]*Matthew* 5:45.

[3]*Matthew* 6:9.

[4]*Matthew* 10:32. My own unscientific, rough estimate is that Jesus used "my father" considerably less than "your father" or "our father."

[5]*Jubilees* 1:24.

[6]*Wisdom of Solomon* 2:16-18.

[7]*Talmud*: Aboth 3:14.

[8]Moore, George Foote: *Judaism in the First Centuries of the Christian Era*, pg. 2:205.

[9]*Ibid.*, at pgs. 203-204.

[10]*Talmud*: Kiddushin 36a.

[11]Graetz, Henrich: *History of the Jews*, pg. II:363.

[12]*Talmud*: Berakoth 60b.

[13]*Ibid.*

[14]Jeremias, Joachim: *The Prayers of Jesus*, pgs. 11-65; Van Den Bussche, Henri: *Understanding the Lord's Prayer*, pgs. 35-51.

[15]See Chapter 1, "*Yom Kippur*: Day of Atonement."

[16]As can be expected, there is a substantial body of literature on "The Lord's Prayer." One of the best descriptions is Klausner, Joseph: *Jesus of Nazareth*, pgs. 396-398.

[17]*Encyclopaedia Judaica*, pgs. 10:660-663; Rowley, H.H.: *Worship in Ancient Israel, pgs. 213-271.*

[18]*Matthew* 6:9-13. *Luke*'s version is shorter (11:2-4). For some reason, he omitted two important themes. Either he did not know them, or part of his original manuscript is lost.

[19]Note 16, *supra*. Since Klausner gives all the appropriate citations, we do not need to list cumulative references to this great body of literature on "The Lord's Prayer." The citations of the two works in Note 14, *supra*, are quite representative.

[20]*Matthew* 9:35-10:16; *Mark* 6:6b-13; *Luke* 10:1-2. The missions of the Twelve: . . . "preach the Kingdom of God and to heal." *Matthew* 10:40: "He who believes in me believes not in me but in him who sent me."

Later, Jesus sent out seventy disciples on similar missions: *Matthew* 9:37-38; *Luke* 10:1-16. *Luke* 10:17-20 describes their return.

Chapter 20

"THEREFORE, CHOOSE LIFE!"

[1]*The Interpreter's Dictionary of the Bible*, pgs. 1:182; 1:440-441.

[2]*Matthew* 7:17.

[3]*Matthew* 6:24.

[4]Moore, George Foote: *Judaism in the First Centuries of the Christian Era*, pg. 1:454.

[5]*Talmud*: Hullin 7b.

[6]*Midrash Rabbah: Ecclesiastes* X:11-1.

[7]*Talmud*: Aboth 3:15 (paraphrased with explanatory footnotes inserted).

[8]*Talmud*: Berakoth 33b; Magillah 25a.

Chapter 21

"THERE IS MORE JOY IN HEAVEN OVER ONE SINNER . . ."

[1]*Luke* 15:2-7.

[2]*Midrash Rabbah: Genesis* VIII:10.

Chapter 22

"THOU ART A GOD READY TO FORGIVE"

[1]*Luke* 14:4.

[2]*Luke* 6:37.

[3]*Talmud*: Yoma 36b; 87a, 87b, 88a.

[4]*Midrash Rabbah: Ecclesiastes* III:11-3.

[5]*Talmud*: Kiddushin 30b.

[6]*Talmud*: Sukkah 52b.

[7]Mowry, Lucetta: *The Dead Sea Scrolls and the Early Church*, pg. 148.

[8]*Talmud*: Baba Bathra 16a.

[9]*Talmud*: Sukkah 52b.

[10]*Talmud*: Kiddushin 30b.

[11]*Talmud*: Berakoth 5a.

[12]*Talmud*: Baba Bathra 16a.

[13]*Luke* 8:2.

[14]*Mark* 3:30.

[15]*Mark* 3:24.

[16]*Luke* 13:3.

[17]*Mark* 6:12.

[18]*Mark* 1:15.

[19]Moore, George Foote: *Judaism in the First Centuries of the Christian Era*, pg. II:509.

[20]*Talmud*: Yoma 8:8.

[21]*The Prayer of Manasseh*: 7, 8, 12-13.

[22]*Numbers* 5:6-7.

[23]*Daniel* 9; 3.

[24]Moore, George Foote: *Judaism in the First Centuries of the Christian Era*, pg. I:517.

[25]*Malachi* 3:6ff.

[26]*Deuteronomy* 4:30-31.

Chapter 23

"DO THIS, AND YOU WILL LIVE"

[1]*Mark* 12:31; *Matthew* 22:39-40; *Luke* 10:27-28.

[2]*Leviticus* 19:18.

[3]*Talmud*: Shabbath 31a.

[4]*Talmud*: Berakoth 16b.

[5]Moore, George Foote: *Judaism in the First Centuries of the Christian Era*, pg. I:495.

[6]*Ibid.*, at pgs. II:201-211.

[7]*Ibid.*, at pgs. I:445-459.

[8]*Amos* 5:24.

[9]*Micah* 6:8.

[10]*Jeremiah* 9:23-24.

[11]*Psalm* 1:1.

[12]*Ezekiel* 18:5-9.

[13]*Midrash Rabbah: Genesis* 24:7 (in footnote on page 204 of the Soncino Press edition).

[14]*Proverbs* 14:31.

[15]*Deuteronomy* 4:8.

Chapter 24

"GIVE TO HIM WHO BEGS FROM YOU . . ."

[1]Moore, George Foote: *Judaism in the First Centuries of the Christian Era*, pg. 11:168.

[2]*Talmud*: Aboth 1:2.

[3]*Deuteronomy* 15:9-11.

[4]*Proverbs* 14:21.

[5]*Proverbs* 21:26.

[6]*Proverbs* 28:27.

[7]*Ecclesiasticus, or the Wisdom of Jesus Son of Sirach* 4:14.

[8]*Ibid.*, 29:14.

[9]*Talmud*: Baba Bathra 10a.

[10]*Ibid.*

[11]*Luke* 14:12-14.

[12]*Matthew* 6:2-4.

[13]*Encyclopaedia Judaica*, pg. 5:343.

[14]*Talmud*: Shabbath 63a.

[15]*Luke* 10:25-37.

Chapter 25

"I HAVE GIVEN TO ALL ABLE MEN ABILITY . . ."

[1]*Matthew* 25:14-30.

[2]*Genesis* 2:15.

[3]*Psalm* 8:3-4.

[4]*Psalm* 102:25.

[5]*Talmud*: Berakoth 8a.

[6]*Talmud*: Kethuboth 59b.

[7]*Talmud*: Aboth 2:2.

[8]*Ecclesiasticus, or the Wisdom of Jesus Son of Sirach*, 7:15.

[9]*Talmud*: Baba Bathra 110a; Pesahim 113a.

[10]*Talmud*: Kethuboth 68a.

[11]*Talmud*: Kiddushin 29a.

[12]*Ecclesiasticus, or the Wisdom of Jesus Son of Sirach*, 38:26-34.

CHAPTER 26

"BESIDE ME THERE IS NO SAVIOR"

[1]Cullman, Oscar: *Salvation in History*; Salm, C. Luke: *Studies in Salvation History*; Smith, Wilbur M.: *The Biblical Doctrine of Heaven*; Fuller, Reginald H.:

The Formation of the Resurrection Narratives.

[2]Moore, George Foote: *Judaism in the First Centuries of the Christian Era,* pgs. 2:289 et seq.

[3]*Isaiah* 38:10.

[4]*Job* 3:17.

[5]*Job* 14:12, 14.

[6]*Ezekiel* 18:21-22, 32-33.

[7]*Psalm* 116:7-9, 15.

[8]*Isaiah* 30:18; see also *Isaiah* 52:10; *Psalm* 14:7.

[9]Moore, George Foote: *Judaism in the First Centuries of the Christian Era,* pg. 2:309.

[10]*Enoch* 50:1-5; Moore, George Foote: *Judaism in the First Centuries of the Christian Era,* pg. 2:304.

[11]*Testament of Benjamin,* Chapter 10.

[12]*Mark* 10:17-31.

[13]*Talmud:* Berakoth 28b.

[14]Guignebert, Charles: *Ancient, Medieval and Modern Christianity,* pg. 68, 69, 70, 73, 79; Cumont, Franz: *The Mysteries of Mirthra; Encyclopaedia Brittanica,* pgs. 7:202, 131; Moore, Note 2, *supra,* at pg. 2:320.

[15]*Isaiah* 43:3-4, 11.

Chapter 27

"... AND THEIR WITNESS DID NOT AGREE"

[1]Pritchard, James B: *Ancient Near Eastern Texts Relating to the Old Testament.*

[2]Houts, Marshall: *From Evidence to Proof,* pgs. 3-42.

[3]Houts, Marshall: *Lawyers' Guide to Medical Proof,* Chapter 1701.

[4]*Deuteronomy* 18:19.

[5]Mendelsohn, S.: *The Criminal Jurisprudence of the Ancient Hebrews;* pgs. 135-138.

[6]Goldin, Hyman E.: *Hebrew Criminal Law and Procedure,* pgs. 97 et seq.; Mendelsohn, Note 5, *supra,* at pgs. 116-119.

[7]Goldin, Note 6, *supra*, at pgs. 236 et seq.; Mendelsohn, Note 5, *supra*, at pgs. 54-55, 129, 137, 139; Gershfield, Edward M.: *Studies in Jewish Jurisprudence*, pgs. 224-225.

[8]*Talmud*: Baba Kamma 74a; Mendelsohn, Note 5, *supra*, pg. 135.

[9]*Mark* 14:5.

[10]*Deuteronomy* 13:1-5.

PART 5

IN THE HOUSES OF THE HIGH PRIESTS

Chapter 28

THIRD ARREST: GETHSEMANE

[1]Grant, Michael: *The Army of the Caesars*, pg. xxxi.

[2]*Matthew* 26:47; *Mark* 14:43; *John* 18:3.

[3]Berger, Adolf: *Encyclopedic Dictionary of Roman Law*, pg. 340.

[4]*John* 18:13, 24.

[5]*Matthew* 26:65-67.

[6]*Mark* 14:63-65.

Chapter 29

"ARE YOU THE CHRIST"

[1]Josephus: *Wars of the Jews*: I:401-402.

[2]*Matthew* 12:5-6.

[3]Kunkel, Wolfgang: *An Introduction to Roman Legal and Constitutional History*, pg. 165.

[4]*Encyclopaedia Judaica*, pgs. 11:1407-1412.

[5]*Leviticus* 8:10, 12.

[6]1 *Samuel* 16:13.

[7]*Encyclopaedia Judaica*, pg. 13:1151.

[8]Klausner, Joseph: *The Messianic Idea in Israel from Its Beginning to the Completion of the Mishnah*.

[9]*Luke* 22:67-68.

[10]*Micah* 6:8.

Chapter 30

"THE SON OF MAN"

[1]*Matthew* 26:64.

[2]*Ezekiel* 21:18.

[3]*Ezekiel* 21:28.

[4]*Ezekiel* 22:1-2.

[5]*Mark* 14:62.

[6]*Matthew* 26:65.

[7]*Matthew* 26:66; *Mark* 14:63.

[8]*Luke* 22:63-65; *Mark* 14:65; *Matthew* 26:67.

PART 6

THE ROMAN PRESENCE IN JUDEA

Chapter 31

HEROD

[1]Josephus: *Histories of the Jews*: XV:8, 1; Avi-Yonah, Michael: *2nd Temple Reconstruction*.

[2]Josephus: *Histories of the Jews*: XV:8, 1.

[3]*Ibid*.

[4]Russell, D.S.: *The Jews from Alexander to Herod*, pgs. 89-90:

> Herod the Great was a man of overpowering personality who contrived to be "everything to all men" and was prepared to use every means to gain his own ends.

> By religion he was a Jew, by race an Idumaean, by cultural sympathies a Greek, and by political allegiance a Roman.
>
> To his inferiors he was utterly ruthless; to the members of his own family he could behave in a most cruel manner; to his superiors he adopted a cunning policy of "playing along with" whichever ruler at that moment found himself in power, and, like his father before him, was ready to change sides at a moment's notice in order to realize his ambitions.

See also *Encyclopaedia Judaica*, pgs. 8:296, 300; 375-385.

[5]Josephus: *Histories of the Jews*: XV:8, 1.

[6]Note 4, *supra*.

[7]Josephus: *Histories of the Jews*: XV:8, 1.

[8]Russell, D.S.: *The Jews from Alexander to Herod*, pgs. 89-102.
I cite Russell frequently because of his brilliant job in summarizing "Herod" succinctly, pulling together the many paragraphs throughout *Josephus*.

[9]Josephus: *Histories of the Jews*: XVII:7, 1.

[10]*The Interpreter's Dictionary of the Bible*, pg. 2:678, also 2:24-26.

[11]Barclay, William: *The Bible and History*, pgs. 23, 24, 26, 27 (and other references in Index).

[12]Josephus: *Histories of the Jews*: XIII:9, 1.

[13]Josephus: *Wars of the Jews*: I:8, 9.

[14]*Encyclopaedia Judaica*, pgs. 3:76-77.

[15]*Encyclopaedia Britannica*, pgs. 15:1084-1106.

[16]*Ibid.*, 15:1105.

[17]Josephus: *Wars of the Jews*: I:10, 2.

[18]*Ibid.*, I:10, 4.

[19]Josephus: *Antiquities of the Jews*: XIV:9, 2.

[20]*Ibid.*

[21]*Ibid.*, XIV:9,4.

[22]*Ibid.*

[23]*Ibid.*

[24]*Ibid.*

[25]*Ibid.*

[26]*Ibid.*, XIV:9, 5.

[27]*Ibid.*, XI:4:9, 3.

[28]Russell, D.S.: *The Jews from Alexander to Herod*, pgs. 86-89.

[29]*Deuteronomy* 1:16-17:

> And I charged your judges at that time, "Hear the cases between your brethren, and judge righteously between a man and his brother or the alien that is with him.

> "You shall not be partial in judgment; you shall hear the small and the great alike; you shall not be afraid of the face of man, for the judgment is God's; and the case that is too hard for you, you shall bring to me, and I will hear it."

Deuteronomy 17:4-7:

> Then you shall inquire diligently, and if it is true and certain that such an abominable thing has been done in Israel, then you shall bring forth to your gates that man or woman who has done this evil thing, and you shall stone that man or woman to death with stones.

> On the evidence of two witnesses or of three witnesses he that is to die shall be put to death; a person shall not be put to death on the evidence of one witness.

> The hand of the witnesses shall be first against him to put him to death, and afterward the hand of all the people. So you shall purge the evil from the midst of you.

[30]Russell, D.S.: *The Jews from Alexander to Herod*, pgs. 86-89; Grayzel, Solomon: *A History of the Jews*, pgs. 92-98; Josephus: *Antiquities of the Jews*: XIV:2.

[31]Josephus: *Antiquities of the Jews*: XIV:9, 5; XIV:11, 1-5.

[32]Josephus: *Histories of the Jews*: XV:6, 1-7.

[33]Josephus: *Histories of the Jews*: XIV:14, 4.

[34]*Ibid.*, XIV:14, 5.

[35]Russell, D.S.: *The Jews from Alexander to Herod*, pg. 89.

[36]Josephus: *Histories of the Jews*: XV:1, 1-2; Russell, D.S.: *The Jews from Alexander to Herod*, pg. 91.

[37]Josephus: *Histories of the Jews*: XV:10, 4; Russell, D.S.: *The Jews from Alexander to Herod*, pg. 91.

[38]*Encyclopaedia Judaica*, pg. 8:376; Russell, D.S.: *The Jews from Alexander to Herod*, pg. 91; Josephus: *Histories of the Jews*: XIV:9, 4.

[39]Josephus: *Histories of the Jews*: XIV:9, 4.

[40]*Encyclopaedia Judaica*, pgs. 8:379-380.

[41]*Encyclopaedia Judaica*, pgs. 8:382, 394; Russell, D.S.:*The Jews from Alexander to Herod*, pgs. 91-93.

[42]Russell, D.S.: *The Jews from Alexander to Herod*, pg. 92; *Encyclopaedia Judaica*, pgs. 8:376, 379.

[43]See Chapter 2, Part 1, *supra*.

[44]*Ibid*.

[45]Russell, D.S.: *The Jews from Alexander to Herod*, pg. 92; *Encyclopaedia Judaica*, pg. 8:379.

[46]Josephus: *Histories of the Jews*: XIV:12, 1.

[47]*Ibid*.

[48]Although Josephus refers to Mariamne many times and is disturbed by the great injustice done her by Herod, he makes no attempt whatsoever to give a physical description of her beauty.

[49]*Encyclopaedia Judaica*, pgs. 7:1455-1459; De Vaux, Roland: *Ancient Israel, Its Life and Institutions*, pgs. 378, 400, 401, 402, and 511; Russell, D.S.: *The Jews from Alexander to Herod*, pgs. 43-81.

[50]Russell, D.S.: *The Jews from Alexander to Herod*, pgs. 60-81.

[51]*Ibid*., pgs. 68-69.

[52]Russell, D.S.: *The Jews from Alexander to Herod*, pgs. 82-102.

[53]Josephus: *Histories of the Jews*: XIV:16, 4.

[54]*Ibid*.

[55]Josephus: *Histories of the Jews*: XV:3, 3.

[56]*Ibid*.

[57]Josephus: *Histories of the Jews*: XV:4, 2.

[58]*Ibid*.

[59]Josephus: *Histories of the Jews*: XIV:7, 4.

[60]*Ibid*., XV:7, 6.

[61]Josephus: *Histories of the Jews*: XIV:13, 8.

[62]*Ibid*., XIV:13, 7.

[63]*Ibid*.

[64]*Ibid*.

[65]Note 8, *supra*.

[66]Russell, D.S.: *The Jews from Alexander to Herod*, pg. 96; *Encyclopaedia Judaica*, pgs. 5:6-13.

[67]Russell, D.S.: *The Jews from Alexander to Herod*, pg. 96; *Encyclopaedia Judaica*, pgs. 14:723-726.

[68]*Encyclopaedia Judaica*, pgs. 8:379, 380, 383; Russell, D.S.: *The Jews from Alexander to Herod*, pgs. 95-100.

[69]Russell, D.S.: *The Jews from Alexander to Herod*, pg. 95.

[70]*Ibid.*, pg. 95.

[71]*Ibid.*, pgs. 95-96.

[72]*Ibid.*, pgs. 95-96.

[73]*Ibid.*, pg. 90; *Encyclopaedia Judaica*, pg. 8:379.

[74]Russell, D.S.: *The Jews from Alexander to Herod*, pgs. 90-91.

[75]*Encyclopaedia Judaica*, pgs. 8:382, 384:

> ... He was a man of unlimited ambition whose opportunism was never restricted by ties of friendship or loyalty (the only exception being his loyalty to his brothers); when in power he brooked no opposition but ruled with cruelty, intensified by his suspicion and jealousy.
>
> Herod's rule destroyed the internal organization of the Jewish community. In contrast to the Hasmonean kings who had ruled jointly with the popular institutions, Herod abolished all traditional autonomous institutions, and in practice he did away with the authority of the Torah, although this never took official form.
>
> He regarded the kingdom as his private property. One of the aims of his policy was to strengthen the foreign element in Erez Israel and to bring the kingdom into the Roman Hellenistic cultural orbit, with the aim of securing it as a sure link in the Roman Empire.
>
> All this however, was of no avail, and far from winning the hearts of the Jewish people and their Sages, Herod was regarded by them as the destroyer of their traditional institutions, the murderer of their kings and leaders, and the agent of a foreign government.
>
> He incurred the wrath of those loyal to the Torah and pledged to national independence; during his time the foundations were already laid for the spiritual climate that was to give rise to the sect of Zealots who opposed all foreign rule and any authority except that of the Kingdom of Heaven.

[76]*Encyclopaedia Judaica*, pgs. 8:381-382; Josephus: *Histories of the Jews*: XVI:11, 4-6.

[77]Josephus: *Histories of the Jews*: XVI:11, 7.

[78]Josephus: *Histories of the Jews*: XVII:7.

[79]*Encyclopaedia Judaica*, pg. 8:382; Macrobius: *Saturnalia* II, 4, 11.

[80]Josephus: *Histories of the Jews*: XVII:6, 5.

[81]Cecil, Russell L. and Loeb, Robert F.: *A Textbook of Medicine*, pgs. 609-632.

[82]Aretaeus (2nd century A.D. Greek physician) who led a revival of Hippocrates' teachings: *On the Causes and Indications of Acute and Chronic Diseases (4 Vol.); On the Treatment of Acute and Chronic Diseases (4 Vol.)*.

[83]Diagnosis made by Dr. Edward Arquilla, professor and head, Department of Pathology, California College of Medicine, University of California, Irvine, an internationally recognized authority and researcher in the field of diabetes.

[84]Schmidt, J.E.: *Attorneys' Dictionary of Medicine and Word Finder*, pg. 1:C-120.

[85]*Ibid.*, pg. 1:E-8.

[86]*Ibid.*

[87]Josephus: *Histories of the Jews*: XVII:6, 5.

[88]*Ibid.*

[89]Russell, D.S.: *The Jews from Alexander to Herod*, pgs. 91, 92, 98.

[90]*Encyclopaedia Judaica*, pg. 8:384:

> The *Talmud* calls Herod "a slave of the Hasmonean dynasty," and recounts the killing of the Jewish scholars and the murder of the Hasmoneans. It even ascribes the building of the Temple to Herod's wish to atone for slaying the scholars (BB 3a-4a; Ta'an 23a).

[91]Russell, D.S.: *The Jews from Alexander to Herod*, pg. 91; *Encyclopaedia Britannica*, pgs. 8:379-380.

[92]Russell, D.S.: *The Jews from Alexander to Herod*, pg. 100.

[93]*Encyclopaedia Judaica*, pgs. 15:579-583.

Chapter 32

PONTIUS PILATE

[1]Flusser, David: *Jesus*, picture on pg. 6.

[2]Reicke, Bo: *The New Testament Era. The World of the Bible from 500 B.C. to A.D. 100*, pg. 78; Durant, Will: *Caesar and Christ*, pg. 21.

[3]*Encyclopaedia Britannica*, pgs. IX:37, 18:371c.

[4]Durant, Will: *Caesar and Christ*, pg. 25.

[5]*Ibid.*

[6]*Ibid.*, at pgs. 216-217.

[7]*Ibid.*, at pg. 33.

[8]*Ibid.*, at pgs. 262-263.

[9]*Ibid.*, at pg. 263; Graetz, Heinrich: *History of the Jews*, pgs. 2:136-137.

[10]Josephus: *Histories of the Jews*: XVIII:170-173; Tacitus: *Annals* IV:6.

[11]Josephus: *Histories of the Jews*: XVIII:174-175.

[12]Graetz, Heinrich: *History of the Jews*, pg. 2:135.

[13]Durant, Will: *Caesar and Christ*, pg. 263.

[14]Josephus: *Histories of the Jews*: XVIII:54-59.

[15]Philo: *The Embassy to Gaius*, X:304-305.

[16]Josephus: *Histories of the Jews*: XVIII:59-62.

[17]For an analysis of the number of Jews in the Roman Empire, in various locations, see Tcherikover, Victor, *Hellenistic Civilization and the Jews*, pgs. 284-295.

[18]Philo: *The Embassy to Gaius*, X:299-301, 302-303.

[19]*Encyclopaedia Britannica*, pg. 18:371.

[20]Philo: *The Embassy to Gaius*, X:160-161; see also Reicke, Bo: *The New Testament Era. The World of the Bible from 500 B.C. to A.D. 100*, pgs. 162, 182-183.

PART 7

THE IMPERIAL ROMAN LEGAL SYSTEM

Chapter 33

THE JUDGMENT SEAT

[1]Josephus: *Wars of the Jews*: II:333, 403, 404; V:238-241. Josephus speaks of the Antonia in several other places. (See general index.)

[2]Berger, Adolf: *Encyclopedic Dictionary of Roman Law*, pg. 565.

[3]*Encyclopaedia Britannica*, pg. 18:369.

[4]Kunkel, Wolfgang: *An Introduction to Roman Legal and Constitutional History*, pg. 18; *The Interpreter's Dictionary of the Bible*, pg. 2:1023; Sherwin-White, A.N.: *Roman Society and Roman Law in the New Testament*, pg. 24; *Matthew* 27:19.

[5]Josephus: *Wars of the Jews*: V:238-241.

[6]We do not know which Centuries and Maniples were in the Antonia at this particular time; but we do have detailed information about their general organization. Grant, Michael: *The Jews and the Roman World*, pg. XXXI.

Chapter 34

THE ACCUSERS

[1]Reicke, Bo: *The New Testament Era. The World of the Bible from 500 B.C. to A.D. 100*, pgs. 228-229.

[2]*Ibid.*, at pg. 84.

[3]Durant, Will: *Caesar and Christ*, pgs. 27-28.

[4]*Ibid.*, at pg. 28.

[5]*Ibid.*, at pgs. 28-30.

[6]*Ibid.*, at pg. 32.

[7]Kunkel, Wolfgang: *An Introduction to Roman Legal and Constitutional History*, pg. 74; Schulz, Fritz: *Classical Roman Law*, pg. 573.

[8]*John* 19:10; Reicke, Bo: *The New Testament Era. The World of the Bible from 500 B.C. to A.D. 100*, pg. 175.

[9]Sherwin-White, A.N.: *Roman Society and Roman Law in the New Testament*, pg. 24; Berger, Adolf: *Encyclopedic Dictionary of Roman Law, pgs. 340, 429.*

[10]*John* 18:29.

[11]See Chapter 29, "Are You The Christ?"

[12]*Matthew* 27:11; *Mark* 15:2; *Luke* 23:3; *John* 18:33.

Chapter 35

THE SEARCH FOR A CHARGE

[1]*Matthew* 27:11; *Mark* 15:2; *Luke* 23:3; *John* 18:33.

[2]*Luke* 23:3; *Matthew* 27:11; *Mark* 15:2.

[3]Sherwin-White, A.N.: *Roman Society and Roman Law in the New Testament*, pgs. 12-13.

[4]*Ibid.*, at pg. 18.

[5]Durant, Will: *Caesar and Christ*, pg. 215.

[6]Hunter, William A.: *Introduction to Roman Law*, pg. 186.

[7]Durant, Will: *Caesar and Christ*, pg. 27.

[8]*Ibid.*, pg. 260.

[9]Kunkel, Wolfgang: *An Introduction to Roman Legal and Constitutional History*, pgs. 156-159; Jolowicz, H.F. and Nicholas, Barry: *Historical Introduction to the Study of Roman Law*, pgs. 387f; Buckland, W.W.: *A Text-Book of Roman Law from Augustus to Justinian*, pgs. 29-30, 38, 40; Hunter, William A.: *Introduction to Roman Law*, pg. 9.

[10]Kunkel, in Note 9, *supra*, pg. 73.

Chapter 36

PILATE'S CHOICES

[1]Berger, Adolf: *Encyclopedic Dictionary of Roman Law*, pg. 418.

[2]See Chapters 16, "The Kingdom of God" and 29, "Are You The Christ?"

[3]Note 1, *supra*, at pg. 382. Also, Sherwin-White, A.N.: *Roman Society and Roman Law in the New Testament*, pg. 27.

[4]Prat, Ferdinand: *Jesus Christ His Life, His Teaching and His Work*, pg. 2:361.

Chapter 37

PILATE'S IMPERIUM

[1]Berger, Adolf: *Encyclopedic Dictionary of Roman Law*, pg. 529.

[2]Derrett, J. Duncan M.: *Law in the New Testament*, pg. 428.

[3]Johnson, Paul: *A History of Christianity*, pg. 6.

[4]Sherwin-White, A.N.: *Roman Society and Roman Law in the New Testament*, pg. 37.

[5]Durant, Will: *Caesar and Christ*, pgs. 27-28.

Chapter 38

THE HEROD AND BARABBAS PERICOPES

[1]*Encyclopaedia Judaica*, pgs. 3:75-76; 8:377-378; *The Interpreter's Dictionary of the Bible*, pgs. 2:592-593; Hoehner, Harold W.: *Herod Antipas*.

[2]*The Interpreter's Dictionary of the Bible*, pg. 2:353.

[3]Brandon, S.G.F.: *Jesus and the Zealots*, pgs. 3-4, 258-64, 273, 283, 334(2), 339(1); Grant, Michael: *A Historian's View of the Gospels,* pgs. 164-166; Guignebert, Charles: *Jesus*, pgs. 468-427.

Chapter 39

SENTENCE: GOLGOTHA

[1]We find a substantial body of literature on the physiology and pathology of death on the cross. One of the most definitive treatments: Barbet, Pierre: *A Doctor at Calvary (translated by the Earl of Wicklow)*. I rely heavily on this book, as well as the scholarly approach of Dr. Theodore Brunner, chair, Department of Classics, University of California, Irvine, who has investigated the subject thoroughly (private conversations).

[2]*Matthew* 27:32; *Mark* 15:21; *Luke* 23:26.

[3]*Matthew* 27:33; *Mark* 15:22; *Luke* 23:33.

[4]Prat, Ferdinand: *Jesus Christ His Life, His Teaching and His Work*, pg. 2:360-364.

[5]Marmor, Leonard: Shock. *Trauma*, pgs. Vol. 13, 1:71-1:84; Kinney, John M., DeCosse, Jerome J., Moody, Frank G. and Zuidema, George D.: *Trauma*, pgs. Vol. 16, 2:55ff.

[6]Prat, Ferdinand: *Jesus Christ His Life, His Teaching and His Work*, pg. 2:374.

[7]*John* 19:19; *Matthew* 27:37; *Mark* 15:26.

[8]*Matthew* 27:27; *Mark* 15:16; *John* 19:23.

[9]Brunner, Theodore: *The Sedecula on the Cross: Literary Evidence in Support of the Giv'at ha mivtar Find.* Private conversations at University of California, Irvine, Department of Classics, and *Thesaurus Linguae Graecae* which Dr. Brunner also directs. Also cited by Daniel Thrapp, *Los Angeles Times*, Aug. 1, 1971, Sec. C, Pg. 1.

[10]*Ibid.*; DePasquale, Nicholas P., Burch, George E.: *Death by Crucifixion.* American Heart Journal 66:9 (1963), pg. 435.

[11]*Ibid.*

[12]Josephus: *Life*: 420-421.

[13]*Mark* 15:29-30.

[14]*Mark* 15:31-32.

[15]*Luke* 23:36-37.

[16]*John* 19:23-25.

[17]*Psalm* 22:16-17.

[18]*Isaiah* 43:1-3.

[19]*Isaiah* 53:3-6.

[20]*Psalm* 22:14-15.

[21]*John* 19:28.

[22]*Isaiah* 43:10.

[23]*Psalm* 22:1; *Matthew* 27:46.

[24]*Psalm* 31:5.

Appendix 2

THE GOSPELS

[1]Neil, William: *Harper's Bible Commentary*, pgs. 351-352.

[2]Craig, Clarence T.: *The Beginning of Christianity*, pgs. 61-62.

[3]Bruce, F.F.: *The New Testament Documents. Are They Reliable?* pg. 39.

[4]Note 2, *supra*, at pg. 60,

[5]Bultmann, Rudolf: *Theology of the New Testament*, pg. 3.

[6]Note 3, *supra*, at pg. 10.

[8]Note 1, *supra*, at pg. 334.

[9]Bratton, Fred G.: *A History of the Bible*, pg. 103.

[10]*Ibid.*, at pgs. 184-197.

[11]*Ibid.*, at pgs. 194-195.

[12]*Ibid.*, at pg. 195.

[13]*Ibid.*

[14]*The Interpreter's Dictionary of the Bible*, pg. 1:520-532.

[15]Brandon, S.G.F.: *The Trial of Jesus of Nazareth*, pgs. 75-76, 79.

[16]Note 9, *supra*, at pgs. 4-7.

[17]Note 9, *supra*, at pgs. 244-279.

Page 279 traces the fascinating in-and-out movement of the words "worschipers," "supersticious" and "religious":

> From Wycliffe to Rieu is a long distance. Some of the changes in English usage may be noted in the forms in which the following sample verse (Acts 17:22) appears:
>
> Wycliffe: Men of Atenes, bi alle thingis, I se zou as veyn worschipers.
>
> Tyndale: Ye men of Attens, I perceave that in all things ye are to supersticious.
>
> Geneva: Ye men of Athens, I perceave that in all things ye are to superstitious.
>
> Rheims: Ye men of Athens, in all things I perceive you as it were superstitious.
>
> Authorized Version: Ye men of Athens, I perceive that in all things ye are too superstitious.
>
> Revised Version: Ye men of Athens, I perceive that in all things that ye are somewhat superstitious.
>
> Weymouth: Men of Athens, I perceive that you are in every respect remarkably religious.
>
> Centenary: Men of Athens, I perceive that in all respects you are remarkably religious.
>
> Twentieth Century: Men of Athens, On every hand I see signs of your being very religious.
>
> Moffatt: Men of Athens, I observe wherever I turn that you are a most religious people.
>
> Ballantine: Men of Athens, I see that you are in every way unusually reverential to the Gods.

Basic English: O men of Athens, I see that you are overmuch given to fear of the Gods.

Godspeed: Men of Athens, from every point of view I see that you are extremely religious.

Phillips: Gentlemen of Athens, my own eyes tell me that you are in all respects an extremely religious people.

Rieu: Men of Athens, I notice that you are in many ways very interested in religion.

[18]Throckmorton, Burton H., Jr.: *Gospel Parallels (A Synopsis of the First Three Gospels)*; Finegan, Jack: *Encountering New Testament Manuscripts (A Working Introduction to Textual Criticism)*.

[19]*Ibid.* See also Negenman, Jan H.: *New Atlas of the Bible* (Ed. by H.H. Rowley); Bratton, Fred G.: *A History of the Bible*.

[20]*Ibid.*

[21]*Ibid.* See also Bratton, Fred G.: *A History of the Bible*; Bruce, F.F.: *The New Testament Documents. Are They Reliable?* pg. 16:

> The best and most important of these go back to somewhere about A.D. 350, the two most important being the *Codex Vaticanus*, the chief treasure of the Vatican Library in Rome, and the well-known *Codex Sinaiticus*, which the British government purchased from the Soviet government for 100,000 on Christmas Day, 1933, and which is now the chief treasure of the British Museum. Two other important early MSS in this country are the *Codex Alexandrinus*, also in the British Museum, written in the Fifth Century, and the *Codex Besae*, in Cambridge University Library, written in the fifth or sixth century, and containing the Gospels and Acts in both Greek and Latin.

[22]Finegan, Jack: *Encountering New Testament Manuscripts (A Working Introduction to Textual Criticism)*; Bratton, Fred G.: *A History of the Bible*; Negenman, Jan H.: *New Atlas of the Bible* (Ed. by H.H. Rowley); Throckmorton, Burton H., Jr.: *Gospel Parallels (A Synopsis of the First Three Gospels)*.

Appendix 3

THE TALMUD

[1]Strack, Hermann L.: *Introduction to the Talmud and Midrash*; Goldin, Judah: *The Living Talmud*; Runes, Dagobart D.: *The Talmud of Jerusalem*; Herford, R. Travers: *The Ethics of the Talmud: Sayings of the Fathers*; Neusner, Jacob: *Invitation to the Talmud*; Cohen, A.: *Everyman's Talmud*; Gersh, Harry: *The Sacred Books of the Jews*; Finkelstein, Louis: *Akiba — Scholar, Saint and Martyr*; *Encyclopaedia Judaica* (general index for multiple related entries).

[2]Ginzberg, Louis: *On Jewish Law and Lore*, pgs. 3-5.

[3]Goldin, Hyman E.: *Hebrew Criminal Law and Procedure*, pgs. 99-100.

[4]Durant, Will: *The Story of Civilization: Part III: Caesar and Christ*, pg. 31.

Appendix 4

JEWISH COURT ORGANIZATION AT THE TIME OF JESUS' TRIALS

[1]*Black's Law Dictionary*, pgs. 991-992.

[2]*Talmud*: Sanhedrin 2a; 32a; 86a. For the best summaries on jurisdiction gleaned from the *talmud* as a whole, see: Mendelsohn, S.: *The Criminal Jurisprudence of the Ancient Hebrews*, pgs. 87-91; Goldin, Hyman E.: *Hebrew Criminal Law and Procedure*, pgs. 63-68; Gershfield, Edward M.: *Studies in Jewish Jurisprudence*, pgs. 188-193.

[3]*Ibid.*

[4]*Ibid.*

[5]*Ibid.* See also, Mantel, Hugo: *Studies in the History of the Sanhedrin*.

[6]Note 2, *supra*.

[7]*Talmud*: Sanhedrin 15b; 18b; *Deuteronomy* 18:20. Also, Note 2, *supra*.

[8]Goldin, Hyman E.: *Hebrew Criminal Law and Procedure*, Note 2, *supra*, at pgs. 76-77.

INDEX